jonah lomu

the autobiography

First published in 2004
by HEADLINE BOOK PUBLISHING

10 9 8 7 6 5 4 3 2 1

Cataloguing in Publication Data is available from the British Library

ISBN 0 7553 1263 5

Typeset in Centaur MT by Palimpsest Book Production Limited,
Polmont, Stirlingshire
Printed and bound in Great Britain by
Clays Ltd, St Ives plc

Headline's policy is to use papers that are natural, renewable and recyclable products and made
from wood grown in sustainable forests. The logging and manufacturing processes are
expected to conform to the environmental regulations of the country of origin.

HEADLINE BOOK PUBLISHING
A division of Hodder Headline
338 Euston Road
London NW1 3BH

www.headline.co.uk
www.hodderheadline.com

jonah lomu

the autobiography

headline

For the friends I made, and for the people
who love the game as much as I do.

CONTENTS

PUBLISHER'S NOTE

The split between Jonah Lomu and Phil Kingsley Jones occurred after this book was sent to the printers. Jonah was given the option of adding words or amending parts of the text at proof stage. He declined, simply saying: 'Why change what I have written. For 14 or 15 years this was the way it was between Phil and me. Nothing can change that.'

WRITER'S NOTE

Within a week of commencing work on this book, Jonah Lomu's kidneys finally succumbed to the ravages of nephrotic syndrome. Apart from the notable exception of an emotion-charged journey through the back streets of Mangere – where the poignancy of the big man's monologue profoundly affected me – all the interviews were conducted from the foot of his bed. It was here, amongst the tangle of tubes and unrelenting drone of the dialysis machine, that Jonah Lomu confided his life story. Throughout nearly 40 hours of taped interviews his cheerful disposition hardly changed. As each week passed and his medical condition ebbed and flowed – quite literally – his concentration never flagged. Jonah Lomu was, you might say, the perfect patient.

It was originally intended that this book would be presented entirely in the 'first person' – that is to say, *exclusively* Jonah Lomu. However, it became apparent very early on that additional 'voices' were required to supplement his words; to put into their true perspective some of the great deeds he performed on the rugby field. Quite simply, the man is altogether too modest. One can only make so many allowances for self-effacement.

Three of the people closest to Jonah's heart played pivotal roles in this book, none more so than his manager Phil Kingsley Jones. Phil was at all times helpful and supportive. He shares a special bond with Jonah which runs deeper than I had ever imagined.

John Mayhew has been Jonah's doctor as well as his close friend for 10 years. No one summed up the big man more succinctly than Doc Mayhew when he said: 'It's almost frightening to think what he could have been had he not played so much of his career with a huge medical handbrake.'

Fiona Taylor became Fiona Lomu on 21 August 2003. Loving, caring and firmly grounded, it seems to me that Jonah could not have found a more special person to share his life with.

As for the actual writing, there were two main go-to guys. The first was Ron Palenski, one of New Zealand's most gifted and respected writers, who kindly consented to read each chapter and offer his comments and thoughts. His support and encouragement helped me far more than he knows. The second was Kevin Chapman, publisher and managing director of Hodder Moa Beckett. He, too, offered great encouragement. Like Ron Palenski, I value his opinion enormously – even if he did take fiendish delight in pointing out mistakes in the first draft.

Thanks also to editor Mike Wagg – one man's comma is another man's semicolon – for his special skills, and to the vastly experienced and respected rugby writer and author Lindsay Knight. When it comes to rugby, his vision remains 20/20.

Likewise, I am indebted to the following people and organisations who also contributed to this book; adidas, Frank Bunce, Jo Caird, Andrew Cornaga, Sean Fitzpatrick, Fotopress, Andrew Gaze, Getty Images, Chris Grinter, John Hart, Gavin Hastings, Paul Holmes, Dr Helen Lee, Sir Brian Lochore, Bob Luxford, Dave McLaren, Laurie Mains, Justine Mezies-Wilsom, Geoff Miller, John Mitchell, The New Zealand Rugby Museum, Glenn Orr, Photosport, Eric Rush, John Selkirk, Wayne Smith, Gordon Tietjens, Tana Umaga, Tony Underwood, Craig Waugh and Jeff Wilson.

WRITER'S NOTE

Several books and publications provided me with valuable research material, most notably *Men In Black* by Ron Palenski, Rod Chester and Neville McMillan (Hodder Moa Beckett), *The Sky Rugby Almanack* — various editions — by Rod Chester, Neville McMillan, Clive Akers and Geoff Miller (Hodder Moa Beckett), *Rugby News* and *NZ Rugby World*.

Finally, thanks to my family — especially my wife Kim and daughter Kate. They put up with a lot over a number of months. Home absenteeism is something I intend to redress.

Warren Adler
Auckland, February 2004

CHAPTER ONE

THE MACHINE AGE

The booing and the jeering of the Wellington crowd rang in my ears. It didn't faze me. When you make mistakes and you play badly you have to accept it. It doesn't matter where it is or what colour the jersey is, it goes with the territory. What I couldn't understand, though – what I couldn't accept – was that this was the end. For the second time in Super 12 2003, the coach had taken me out of the game at half-time. Replaced, substituted, dragged. Call it what you like, it's never a good feeling. I have lived for a long time in the knowledge that my kidneys would one day get the better of me, but this was World Cup year. I was only twenty-seven. I wanted one more chance on the big stage. I desperately wanted to be part of the All Blacks again. Four games of Super 12 rugby – two as a replacement player in South Africa and twice substituted in Wellington. Surely it wasn't meant to end like this?

For the past eight years or so the doctors have been able to manage my kidney condition. Each year I've had my ups and downs and, with the exception of 1997 when I was out of rugby for about eight months as the doctors put me on a tough regime to try and correct the disorder, I've always bounced back. This time, though, it was different. The signs that my health was beginning to deteriorate badly happened during that handful of Super 12 matches at the start of 2003. It was the same in all four games. I felt fine to start off with, but as soon as I did something strenuous the lethargy would set in. My 'recovery time' has always been longer than that of other players. In 2003 it seemed to take forever. I found it difficult to cope with even the smallest things, like running back to position. My concentration was completely shot.

When I returned from South Africa with the Hurricanes at the end of March, the doctors ran a series of blood tests, but I knew even before Doc Mayhew rang me with the results that things were bad. The kidney failure had caused my haemoglobin to drop to a dangerously low level. The normal blood count for haemoglobin in a male is between 135–180 milligrams per millilitre. In 2001 and 2002 my count had hovered around 90–95. This time it had dropped to around 68. This was it. Verging on complete renal failure. Machine time.

D-day – dialysis day – was 31 May 2003. The possibility of one day having to go on to dialysis is something I had come to terms with years ago. Mentally it was never a burden. I've known since my early twenties that at some point in my life it was always going to be me and the machine. Not such a big deal, really. You just sit there for two or three hours every few days with a couple of needles in your arm while the blood is sucked out of your body, cleaned and then replaced. No sweat. The trouble was that it wasn't as straightforward as the doctors had imagined or as they had told me it would be. My body – my metabolism – is so different from other people's. For a start, it's a lot bigger, so the time I had to spend on the machine was longer than is normally the case. Getting the dialysis levels right proved a problem from day one. Then . . . then came the numbness in my legs and feet. It started like pins and needles. Then I began losing my balance. Couldn't find my feet. The doctors changed my dialysis routine about a dozen times to try and correct the problem, but nothing worked.

Talk to me about kidney disease and there's not much I don't know. Talk to me about neuropathy and it's all a bit of a mystery. It sometimes happens to people with kidney disease. It sometimes happens after two or three years on dialysis. It doesn't usually happen after just two or three months on a machine. With me, it came on quickly. Just my luck . . . It seems that during dialysis some proteins in my blood weren't being properly metabolised or cleaned out. These proteins were eating away at the myelin sheaths around the nerves — nerves in my legs that send and receive messages to and from my brain. The nerve fibres became exposed. They became hypersensitive. The doctors said the condition is dangerous. It can lead to paralysis. The doctors also said the condition is reversible. It's Christmas 2003. I've just gone on to night dialysis. Eight hours while I sleep. Mmmm . . . The first night I got an hour's sleep, the second two. I'll give it another month or so, I think. Christmas — it's a time of hope and cheer . . .

It's a strange thing that in a year in which my rugby career stalled, I found great happiness in another area of my life. I got to know Fiona Taylor in 2003. We fell in love and we got married. We first met about five years ago through a mutual friend. Up until early in 2003 she was, I guess you could say, just a casual acquaintance. It was always like, 'Hi, how are you going?' Nothing more. Then it just happened one day. Click. Straight out of the movies, Fiona reckons. She is a special woman and, as I've discovered, she is a strong woman. She has had to be.

Fiona has helped me face up to the biggest challenge of my life. She has been with me since the very first day I was put on the dialysis machine. She was with me when I was told that a kidney transplant was no longer just a possibility but a necessity. What Fiona didn't know was that I would start out just like any other dialysis patient, but eventually finish up being hooked on to a machine for up to eight hours a day, six days a week. She didn't know that after only a couple of months I would develop a form of neuropathy and I would struggle to walk properly. She has had to deal with a lot.

Fiona has worked in the healthcare industry for a long time. She spent five years with a company called Baxter Healthcare. Ironic, I suppose, that in her job she has provided many of the same products I'm now using. She's seen it all before. Renal supplies are a big part of Baxter. She knows how it all works. If necessary, she can put the needles into my arm and make it all happen. Blood doesn't bother her. We laugh about it now – laugh that we entered each other's lives at this particular point. Now she works from home, doing consultancy work. In our first year together we've hardly been apart. Never more than an hour or two. When I first went on to home dialysis she was by my side virtually the whole time. Whenever the machine has hiccupped it's been all hands on deck – well, at least two on deck and two on the bed. We're not like a normal married couple. We've crammed five years of marriage into one. It could have been a recipe for disaster. Instead, we've become closer. Yeah, she's a strong woman all right. I don't think I could have coped on my own. I know our love grows stronger by the day and this is what Fiona herself has to say about our relationship: 'I knew Jonah had a kidney disease when we got together. I knew it was inevitable that he would one day go on to dialysis. I just didn't know it would happen so soon. The first year has been stressful. No doubt about that. But we got through the tough times – we got through by talking all the time. Even though we're never far from each other, we check in constantly. We ask each other if we're doing all right. Because we are so stressed, sometimes it's easy for the little things to get on top of you. We handle it by putting a lid on those things straightaway. We've learned how to diffuse the tension.

Fiona Lomu: In saying all that, nothing has changed about the way I feel about him. The same things that first drew me to him are still there. He's a big, loving person with a huge heart. I admire so many things about him. I admire how he deals with all the issues in his life. I admire his inner strength. I admire what he's made of his life after where he came from. For outsiders looking in, it must be hard to understand the bond we share. It would be difficult to understand that we are so much alike. We came from different worlds and yet we have so much in common. Sometimes he does things and I think, 'That's just what I would have done.'

Fiona has also had to put up with all the other things that go on in my life. She has had to read all the crap that's been printed in the papers about my personal life. She has had to cope with the fallout from the break-up of my long-time relationship with Teina Stace and all the endless stories about how I didn't do the right thing by Teina; about how I was supposed to have guaranteed the deposit on a house for her; about how I left her broke and broken-hearted. It's always been the same. The media latches on to stories about me and they don't seem to care whether they're right or wrong. In the past I have got angry, but eventually brushed the stories aside. For Fiona, though, it was hard.

The truth about my relationship with Teina is that I realised I was no longer in love with her. It's sad, but it happens to lots of people. Because it was me, though, the whole thing became very public. I did what I thought was the right thing. I was honest with Teina and I told her exactly how I felt. She deserved that.

We parted in our own way, but the media wouldn't drop it. Teina decided she didn't want to say anything publicly, but when she was silent the papers started hassling her. They should have left her alone. They started writing stories. It pissed me off because more often than not those stories were just bullshit.

As if all the stuff about the break-up wasn't enough, Fiona and I had our engagement announced publicly in the newspaper. Not in the engagement notices, but on the front page. We didn't want that. We had my father quoted as saying that there had been a big family gathering to celebrate the event. It was news to us. As Fiona said at the time, we must have been the only people not to be invited to our own engagement party. We wanted a small wedding. There were only sixteen guests. No best man, no bridesmaids or flower girls, and none of my relatives.

I am not ashamed of my family like some people may have suggested. My mother and father live in a house in Karaka in South Auckland that belongs to me. I am happy for them. There are many good things going on with my brothers and sisters. Sela has just completed her third year at medical school. John and Talanoa are doing just fine. Then there's Irene — little Irene who is so happy and enjoying school. That gives me a lot of pleasure. I know it's hard for people to accept that I could get married and not invite any members of my immediate family. The thing is, I have not made peace with my father. I would love to have had my mother at the wedding, but it would have almost certainly meant war between her and my father. I may some day forgive him for what happened to me as a child, but I will never forget. Maybe people will see things differently after they have read the story of my early childhood. Fiona and I do not owe anyone any further explanation as to the way we got married and even after all the bad publicity we received, we wouldn't change a thing. It was our day.

I have lost count of how many medical people I have seen over the past year. Neuropathy seems such a hard thing to get a line on. Some specialists say it is reversible after a kidney transplant; some say that in the meantime I could lose the use of my limbs. The irony is that from my knees up, I feel fantastic — the best I have felt in, well, I don't know how many years. The waiting list for a kidney transplant in New Zealand is at least a couple of years. Unless, of course, you have a live kidney donor. Then the wait is about three or four months. At the moment I continue to dialyse, I stay positive . . . and I wait.

A long time ago, when I was first diagnosed with kidney problems, someone asked me what rugby meant to me. I gave the same answer then as I do now. To me, rugby is life. It's what I know — it's all I know. I have been criticised for not choosing to have a transplant a long time ago: 'Jonah's mad. Why doesn't he give it all away? His health is far more important.' I can understand this criticism. I guess it shows that people care about me. Most people, though, will never understand why I have wanted to keep playing all these years — why I still want to play. You see, most people never get to pull on the black jersey. I want to do it again. It's not about money. I want to leave the game on my terms. If the doctors say I can play after a kidney transplant, then I will play.

With my right arm — my 'dialysis arm' — heavily bandaged I made one last attempt to make the All Blacks World Cup squad in 2003. I got half a game for Wellington in a National Provincial Championship warm-up match against Taranaki. It was a game that counted for nothing. Still, 5,000 people turned up that day at Porirua Park. For me, that was very moving. I think a lot of them came along because they wanted to see me succeed. It was early August and, while my legs were still okay, deep down I knew my dreams of playing in a third World Cup were gone.

Instead, I got to the World Cup in Australia not as a player, but as a special guest of the International Rugby Players' Association. I was flown there to receive the Investec Special Merit Award for services to rugby at a big dinner in Sydney. It was mid-November, four days before the World Cup final. By then, walking had become difficult. As I shuffled to the stage to collect my award, Fiona cried. She told me later that she had sensed a lot of emotion in the room – a lot of love. For me, though, it was one of the proudest moments of my life. To be acknowledged by your fellow players is the greatest honour of all.

Footnote: The rugby statisticians tell me I have played 199 games of first-class rugby. This, I am told, is the same number as the great All Black Jeff Wilson played before he retired from rugby after the Super 12 of 2000. To me, Jeff was the most complete rugby player I ever saw. Strong, fast, beautifully balanced. A magic player to have on your side and a real handful to mark. Jeff Wilson came out of retirement in 2001. He played for the All Blacks again. He got his 200th game. I'd love to be like Jeff. I'd love just one more taste.

CHAPTER TWO

LOOK BACK IN ANGER

I will never forget that day at our home in Mangere in South Auckland. Something inside me just snapped. Something inside me decided enough was enough. I was only fifteen years old, but I was already much bigger than my father. Bigger and stronger. That day in Mangere I decided I would get my retaliation in first. Although I didn't know it back then, that day I would rip apart the last remaining bond between father and son.

The hate had been brewing inside me for years – hate which had started the day I was taken away from Tonga. Taken by parents I never knew. Taken back to a country I had been born in, but had been sent away from as a small baby. Taken by a mother who loved me dearly, but a father who never showed me any love at all.

That day my father had been on the 'juice'. That day he raised his hand to hit me – again. That day I grabbed him, picked him up and threw him across the room and on to the floor. 'I'm not taking this any more!' I stood over him and yelled. 'If you ever lay a hand on me or any of the other kids again you'll have me to answer to!'

'You are no longer my son! You are not mine! Get out of my house!' he roared. He was in a rage. He was totally wild. That day I packed my things and I left my father's house. That day was the last I ever spent as a son under the roof of my parents' home. That day my life changed forever.

Aunty Ruby was a religious woman. A Methodist. She was reading the Bible at the National Women's Hospital and I guess she just fell upon the page. She was reading the story of the man and the whale. She named me Jonah. Jonah Tali Lomu, born in Greenlane, Auckland, on 12 May 1975. Because I had not been a well baby, I was kept in hospital for a number of weeks after the birth. For the first two weeks I was a baby without a name. Trying to understand why it took so long to name me is still a bit of a mystery. I know something of Tongan culture. I know about the extended family set-up, but despite years of asking I'm still not sure I have all the answers. Under normal circumstances, I would have been named by my father's side of the family, after my grandfather. I was the first-born child of Semisi and Hepi Lomu. I was not, however, my father's first child. He already had a son from another relationship, and this is where the real mystery for me lies. To the best of my knowledge, the fact that my father had another child from a previous relationship should not have been a reason why Aunty Ruby named me. You see, Aunty Ruby was a relative from my mother's side of the family. After all these years, no one has given me an acceptable explanation as to why no one from my father's side of the family was willing to step forward and name me. After all these years, I still don't know why my father's side of the family wanted nothing to do with Jonah Lomu . . .

My father came to New Zealand in 1973. Like so many Pacific Islanders, he was looking for a better life for himself and his family. He lived there for a time before my mother came over. Mum was actually pregnant with me when she arrived in Auckland. She had always wanted me to be born in New Zealand and she also wanted a good education for me and my brothers and sisters. I was to live in New Zealand, though, only until I was one, until the birth of my brother, John. He was born on 12 May 1976, exactly one year after me. *He* was named by my father's side of the family. Then *I* was given away. My mother's older sister, Longo, came to New Zealand and she and my mother took me to Tonga, to the Ha'apai Islands, where my mother's roots are.

For almost six years, until just before my seventh birthday, Longo and her husband Moses became my parents. They were good people. They treated me with kindness. I called them Mum and Dad. I spent those early years in a little village called Holopeka. Although the island was relatively isolated, for a young child growing up, this was the good life. It didn't matter, for instance, that to get to the capital, Nuku'alofa, it could take a full day by boat. Like so many Tongan kids, I didn't have a care in the world. Money wasn't a concern. Apart from a few land taxes there was little need for money in the islands. As long as you had a roof over your head you could live off the land, and as long as the crops kept turning over things were sweet.

The memories I have of life in the islands are pretty sketchy now. Sure, I remember the carefree days on the beach and playing in the water with the other kids. I remember the beautiful weather and I remember the love of Longo and Moses, who, sadly, has since passed away. There was no schooling, but I did go to church and, at the same time, I learned about the myths and legends of the Tongan people. As I grew older I often wondered about the stories that had scared and excited me as a young boy in Ha'apai. Stories of souls crying out to you as you walked past graveyards in the town; stories of relatives being possessed by ghosts. But the one memory that freaks me out the most actually happened right in front of my eyes. I must have been about six years old and I walked into a room and was confronted by the frightening sight of an aunty who was literally hanging upside down against a wall. It was like her feet were glued to that wall. She was screaming and her body was twisting and shaking. Longo and Moses told me to get out of the room. They said her body had been possessed. I will never forget that sight.

In my time in Ha'apai, Christian beliefs were strong. They still are, but the old myths and legends remain. Tongan people are very spiritual. There are hundreds of stories about gods and one that particularly sticks in my mind is of *Pekepekātama*, the flying fox god. It was told to me many times. Unlike other flying foxes, this one was white and its appearance meant that a chief might soon die. A big, white, scary bat! What kid wouldn't remember a story like that?

Just before I turned seven my mother and father came to Tonga to collect me from Longo and Moses. They came to bring me back to New Zealand. In Tongan culture this is not unusual and it's sometimes just the way that the extended family works. Children are often shifted from one house to another, but I'm still not sure why my parents decided at that particular time that I should go back to New Zealand. It has never been properly explained to me. I didn't want to leave Tonga. I didn't want to leave Longo and Moses and move to a strange new country. I was six years old and Longo and Moses had been parents to me for as long as I could remember. I didn't want to leave with people I didn't know. I knew Hepi Lomu was my natural mother, but I didn't know her as 'Mum'.

For the first couple of years after I left Tonga everything was so strange that an anger began to build inside me. I didn't want to be in New Zealand. For a start, I had never been to school. When I began my education at Oranga Primary School in Onehunga I couldn't even speak English. Not a single word. I spoke Tongan fluently and, not surprisingly, I found it hugely difficult to make friends. By the time I entered Favona Primary School, after my parents moved to Mangere, I was depressed and becoming a bit of a problem child. Back then, my parents shifted around a lot, which, I guess, was also unsettling. At various times the family lived in Newmarket, Penrose and Onehunga, before we finally settled down in Maitland Place, Mangere.

My problems at school weren't helped by the fact I couldn't get on with my father. I didn't have a problem with my mother. I loved her then, just as I love her now. Anything good I did back then I did for my mother. But I just couldn't get along with my father. He was always very strict on the family, especially me and my brother John. My sister, Sela, was just a baby and my brother, Talanoa, and youngest sister, Irene, had not yet been born when I came back to New Zealand. Right from the day I returned it seemed there was a lot of bad blood between my father and me. He gave me no freedom and I never got the feeling that he loved me.

There was also another problem. My father was a drinker. Not just a glass here or a glass there. He was a problem drinker. When he wasn't drinking he could be a reasonable guy, but when he drank he was the worst person in the world to be around. He would often become violent. I hated it when he came home drunk as anything. I hated it when he yelled and screamed and took his frustrations out on the family. I hated it most of all when he beat me or my brother or when he hit my mother. This is the hardest thing to explain to anyone because, as much as he was a bad man on the drink, he could also be a good person. I wanted him so much to be a good person and I desperately wanted him to be a loving father.

Yet for all his faults in those days, my father was a hard worker, a mechanic. He always put food on the table and us kids never went hungry. Booze, though, was always the problem. My brother

John and I lived in fear of him coming home late. It was usually on payday or at weekends. On those nights we would go to bed early, snuggle up and try and block out the ranting and the raving. I can still hear him yelling for someone to cook him something. Years later, when I went to see the New Zealand movie, *Once Were Warriors*, I got really choked up. As I watched the film I found myself reliving my childhood. I felt those same old emotions being drawn up inside me. It was awful and very hard to watch.

The beatings I received were bad. Sometimes before I went to school I would have to make sure I was covered up, so people couldn't see the marks from the hidings. One time I got beaten with an electric cord and you could see the bruise marks all over my back. They stayed with me for days. In the face of all this, though, I remained defiant. I never cried when my father hit me. I knew this annoyed the hell out of him. I just sat there and took it. That was something that really got to him. I would just look at him the whole time he was belting me. He hated it.

The one thing I can look back on now and be thankful for is that my sisters, Sela and Irene, and brother, Talanoa, did not have to put up with what John and I and my mother had to. Mum has always been a regular churchgoer and, fortunately for everyone, my father finally found religion. That saved him from going right off the rails. The other kids got to see a father who was a better man than the one John and I had known. They're lucky in that respect and I'm pleased for them. It came too late for John and me though . . .

There have been many stories written and even the odd book published dealing with my early life growing up in South Auckland. Some of the stories are true, some of them have greatly exaggerated certain aspects of my life and then, of course, there are a number of stories which are just plain rubbish. It's true that I was no angel as I grew into my early teens. I was never exactly a street kid, but I knew about life on the streets. I hung out with what some people might call the wrong crowd. I had made friends with lots of people who lived on the streets and many of them, in fact, were relatives. Part of the reason I hung out on the street is because it was a way of getting away from the problems at home. My mother tried her best, but because of my relationship with my father I never felt like I was truly wanted at home, so I turned to my street friends.

I hung out with all sorts of groups back in the late 1980s. It was mainly about being wanted and, I suppose, it was also about wanting to be a bit of a gangster. Like so many kids, I enjoyed being part of the cool group. I wanted to be part of the 'A' team. One of those groups was called the CCB – the City Crip Boys. They were based in Onehunga and I would walk all the way from home, in Mangere, just to be with them. The CCB were made up predominantly of Tongans, but I never became a fully-fledged member of the gang. At the time, I had relatives in another group, so I just hung out with them. The funny thing was that there was a fair amount of bad blood in South Auckland between the Tongans and the Samoans back then, yet there were also a number of Samoans in the CCB.

There were some really stupid things going down. Dangerous things. Like going into the city and just picking out some person and beating him up for a piece of clothing or some money. If you laid into him and he was still standing, you just turned and ran. We also stole cars, jump-started them and took them for joyrides. That was a big buzz. The boys would cruise into town and usually end up in a fight. BMX bikes were also a big go. We'd pinch them from anywhere. From inside shops for the top-of-the-range bikes. From outside shops for parts. It didn't matter. Sometimes we'd carry two or three bikes back with us from town. Then we'd head down to Mangere Bridge, strip them on the bridge, take the parts we wanted and chuck what was left over the side. I hate to think how many bikes we took in those days.

As we got a bit older, the guys I hung out with fought more and we did our share of drinking. Sometimes the boys would find a field somewhere and sit around drinking home-brewed beer out of a bucket. I got into my share of fights back then, too. I don't think I ever really went looking for a fight, but I was cheeky and I was aggressive. I was also a bit of a show-off. Because I was usually the youngest guy in the group I was always trying to prove myself — to show everyone I could handle myself. I wanted to be like the others. I wanted to be staunch. When I fought, I almost always thought of my father. I imagined I was fighting him — that I was beating him up. Sometimes I would completely lose control — I didn't know when to stop. When I think back to those times, all that anger and all that hatred frightens me.

I also took my share of beatings on the street. I got a really bad kicking once from some guys wearing steel-capped boots. My chest and stomach were bruised for weeks. I was stabbed in the leg with a knife and in one fight I was stabbed with a broken beer bottle. It was a violent time. Those fights were deadly serious and there were occasions when I lost and found myself having to run for my life. We didn't just fight on the streets, either. A favourite haunt for fights after school was a field next to the local rugby league ground. If there was something said during school that you didn't like, then you would almost always end up in this field. That's where all the school problems were sorted out.

Things erupted big-time on the tough streets of South Auckland just before my thirteenth birthday. My uncle, David Fuko, was hacked to death with a machete by some Samoans in the middle of Otara Shopping Centre. They chopped off his head and his arms. A cousin of mine was lucky to get away with his life. I'm not entirely sure what happened that day, but I do believe that the attack came down to a case of mistaken identity. There were all sorts of stories flying around at the time that the killing was some kind of revenge hit. That's just rubbish. My uncle was simply in the wrong place at the wrong time. The South Auckland suburbs of Otara and Mangere could be dangerous places back then. He was basically the victim of something he was never really a part of. Whatever, the murder did spark things up between the Samoans and the Tongans.

The media had a great time after David Fuko's death, but I think they overplayed the hatred thing between the two races. I had a lot of Samoan friends on the street and I personally felt I had a really good handle on what was going on. There was anger, no doubt about that, but I don't think it ever developed into out-and-out hatred. I certainly never went looking for revenge or anything like that. Around that time there were groups like the Sons of Samoa and the Tongan Lynch Mob and, sure, things did get heated. Sometimes they would meet in town for a rumble. Sometimes I was involved. But at the same time there were also loads of other groups involved in fights in the middle of Auckland – punks, boot boys, all sorts.

By the end of 1988, I was well known to the police. My mother could see the writing on the wall. As I've said, she had always wanted me to get a good education. By now, though, she was beginning to think I mightn't live long enough to get one. She needed to act and she needed to act quickly. She managed to get me enrolled on a full scholarship as a boarder at Wesley College in Paerata, in the country, on the outskirts of South Auckland. Wesley is the oldest school in New Zealand. It's attached to the Methodist Church and is a multicultural school with a large number of Pacific Island pupils. It's also a school that is strong on two things which I knew little about back then – discipline and rugby union. I would learn much more about them both over the next few years.

I had never played rugby union before starting at Wesley as a third-former in 1989. At primary school and at Arahanga Intermediate School in Mangere, my game was league. I played for the Manukau Magpies club. I loved league in those days. Despite my father not allowing me to play on Sundays, I still managed to make all the age-grade teams. At intermediate I also discovered that I had a talent for athletics. It was an ability that I stumbled upon by complete accident. One day I saw a sign in class saying there was a high-jump competition happening in the school hall. Two of my mates were quite good at the event and they invited me to come along. I liked being with my friends and I particularly loved the idea of missing class to do sport.

The competition was quite simple. You had your name called and you made your jump. If you missed, you were out. I made it through the first round and never looked back. They kept raising the bar and I just kept clearing the height. Before I knew it there were just four of us left, including both my mates. I never thought I had a chance when the competition started – it was all a bit of a laugh – but when it got down to just two of us, I decided to give it everything. My approach to the bar was unsophisticated. None of that Fosbury flop stuff for me. In the end, my untrained, old-fashioned approach was enough. I won the competition and in doing so launched my schoolboy athletics career. My music teacher at Arahanga was Miss L'Estrange. She was also the high-jump instructor. She talked to me afterwards and said that with a bit of training she thought I could go even higher. She started to train me and she taught me the flop. I went on to win the Auckland Intermediate title.

As a young South Auckland kid used to roaming the streets and playing by his own rules, the prospect of going to a church-oriented school, which was heavy on discipline, was not one I was looking forward to. When I arrived at Wesley College, I was a very angry boy and at first I rebelled against the discipline. The whole school system came as a massive culture shock and I resented being there. On my first day I whacked a kid much older than me after he made a remark I didn't like. At the end of my second day I had picked up something like six detentions. It was going to take a long time for all that anger inside of me to go away.

The one thing that kept me from losing it completely at Wesley was sport. For as much as I'd become used to the thrills of an ill-disciplined street life, sport was becoming a powerful magnet in my life. For this I have one man to thank. Chris Grinter was the deputy headmaster at Wesley. Mr Grinter was a rugby union man. When I arrived he was in charge of the First XV and, before that, from 1986 to 1988, he had been hugely successful as coach of the New Zealand Secondary Schools side. Chris was also a great listener, a man who had this special ability to 'connect' with his students and his players. At Wesley the whole discipline thing revolved around the deputy principal and, as a result, I spent many hours with Mr Grinter.

It didn't take Chris long to recognise that I had arrived at Wesley with an 'attitude'. He decided I needed to channel my anger and aggression in a more positive way. The answer was simple. He went out and bought me a punching bag. There was no gymnasium at Wesley in those days, so I had to make use of an old storeroom. Whenever I felt angry I'd go and grab the key off Chris and head off to the big bag. I used to just belt the crap out of that thing. On my worst days I'd be in there three or four times before lunch. I always felt better after those sessions. As time wore on and the anger subsided, I found myself going to the big bag purely for a workout.

However, one thing Chris couldn't get me interested in during my first year at college was rugby union. Wesley was a traditional New Zealand school where union was the only kind of rugby played. The trouble for me was that it was the wrong kind. I had a league background and I wanted to keep playing. There were generally no exceptions to the union rule. You either played rugby for the school or you didn't play at all. Despite this, I went to see Chris and told him I wanted to be excused to play club league on the weekends. I got a hell of a shock when he agreed. I think Chris felt at the time it was better to have me doing something I loved rather than have me rebel against the school and its rules. We struck a deal. Chris agreed to give me one year of rugby league, provided I came back to play school rugby in my fourth-form year.

The following year I had no problem fulfilling my part of the deal. I had just come to respect Chris so much during my first year at Wesley. He was much more than a coach. He was my first real father figure since I had left Tonga. Over the course of many conversations during my early days at Wesley he, more than anyone, was able to get inside my head. It was strange at first. I wasn't used to this sort of caring approach. He had this amazing ability to talk to me in a grown-up way, yet still make me see that I was just a child. I probably didn't realise it at the time, but I needed this sort of interaction. He taught me to think more deeply about things and to be positive in everything I did; to get rid of the negatives and to take in only what I needed. There would be some tough times ahead for me at Wesley. I still hadn't got the streets out of my system, but Chris had shown me the way.

CHAPTER THREE

SAVED BY THE BELL

Athletics was my thing in that first year at Wesley College. I was pretty raw back then, but I had natural speed for the sprints and in the field events my size and strength were obviously an advantage. At the school championships in 1989 I won all the junior sprints, from the 100m through to the 400m, and anchored the winning 4 x 100m relay team. I took all the jumps as well – high, long and triple – and in the field I won the discus, shot and javelin. Hurdling was one event I really took to and I spent hours analysing the style of the great Welshman, Colin Jackson. I had a video of Jackson in action and I watched it over and over. Play . . . stop . . . rewind . . . play. Eventually I got it down to a fine art. At one stage I even had visions of becoming an international-class hurdler.

Over the next five years I won virtually every athletics event I entered at school and on the regional and national scene I also picked up my share of titles. Everything came naturally. The fact that I had virtually no formal training was never a problem. Here are some results from the 1989 school magazine:

The days were long, but I loved every minute of those athletics meets. I'd run the 100m, then shoot across to the shot put. Then

Athletics 1989

Junior Boys

Championship	First	Second	Third	Time	Record	
100m	J. Lomu Si	C. Doyle Wi	G. Purcell Si	12.8s	G. Watene St 12.6s	1975
100m						
hurdles	J. Lomu Si	A. Hook Sc	J. Bagley Sc	16.4s	C. Cheeseman Sc 17.3s	1981
200m	J. Lomu Si	C. Doyle Wi	J. Bagley Sc	28.3s	C. Cheeseman Sc 26.9s	1981
400m	J. Lomu Si	J. Steedman St	J. Bagley Sc	1m 02.6s	C. Cheeseman Sc 59.1s	1981
800m	J. Steedman St	C. Doyle Wi	A. Laker Si	2m 33.4s	M. Johnstone Sc 2m 20.4s	1982
1500m	J. Steedman St	A. Laker Si	J. Webster Wi	5m 27.4s	A. Mabey Si 5m 18.6s	1987
Discus	J. Lomou Si	C. Doyle Wi	J. Steedman St	22.61m	A. Tuora Sc 34.33m	1968
Shot	J. Lomu Si	J. Steedman St	S. Mabey Si	12.01.m	B. Marrah Sc 11.54m	1973
Javelin	J. Lomu Si	J. Bagley Sc	T. Huirama St	26.85m	C. Cheeseman Sc 28.7m	1981
Cricket Ball	S. Bradley Wi	J. Bagley Sc	C. Campbell Si	59.3m	J. Neale Si 78.69m	1963
Long Jump	J. Lomu Si	M. Stowell St	M. Stowell St	4.71m	D. Kimpton Sc 5.51m	1951
High Jump	J. Lomu Si	G. Purcell Si	T. Huirama St	1.54m	H. Morrison Wi 1.53m	1976
Triple Jump	J. Lomu Si	C. Doyle Wi	J. Bagley Sc	10.42m	J. Neale Si 11.00m	1965
4 x 100m Relay	Simmonds	Winstone	Stanton	54.9s	St 1973, Si 1978, Sc 1982 54.8s	

28

it was off to the javelin, the high jump, hurdles, relay . . . magic. There were quite a few coaches back then who thought I had a real future as a decathlete. Trouble was, I had a problem competing in one particular event. At Wesley we weren't well off equipment-wise and to be a good decathlete you have to master all the events. Pole-vaulting was the stumbling block – the school didn't own a suitable pole. In fact, the biggest one I could ever find was only made to take the weight of an athlete up to about 90kg. Hell, the last time I weighed 90kg I would have been about eleven.

By 1993, my last year at Wesley, it's fair to say that rugby had taken over as my first sporting love. However, that didn't stop me competing full-out in athletics. I took the Wesley senior athletics title and won seven events at the Manukau Interschools Championships. In the North Island Champs I won the shot put, finished third in the discus and fifth in the triple jump. I'm often asked about my 100m times. The quickest time I ever posted in competition was 11.2 seconds in that final year at Wesley, but I am proud of the fact that I once stopped the clock at school in 10.89 seconds. Sure, it was hand-timed, but it was still very satisfying.

Physically, athletics proved a great outlet for me in my early days at Wesley. At heart, though, I was still a bit of a wild boy. During the school week everything was fine, but at weekends I often found myself getting into trouble. The exeat passes students received every three or four weeks were a licence to hit the Pukekohe shopping centre or downtown Auckland – off with the school uniform and on with the street clothes. How does that song go? 'Saturday night's all right for fighting?' Old habits died hard.

The kind of street clothes I wore back in those days were often a magnet for gangs of kids we called label bashers: adidas shoes, All Stars track pants and bomber jackets. Like so many kids on the street, that was my get-up. One night I was sitting at a bus stop near Albert Park in Auckland when a guy came up to me and told me to give him my jacket. Yeah, right. It was my prized possession – a British Knight jacket one of my relatives had bought for me in the States. When I refused, he hit me. I was only fourteen, but I was wise to the way of the streets and I could handle myself. I got to my feet and gave him a warning. When he tried to hit me again I lost it. I just snapped. This guy must have been eighteen, but it didn't matter. I gave him the beating of his life. When he went down I literally kicked hell out of him. It's not an incident I look back on with any sense of pride.

After the fight I was scared. I went looking for my cousins, who I'd been with earlier in the evening. I was covered in blood when I finally caught up with them. We found a public toilet and managed to wash most of the blood off, but as we headed back towards the middle of town a police officer pulled up and called me over. 'Excuse me, Sir, have you been near Albert Park this evening? Someone has been badly beaten.' The cop said the guy had described me to a T and that I'd beaten him up and stolen his shoes. The last thing I needed was trouble with the law, so I admitted that I had beaten the guy up, but explained that I'd just been defending myself. The cop wasn't convinced and he decided to take me back to Albert Park. 'What about the missing shoes?' he asked. 'You've got to be kidding,' I replied. 'Look at the size of his feet.' I was a size thirteen. The other guy would have been a size eight or nine at the most. The cop thought about it for a while before letting me go with a warning.

I didn't forget my promise to Chris Grinter when I returned to school to begin my fourth-form year. It's more that I just didn't remind him about our agreement that I would play rugby in my second year at Wesley. In fact, at the start of the year, rugby couldn't have been further from my mind. I was still thinking league and I was heavily involved in athletics. I became junior boys athletics champion for the second year and again represented the school at the North Island Secondary Schools Championships. I was also getting into basketball. At fourteen, I could already slam-dunk the ball. I remember Chris wandering into the school hall one day while I was playing with some mates. He stood and watched for a while and must have liked what he saw. Chris was looking for another lock for the First XV. I had a pretty fair vertical jump – there was no lifting in rugby line-outs back in those days – and he said, 'Jonah, why don't you come down and try out for the First XV?' I liked Chris and I owed him. 'Why not,' I replied.

Chris Grinter: I already knew Jonah well by the time he returned to Wesley for his fourth-form year. I knew of his reputation as a bit of an angry kid and, of course, I knew of his reputation as an athlete. I've seen a lot of kids over the years, some truly remarkable athletes, but what you had in Jonah was this incredible combination. Size, strength and speed – amazing speed for a boy that big. I always felt he would make a great rugby player, but I never expected he would walk straight into the First XV – not without any experience and certainly not at fourteen years of age. Even after he took to rugby, he never ceased to amaze me with his athletic prowess. I genuinely believed he could have become a seriously good decathlete – so strong in the throwing events and absolutely explosive in the sprints.

Personally, I never found Jonah that difficult to handle at school. Sure, he was tough, but he was never a bully. The only potentially ugly incident that really sticks in my mind came in his fourth-form year, when a student burst into my office. His eyes were nearly popping out of his head and he could hardly get his words out. He said Jonah was off to give another boy a hiding. I rushed out of my office and across the quadrangle and finally caught up with Jonah – a very focused Jonah. I suggested he should not continue. He just kept walking. Eventually I grabbed him in a bear hug and held him up as best I could while his anger subsided. I gather this other student had given one of Jonah's relatives a hard time. He could have broken free of my hold and he could have done some awful damage, but we had built this mutual respect. In the end, I think that was what saved the day.

As time went on, I watched with pride as all that pent-up anger disappeared. The school environment was good for Jonah. Even as a rugby player I never once saw his temper get the better of him. That's quite incredible for a boy who had come to Wesley from an obviously troubled and angry background.

There were a few mixed emotions for me when I got my first start for the Wesley College First XV. Chris decided after the team had strung a few wins together that he would rest a number of his top players for the next game. A good mate of mine, Jason Walker, was one of the school's top locks, and he was one of the players Chris decided to rest. To be fair, Chris asked Jason if he minded if I got a run in his spot. Mmm . . . What do they say about never giving a sucker an even break? I had a pretty useful game. Got all my line-out ball, scored a couple of tries and cemented my position in the side. I played twenty-one games that season and poor Jason got relegated to the bench.

I guess you could say Wesley College came of age as a rugby school in 1990. We lost only one match and that was against Auckland's traditionally powerful Mt Albert Grammar. The forwards that year were enormous and I was by no means the biggest player. One of our props tipped the scales at just under 130kg. Hell, our combined weight was more than that of the All Blacks pack. The highlight of the season was winning the New Zealand Schools Championship – the Top Four tournament – in Invercargill. After being beaten in the final the previous year, the win was special for many of the older guys in the team.

It was in my fourth-form year that I first came into contact with a man who would help shape the rest of my life. All the school's rugby players were assembled in the hall one day to listen to this joker with a funny accent talk to us about the game. He was running the Coca-Cola Rugby in Schools programme for the Counties area and he'd brought along two or three All Blacks, including Inga the Winger, the great Va'aiga Tuigamala. I was fourteen, I was cheeky and I wasn't really interested in what Phil or his players had to say. I had gone along mainly because I knew there was free Coke on offer. If you answered questions correctly, your prize was a can of Coke. I positioned myself behind one of the pillars in the hall and just heckled this bloke the whole time. 'Just hand over the Coke,' I kept yelling. In the end he was pretty pissed off. He couldn't work out which boy was giving him a hard time. Welcome to Jonah's world . . . Mr Phil Kingsley Jones.

Before he became world famous as a manager, Phil was a rugby coach. Not a bad one, either. Back in those days he was also in charge of rugby development for the Counties Rugby Union. Chris Grinter apparently rang him one day and said he should come down to Wesley and take a look at a young lock he had just brought into the First XV. Sure enough, Phil turned up to have a look at me – nowadays, though, he tells everyone he was looking at other players – and the next thing I knew I was put into a development squad and then included in the Counties Secondary Schools team. Phil and I became close that year. I travelled to all the tournaments with him. What a circus . . .

The first time I hopped in the car with him he had Elvis Presley blaring from the cassette player. 'Oh, man. What have I got myself into?' I thought. I went straight for the eject button and popped in a rap music tape I had on me. 'What the hell is that?' Phil said. 'That, Mr Kingsley Jones, is music,' I replied. After that, Phil made a rule that he reckoned we were going to stick by for the rest of the year. I could play my stuff on the way to the games and he would play his music on the way back.

I don't like to admit it, but I got to quite like Elvis and some of the other old stuff Phil used to play. In fact, in the end, I was quite happy to let him have his way on both legs of the trip and after a few months we were both singing along, Elvis Presley cranked up to the max. A Welsh Kiwi and a young Pacific Island boy singing off the same song sheet. It was classic. Phil reckons I liked the music loud because that's the way all the 'bros' liked it. In truth, the volume was always up loud to try and drown out the constant pinging noise coming from the dashboard every time Phil got over 90km/h in that crappy old car he used to drive.

Phil Kingsley Jones (personal manager to Jonah Lomu): Despite the fact I recognised real talent in Jonah as a youngster, I never treated him any differently than any of the other players, but it's fair to say I did spend more time with him than most of the others. In those early days he wasn't the easiest boy to communicate with. He was different. He still is. He liked to dress differently and back then he sure as hell acted differently to most kids. Often he would turn up for training wearing what I thought were outrageous clothes. Bandanas were always a favourite. I'd say to him, 'You can't come here dressed like that. Are you off to rob a bank, or what?' Depending on his mood, he'd either go back to college and change or he just wouldn't come back at all.

I remember selecting him very early on in the piece for a development side to play in a senior sevens tournament run by the Counties Rugby Union. The organisers were short of one team and, to avoid the bye, I got a pick-up side together from a bunch of schools in South Auckland. Once I told everyone that Jonah was in the team, I had no problem getting players. We trained on the Tuesday and Thursday prior to the big event at Pukekohe Stadium on the Sunday. Well, ten minutes before kick-off there was no sign of Jonah. My worst fears were realised when a little boy wearing a black and white Wesley College blazer raced up to me and said that Jonah's aunty was ill and he wouldn't be able to make it. The other boys were hugely disappointed. I was gutted myself, but I tried to act like it wasn't a problem for us. God, if they'd only known. I mean, this was a kids' team playing in a men's competition.

Just before the players ran out for the start of the match – a big one first up against the teak-tough Army boys – I caught sight of Jonah charging towards me. He was sweating and breathing heavily. I think he'd run about 20km to get to the tournament. 'Sorry mate,' he said. I wasn't listening. I let him stew for a couple of minutes before I pulled him aside and said, 'This isn't good enough. This is a team, son, and the guys here are relying on you. You can't just turn up when it suits you. Sit out this game.'

A few minutes into the game I looked over at the big fella and I could see the hurt written all over his face. He was genuinely sorry. In the finish I relented and put him on. Call me soft – or call me realistic. By the time I put him on we were down 16–0 and, it appeared, we didn't have a prayer. That was until the boy started getting the ball. I'm not exaggerating when I say he almost single-handedly buried the opposition. Those big Army boys just couldn't handle him. At the final whistle we had lost by just a couple of points. Army went on to win the tournament. We went into the shield competition for first-round losers and won our remaining matches by wide margins. Boys against men. That day the people of Counties got their first real taste of Jonah Lomu. He was fifteen.

My first taste of international rugby came in 1991, when I was picked for the New Zealand Under-17 team to play Australia. We beat the Aussies 25–0 that year, but really it was in my final couple of years at school that things started to happen for me on the rugby field. By then I had switched to No. 8 and because of Wesley's success, particularly in sevens and the Top Four competition, we were starting to get noticed. In 1992, I had a pretty big year for Wesley. The thirty tries I scored in seventeen matches I'm sure helped when it came to selection for the New Zealand Secondary Schools side. That year, the schools side played a Test against Ireland before going on a short tour of Australia.

The star of the side was a blond-headed fullback from Southland called Jeff Wilson. I had heard of his reputation before we assembled for the Ireland Test in New Plymouth, but I had never seen him play. With time almost up against Ireland, we were awarded a penalty about 45m out from the Irish line and about 5m in from the touchline. We were one point behind the visitors and it was blowing an absolute gale. Jeff was a wonderful kicker, but even so, I still gave him almost no chance of slotting the goal. I was standing behind him as he lined the kick up. It was like watching Tiger Woods over a putt. The wind was so strong that he aimed way outside the right-hand upright. In the end, he judged it perfectly. It swung back from a mile outside the posts and went straight through the middle to give us the win.

The Irish were gutted as the final whistle sounded. Many of them just dropped to their knees and some of them were in tears. I was still nodding my head when I went up to Jeff at the end of the match. 'You are the man,' I said. After the Australian tour, where we won all three games, I knew Jeff was destined to become an All Black — I just didn't realise it would be the following year.

I was on a weekend home pass from Wesley that day when my father threw me out of home. Once I had questioned his authority it was all over for me. From that day on, I spent all my free weekends and holidays at the homes of friends and learned very early on to fend for myself. Life at Wesley College was beginning to treat me just fine, but I still missed seeing my family and friends in Mangere. I missed those days of cricket and longball and rugby league out on the streets. I missed the little stuff. Nicking fruit with other kids from an orchard and sprinting off and laughing as the owner yelled insults at us. I missed those games of volleyball at the park. Tongans, Europeans and Samoans. Sometimes we couldn't understand each other, but we were all there for just one reason — to have fun. On those occasions we all mixed so well.

Religion has always played a big part in my life. When I was growing up there were always church groups organising gatherings in South Auckland. Summer barbecues where the kids would laugh and play and get a bit of stability into their lives. Like many Tongans, I worshipped at the Methodist church in Mangere. It was a weird environment in many ways. You see, the church is right next to a pub and booze wholesaler. The betting shop, the TAB, is part of the same complex. Sitting on the steps of the church, I would often watch drunks stagger out of the pub and I can't begin to recall how many fights I witnessed from those steps. One day I remember the minister's son getting chucked out of the pub. He was literally thrown through a window. All this sort of stuff was taking place only a few metres from the church door. This was South Auckland . . . and this was just part of life.

Nowadays, I'm not a great churchgoer, but my faith is still important to me. In day-to-day life, I take on board what I think is important from the religious beliefs I was taught when I was young. I pray to God for guidance and protection. I sometimes pray to God for help. If I get a chance these days, I'll go to church. For me, though, my religion is much more of a personal thing.

In 1993, I was head-hunted by a number of schools. I had, I suppose, built up this reputation as a pretty useful rugby player and I was continually being asked to change schools. But I never once gave any serious consideration to the offers. I enjoyed Wesley and in my final year I was rewarded with the honour of being made head boy and captain of the First XV. The rugby we played that year was fantastic. Although we lost a couple of games along the way, we took some of New Zealand schoolboy rugby's greatest prizes, including the Top Four title, when we beat St Paul's in the tournament final at Hamilton. We also won the Condor National Sevens title in Auckland. I had a ball at that event, scoring three tries in the semi-final against St Kentigern College, and four against Te Awamutu College in the final. One especially satisfying game of fifteens for me came against Rotorua Boys High School. They had been on an impressive winning roll which we halted by 43–10. My five tries that day sure helped.

Many of the country's rugby stars of the future were selected for the New Zealand Secondary Schools side to play 'Tests' against England and Australia late in the 1993 season. Anton Oliver captained the New Zealand team from hooker, while in the backs a couple of the up-and-comers were Carlos Spencer and Christian Cullen. We scored big wins in both matches. I had a pretty good game against England Schoolboys in Dunedin. I scored a try and made quite a few busts. I think I decided pretty early on in my career that I enjoyed playing against the English . . .

Right through those school years my biggest supporter was my mother. You know, as much as I hold a grudge against my father, Mum was always there for me. When I wasn't with Phil, it was Mum who would take me to all the trials. My parents had this beat-up little Mazda 323 back then and Mum followed me all over the North Island in that old car. She even drove down to Gisborne once to watch me play. How the hell the car lasted the six- or seven-hour trip, I'll never know. Right to this day Mum has remained my greatest supporter and my number one fan. Things have never been easy for her, but through everything she has remained the rock of the Lomu family. She wasn't just there for me, she was there for all the kids, too. She suffered a lot in the early days when my father was drinking heavily, and it was tough on her when John and I left home, but she has never complained. She is a great woman.

I returned to school for only a month or so in 1994, but my heart wasn't really in it. There was mounting pressure from a number of provinces, especially Auckland, to switch unions. For me, though, the decision to stick with Counties wasn't that hard. I just walked into Phil Kingsley Jones's office one day and said, 'I want to play for Counties.' There was no emotion on Phil's face. He just said, 'Okay.' I knew deep down, though, he was delighted. I owed Counties and I owed Phil.

Rugby was still an amateur game back in 1994. I came out of Wesley College with the School Certificate and my Sixth Form Certificate. I had no money and I needed a job. Phil sat me down and told me it was time to write up my CV. It took me three hours to list my sporting achievements. It took about two minutes to list my academic ones. When Phil took me for my first job interview I couldn't have been more nervous. Despite the fact the guy we were going to meet at the Auckland Savings Bank was a mate of Phil's, I was nervous as hell. However, the couple of tips

Phil gave me before the interview would stand me in good stead — not just for the interview, but for the rest of my life. Polynesians are naturally shy. Eye contact with strangers is not the norm. When I met Mr Jim Anderson of the ASB I greeted him with a firm handshake and I looked him squarely in the eye.

Two weeks after sitting a customer service officer's test I was working in the Pakuranga branch of the ASB. When I started, I knew bugger all about the banking world, but I grew to love life in the bank and, as well, I loved meeting people. The staff at Pakuranga were good people and really made me feel welcome. I had no idea at the time that I would remain with the bank for four or five years and that I would eventually move into the marketing office in town. For the moment, though, I was earning some money and living for the day when I could break into provincial rugby. Life was pretty sweet after five years at boarding school.

CHAPTER FOUR

11 IS THE LONELIEST NUMBER

The call from Counties coach, Ross Cooper, came early in 1994. It must have been after midnight and I was asleep. He asked me if I'd like to play some sevens for the union. I barely remember the conversation, but somewhere along the line I must have mumbled a 'yes'. When he rang back the next morning he confirmed I hadn't been dreaming and I was on my way to Palmerston North for my first national sevens tournament.

In those days, I thought this was as good as it gets. Sure, I'd played for plenty of New Zealand and provincial age-group sides, but this was senior footie. Never mind that it was only sevens. Counties could field a side of real stars in those days – speedy, skilful players like Joeli Vidiri, Luke Erenavula and Junior Paramore. Despite a few close calls, we progressed through the pool matches and quarter-finals. By the time we met Otago in the semis we were really firing. I was having a good time and in the final I managed three tries as we put Waikato away and grabbed the Telecom Cup – Counties' first win at the nationals since 1985.

That sevens event, I'm sure, was when I first came to the attention of the All Blacks selectors. I'd played well and was actually named player of the tournament. I know that All Blacks coach, Laurie Mains, spoke to Ross Cooper just after the tournament and suggested he'd like to see me on the wing for the Counties representative side in its opening few matches. I'm not sure if Ross was all that thrilled with the idea, but I certainly didn't have a problem when he asked me. All my fifteens rugby had been played in the forwards and I kind of liked the idea of mixing it out on the wing for a change. For the moment, though, my attention was totally on sevens.

A few days after the nationals I was picked for the full New Zealand team to play a tournament in Fiji and then to go on to Hong Kong for the big annual event. We got beaten in extra time in the semi-finals in Suva by an Eastern Fijian XV which went on to beat the full Fijian side in the final. Our team was full of great sevens players, including Eric Rush, Dallas Seymour and Graeme Bachop. I picked up four tries and was pretty satisfied with my effort. At eighteen, I was the baby on the trip – something I would get used to over the next few years.

Despite coming down with food poisoning early on, my first trip to Hong Kong was a blast. I'm not sure what I picked up, but I was certainly feeling crook just after we arrived. I clearly remember Rushie and coach Gordon Tietjens coming to my room and asking me whether I thought I'd be okay to play. I just said, 'You give me that black jersey and I'll be right – sweet as.' I got straight out of bed, made it through the first training session and went on to play every game. Food poisoning or not, this was a New Zealand jumper and I wasn't going to miss the opportunity. Not only did we win the tournament, but I had the time of my life. Fiji was great, but it was in Hong Kong that I really started to feel like I was representing New Zealand in a truly international competition. I just fell in love with the place. The atmosphere and excitement the city generates during sevens week are like nothing else on the circuit. Only Wellington gets close to the buzz of the Hong Kong tournament.

By now I had become firm friends with many of the players in the New Zealand side. Rushie was becoming more like an older brother to me and I was in awe of Gordon Titch Tietjens. Even back then, his fitness sessions were tough. Now they are legendary. Like a great horse trainer, he makes sure his players are always ready to race. In addition, he has a unique ability to re-create game situations on the training field. Players have always wanted to play for Titch and that's something that not all coaches can claim. It's a special gift.

However, Hong Kong in 1994 belonged to Glen Osborne. Oz is one of the great characters off the field. He's got a marvellous sense of humour and is always taking the mickey, often out of himself. Come game time, though, he switches on. And in Hong Kong that year he switched on big-time. Oz was the key to New Zealand's win in the tournament. There are some guys who just can't get to grips with the open spaces in sevens rugby. Not Oz. He's a natural. His running that year was some of the best I've ever seen and although he scored only four tries, he set up heaps of others. He also got plenty of points with his boot and was deservedly named player of the tournament as we beat Fiji in the semis, then Australia in the final. It was a special moment for Rushie, too, who hadn't tasted success in Hong Kong since 1989, and for Titch, as well. This was his first year in charge of New Zealand and the beginning of an amazing coaching career.

I fell in love with sevens that year and it's something I've never quite got out of my system. Part of the attraction, of course, has been the space the game allows me and part of it has been the mates I've made in the New Zealand team and the great adventures we've enjoyed all over the world. There has been plenty of success, too — in Hong Kong in the mid-nineties, in Kuala Lumpur in 1998 when I was part of the New Zealand team which struck

gold at the Commonwealth Games, and the World Cup in
Argentina in 2001.

Actually, my first taste of big-time sevens came a couple of
years before breaking into the New Zealand team. When I say
big-time, I mean it, well, in the loosest possible sense. I was playing
in a touch competition at the Weymouth Rugby Club in Counties
and in one match I came up against Rushie, who by then was
already a sevens legend. I got the drop on Rushie in this game,
sidestepped him and scooted away to score. Incidentally, he hates
being reminded of that! After the match he introduced himself
and asked me if I'd like to play sevens with him in Singapore. I
jumped at the chance. 'When can you be ready?' he asked. 'We
fly out in two days – you got a passport?' I rushed straight home
and packed. I wasn't going to miss this opportunity. Two days
later I'm at the airport early and raring to go. I hand Rushie my
passport and he looks at it in total disbelief. 'Sixteen! You're sixteen
years old?' At that time I didn't think it was such a big deal. 'Yes,
Mr Rush, I've always looked older than what I really am,' I replied.
Rushie shrugged his shoulders. 'We'd better keep this one quiet,
bro,' he said.

The team was called the Mongrels. It was an unofficial pick-
up side that used to play various tournaments around the world.
This particular tour included players like Glen Osborne and Peter
Woods, two of New Zealand's greatest sevens players, and the
street-smart and, as I was to find out, highly dangerous Lindsay
Raki, known as the Croc. Raki loved practical jokes and most of
all he loved young blood to practise on. The first thing he told
me at the airport was that I was not to utter a word to Rushie
during the whole trip. If he talks to you, Raki said, you musn't
answer. I'm thinking this must be some sort of respect thing.
Little did I know it was Raki's bizarre idea of initiation into the
Mongrels. So Rushie's talking to me throughout the tour and I

just don't say a word back. I nod politely and mumble at the ground. I followed this routine for days. Rushie, of course, was in on the game, but he never let on. He would say to me, 'Why aren't you talking to me?' I couldn't answer. Respect, I'm thinking, respect. Eventually they let me in on the joke. The whole team cracked up. I'm still waiting to get one back on Raki.

Eric Rush (All Black 1992, 93, 95, 96, New Zealand Sevens 1989–2003): From the first moment I saw the big man – hell, he was just a boy back then – I knew he could be anything he wanted in sevens. Absolutely awesome. The most destructive player the game has seen. On that Mongrels trip to Singapore, back in 1992, we were due to meet a local side in our final pool match. They had been thrashed by everyone else and we knew we'd do it easy against them. Well, Jonah being the new kid on the block, we gave him his instructions before the match: 'Jonah, you're on your own in this one. We'll help you with the first kick-off, but after that it's up to you.' And that's exactly the way it happened. The rest of the team just ran around doing nothing. Jonah would score the try, kick the conversion, trot back, catch their kick-off and go again. We never tackled anyone and none of us had one run with the ball. Nothing. Final score: Jonah Lomu 36, Locals 0. Unbelievable. Sure, the local side wasn't exactly full of giants, but this kid was just sixteen.

Things have always been the same since that first tournament. The constant has been the destruction and sheer power. He gave us a psychological edge over the Fijians from his very first encounter with them. They had been the kings at Hong Kong, but Jonah's introduction to them in 1994 changed all that and for three years running we took the title. It's not that they were scared of him, but I'm sure if they'd had a choice they'd have run the other way. I clearly remember one of the Fijian forwards — a good player and a bit of a hit man — lining Jonah up early in the final. He tried to put in a shot on the big boy, who was going at full pace. He was nearly knocked out. After that, they just didn't want to know him.

After my return from Hong Kong things got serious. Ross Cooper selected me — on the wing — for my first first-class game, against Horowhenua in Levin. That game is still a bit of a blur to me — free-flowing and heaps of tries. I got three as we scored over a hundred points. It was satisfying in that respect, but wing was still a completely new deal and it was hard to judge my own perform-ance in a match like that. I really didn't have a clue what I was doing. Christian Cullen was at fullback for Horowhenua that day in only his second first-class game. To be fair, it was probably a lot harder for him being on the end of a hiding like that.

When Ross told me after the game that the All Blacks selec-tors had me in their sights as a wing I couldn't believe it. I was still only eighteen and had played just one game in that position. When I got the call-up for the first All Blacks trial in Gisborne, I was staggered. Hong Kong sevens, provincial football, All Blacks trial. Everything was moving so fast — it was like a never-ending fairytale.

One thing I quickly found when I got to Gisborne was that the national set-up was far removed from what I'd experienced in my short time with Counties. My team — the Possibles — included some of the greatest names in New Zealand rugby. Sean Fitzpatrick was captain and around him he had guys like Mike Brewer and Richard Loe. Whereas I had been able to handle the transition comfortably enough at Counties, here it was different. This was the real deal.

Instead of trying to soak up everything, I kept to myself. The training sessions were more physical than anything I'd been used to. Players were hitting very hard and for a while I thought a lot of the aggression was centred on me. I began to have doubts. Was I really wanted? It's a thought I would carry with me for a long time. It's easy enough for me to look back now and say, 'Hey, that's just the All Blacks way. You train the way you're going to play. No holding back.' Back then, though, I was the new kid in every sense and I didn't know how to take it. As if the training and this new environment weren't scary enough, in the back of my mind was the thought of marking one of my childhood heroes.

In 1994, John Kirwan was coming to the end of his All Blacks career, but to me he was still the greatest. I had just turned twelve when he was starring for New Zealand at the 1987 World Cup. Now he would be on the right wing, opposing me in my first All Blacks trial, just ten days after my nineteenth birthday. With only eighty minutes' experience on the wing in just one first-class game, I was having some nervous moments. However, as it turned out, my Possibles side won the match comfortably and I thought I performed well enough. While I was exposed defensively a few times, I didn't get many opportunities on attack. There were a couple of line breaks which lifted my confidence, but I was mostly concerned with my tussle with JK. The fact that I didn't get a try in our 50-point win was offset by the fact that he didn't get one, either.

The excitement of my first All Blacks trial in some ways over-shadowed some of the self-doubt I was having about my switch to the backs. The truth is that I was absolutely lost at times. My schoolboy rugby had been confined mainly to the loose forwards, apart from odd stints at lock. Stay tight, get loose? That was all so natural. Playing on the left wing at provincial level in New Zealand was a completely foreign experience. Counties' next match would be my first game at home, against Hawke's Bay at Pukekohe, and while I managed a try in our win, the whole wing thing was still causing me headaches. I knew deep down that I was just getting by.

When I was named in the final trial to pick the All Blacks team to play France in Christchurch, I made a mental decision to just put everything else out of my mind. I told myself that the selectors were showing faith in me and that I had to perform to the best of my abilities. Forget all that stuff about not being good enough. I had to get rid of any negative thoughts and simply try to fit in. Here was my chance to press for the ultimate honour. Although I tried not to take too much notice of it at the time, there was a lot of media hype around that trial. Much of it concerned me and that the Probables side I had been selected in was close to Laurie Mains's shadow Test team.

The final trial at Napier was very different to Gisborne. Whereas many of New Zealand's top players had been missing from the first trial, all the stars were on show at Napier. One of those players, Eric Rush, was already figuring prominently in my life. Another, Jeff Goldie Wilson, had already been an All Black and would go on to be my wing partner in countless Tests. They had not been at Gisborne because their respective provincial sides had been involved in a national championship match the day before. This time they were in the opposing Possibles team. I would mark Goldie and John Kirwan would mark Rushie.

Eric Rush: My advice to Jonah has always been the same: 'Never give anyone a second chance, bro.' Before that trial in Napier it was no different. I told him I expected him to go hard against me. I said that next time we might be in the same team, and we might have a mate playing for the oposition, and I didn't want to be looking over my shoulder and wondering whether he was giving it a hundred per cent. 'Just smash 'em, Jonah, and don't be afraid to give it to me, either,' I told him. Yeah . . . famous last words, those were.

Early in the trial a high kick went up. It was my ball. I knew I had to take it. And then the ground shook. Boom, boom, boom – it was like rolling thunder. I knew he was coming – the big boy was bearing down on me. Shit! This is a bloody All Blacks trial. Catch it, Eric, just bloody catch it. And still I hear boom, boom, boom . . . Up I went and I'm thinking, I'm dead. I'm friggin' dead. And then I've caught the ball and it's just like slow motion as I'm coming back down. This huge shadow's right on top of me. I'm thinking about all the advice I've handed out. 'Just smash 'em, Jonah,' I'd said. Eric, you big-mouth. And then he's on me. I'm waiting for the lights to go out and the scream of the ambulance siren. But no. He wraps his big arms around me and says, 'You're lucky this time, old man.' I've never been so grateful in all my life.

Under the bright lights in Napier, JK and I both got amongst the tries. He scored twice and I got over the line once as we put the Possibles away. I was satisfied with my performance, but as I headed for the traditional after-match function I had few expectations. Waiting for the announcement of an All Blacks team is, I suppose, a bit like waiting for exam results. There is no middle ground. You've either passed or failed. Given that I had simply refused to believe I'd be selected, the announcement came like an almighty bolt. When I heard my name read out I was ecstatic. I tried to look calm and composed, but inwardly I wanted to jump up and scream and shout. I was young and naïve about many things concerning the All Blacks, but I did realise that a lot of other players with similar dreams to mine had missed out.

One of them was Rushie. After the team announcement he was the first person to congratulate me. He has always been such a great supporter of mine. We were both vying for the same position, but it never seemed to concern him that he was offering free advice to a player who was going after exactly the same spot. Rushie had been an All Black since 1992. He'd had a dozen games in the black jersey, but not one of them had been a Test match. I knew just how much that Test jersey meant to him. What can I say? The man is gold.

Sure enough, that shadow Test team from Napier was selected in its entirety to meet France in the first Test. For Jonah Lomu, the rocket-ship ride continued. Four first-class games — two of them All Blacks trials — and four victories. Could nothing go wrong? I was about to find out.

The intensity of Test week is as demanding mentally as it is physically. Right from the first team meeting your senses are on high alert. For my first Test in Christchurch they roomed me with John Kirwan. It was a fairly logical decision by team management. JK had played nearly sixty Tests by this stage and his knowledge and experience proved a great help to me. He tried his best all week to keep me relaxed and make me feel comfortable in the All Blacks environment.

I trained hard in the days leading up to the Test and tried to absorb as much as I could. I knew Laurie Mains and Earle Kirton were watching me closely and I was aware that I was also coming to the attention of another person making his debut that week, none other than the legendary Colin Meads. This was Colin's first Test as All Blacks manager. He wasn't just the manager, though. He was the man and we would develop a great relationship over the next couple of years.

Receiving my first All Blacks jersey was something I'll never forget. To receive it from Colin Meads was a huge honour. On the morning of the match I knocked on the great man's door. It's fair to say I was shitting myself. Colin opened the door and there before me were all the Test jerseys, carefully laid out. I was so nervous I can't recall exactly what he said to me. What I do remember, though, is him grabbing my hand in that great mitt of his and wishing me well for the Test. We were staying at the sprawling Russley Hotel and it was a fair hike between rooms. I clutched that jersey tight and on the way back to my room wondered whether I was really an All Black. When I got there I sat on the bed and stared at the No. 11 on the back of the black shirt. I thought about the game ahead and I thought about my performance. I didn't want to let myself down. I desperately wanted to play well in that jersey.

Before kick-off I was, not surprisingly, having difficulty keeping my emotions in check. The anthem made it worse and I was close to breaking up. It was the realisation of a dream which, in reality, had only started a month or so earlier, when I was unexpectedly given an All Blacks trial. The hype about my age – youngest Test All Black and all that – was something I never worried about and, to be honest, when you're in the All Blacks environment those sorts of things become secondary to the job at hand. Besides, right through my school days I was used to playing in teams where I was often the youngest player. I gave it little thought before the match against France. It was really no different for me than for any other member of the All Blacks side that day. I wanted to play well, of course, but most of all I wanted to win. That's always been my focus.

However, what began as a day of great expectations for me turned into a disaster. The game was disappointing; the loss embarrassing. The All Blacks are never expected to lose and they're certainly not supposed to lose at home. It is simply not tolerated. In Christchurch that day we never really got into the game and, although there was only a try apiece in it, the French converted all their kicks, including three dropped goals, and were deserving winners. I envied them. They had turned the hundredth Test match of their great centre, Philippe Sella, into a party. For Jonah Lomu, in his first Test, there would be no celebration.

After the match, the mood in the dressing room was low, to say the least. Laurie Mains was as straight and direct as only Laurie can be. As far as my performance went, he told me that he didn't believe I'd done too much wrong in the game, but that I'd have to work on getting all the little things right. He put my mistakes down to a lack of experience in the position, but there was no ranting or raving. His words gave me encouragement but they couldn't take away all the pain of the loss. As I walked out of the dressing room I was reminded by several players that All Blacks always hold their heads high win or lose. It's something I've tried to carry with me throughout my career. Sometimes it's not easy . . .

Laurie Mains (All Blacks coach 1992–1995): 'We knew Jonah wasn't really ready for that level of rugby back in 1994, but we were, I believe, realistic in our expectations. There was huge potential in the young man to do something outstanding for the World Cup in 1995. We were prepared, at that stage, to go through the pain of introducing him to Test rugby. The selectors never expected him to play like an experienced Test campaigner, especially given that he was in a completely new position.

Before the match, assistant coach Earle Kirton and myself were reluctant to try and fill his head up with too much. Sure, we talked about defensive lines and told him to run hard when he got the ball in hand. Mostly, though, we encouraged him to just be himself. We had seen this huge potential in him and that's why we selected him through those trial games. Jonah wasn't easy to communicate with back then, because he was just so shy. He had great respect for the team and the management but, again, the communication thing tended to be one way.

Any failings in Jonah's game that day were our responsibility, not his. We had placed him in a position that really was way ahead of what he'd been prepared for. For our part, we saw it as a learning experience. Anything he did do well would be a positive and we could always build on things that went wrong. We were convincingly beaten in Christchurch, but it wasn't because of Jonah. The forwards lacked control and we lost a lot of ball. Afterwards we were conscious about tidying up our whole game and getting stronger field position. Remember, this was a very good French side. We knew we had to lift our game as a team.

Despite our loss in Christchurch, confidence was high for the second Test in Auckland. By the end of the week, I was believing in myself again. The experienced players in the side kept telling me I was the best player for the position. The message was simple: 'Get out there and play your natural game. If you weren't the best left wing you wouldn't have been selected.' That's the thing about the All Blacks — there are never any negatives when you're preparing for a Test, even if you have just dropped the first game of a series. No side beats us before the match. We could get stuffed by forty points, but we always come off the park believing that we'll get 'em next week. Losing is not an option. It's just not in the All Blacks culture. Everything is about belief — belief in yourself, belief in your team-mates and, above all, it's about belief in the jersey. If that sounds a bit corny, then I'm sorry. It's the truth. I've never prepared for a match in the black jersey any other way.

I can't remember having any one-on-ones with the coaches before the Auckland Test. Any advice from Laurie and Earle was given to me in the team environment. I was inexperienced, end of story, but still I was encouraged to be myself and work on the basics. We dominated the French in the second Test at Eden Park. For about seventy minutes we owned the game. The forwards were fantastic and we had enough ball and territory to win the match easily. I was still finding life difficult in my positional play, but I was confident right to the death – right until that final kick from Stephen Bachop. The whole movement is still so clear in my mind – from Saint-Andre through all those pairs of hands to the final touchdown by Sadourny. The try from the end of the world, the French called it. The end of the world? I wished the world had opened up and swallowed me. What can I say? I missed a tackle that was there to be made. I had to make a decision and in the end I didn't. No-man's-land. In rugby, especially Test rugby, those decisions have to be made, and when you're on the wing they have to be made in a split second. France 23, New Zealand 20.

Even to this day, I think about it. I could have stopped that try and we'd have squared the series. In the end, I didn't tackle anyone. I still feel I cost the All Blacks that game.

Laurie Mains: Jonah has always been too tough on himself when it comes to that particular try. Stephen Bachop put in a very good kick. It went deep into the corner and simply took a rotten bounce. There were any number of players in that counter-attack by France who had opportunities to snuff out the movement. They didn't do their jobs, either. Management never apportioned any more blame to Jonah than to any other player who could have made a crucial tackle; made the French run down a channel where they would have been picked up. It was late in the game and the players were tired. Jonah is wrong to beat himself up over his part in the try.

If I thought the feeling was bad after Christchurch, it got even worse after Auckland. The media had a field day and reminded the whole country that this was the first time in history that the All Blacks had lost a series to France. I found it difficult to get a line on what the coaches were thinking about me. I didn't know where I stood and I felt quite alone. I'm certainly not blaming Laurie. His style has always been to separate himself from the players. He's always been a hard-arse when it comes to player/coach relationships, but at that stage of my career I didn't understand him. I never questioned myself about whether I was good enough to play at that level. I believed that in time I could come to grips with the position. The feeling was more one of loneliness: am I wanted? I've never been a great talker about a game once it's over. No post-mortems for me. I kept a lot of what I thought to myself and that's when the self-doubt creeps in – when you start to think you're on your own.

Meanwhile, as we were playing the French, South Africa had arrived in New Zealand for a three-Test series. It was their first tour since 1981 and the whole country seemed to be talking about it. The first Test was to be played just days after the second Test against the French. I had expected the news that I wouldn't be involved against the Springboks even before Laurie delivered it to me. He told me before the team meeting at the Poenamo Hotel in Auckland the day after the Test. He grabbed me and Matthew Cooper, who had partnered Frank Bunce in the centres against France, and took us outside. He pulled me aside first and I knew what was coming. He said he wanted me to get more experience on the wing and that he and the other selectors felt the best way I could get that was by playing for the New Zealand Colts and then returning to provincial rugby. It was sad knowing I wasn't going to be part of the All Blacks set-up, but hardly a shock. I simply made a pledge to myself that next time around I would make sure I was a more complete player – a better player than I had been against the French.

Laurie Mains: If things had gone more smoothly in the French series we would have retained Jonah, but not keeping him on wasn't a reflection of what we thought of him at that time. More, it was a case of saying, 'We've got a great deal of potential here. We don't want to destroy this kid.' The Springboks were a very good team and the series against them was to be followed by a one-off test against Australia, the reigning World Champions. We felt it was better to let Jonah settle down and learn the position through the National Championship. We were simply not willing to push him over the edge and knock his confidence and belief in his ability to play wing. The World Cup was looming large and Earle and I knew we had something very special in Jonah Lomu. We had to manage him the best way possible.

Rugby Park, Te Kuiti, is about as far removed from Eden Park or Lancaster Park as you can get, but that's where I found myself after the French series. My first game back for Counties was in its National Provincial Championship (NPC) opener against King Country. I'd have to say it was a refreshing change to have all the pressure taken off me. Ross Cooper told me he expected me to play to my potential, but really it was nothing like the pressure-cooker stuff I'd just experienced with the All Blacks. The game gave me the opportunity to be myself again. I was back in a more relaxed, familiar environment, with players that I knew. I picked up a try in the match, but more than anything I just enjoyed the chance of having a run with the ball. It was like a huge weight had come off my shoulders.

By the time the New Zealand Colts tour came around at the end of July, I was itching to be part of the action. The team headed to Australia, where we played three matches, including a game against Australia Under-21. It was a New Zealand side packed with players who would go on to represent the All Blacks. In the backs we had Andrew Mehrtens, Justin Marshall and Tana Umaga, and among the forwards were Anton Oliver, Kees Meeuws and captain, Taine Randell. Tana and I were the wings for all three matches and we had a ball in the two lead-up games before the match against Australia, picking up ten tries between us. Our 'Test' against Australia was played as the curtain-raiser to the Wallabies–Western Samoa match at the Sydney Football Stadium and, while neither of us scored in that match, we were delighted to beat the arch-enemy. Very satisfying, too, for guys like Mehrts, Adrian Cashmore and Taine, who, a year earlier, had been in the Colts side which had been thrashed by Australia in Auckland.

On my return from the Australian tour I was determined to play well and soak up as much experience as I could. The National Championship would give me that chance. Counties had a decent sort of a side back then with a competitive forward pack and pace to burn in the backs. Things looked good when we beat Otago at Carisbrook in Dunedin and followed that up with a win at home against Wellington. I was loving it. With the win against King Country thrown in, Counties was three for three and riding high at the top of the NPC table. I'd scored tries in all three matches and was looking forward to facing North Harbour at Takapuna.

To say I was brought back to earth at Onewa Domain would be an understatement. Counties had a set midfield move which wasn't really that complicated. Suffice to say, it went horribly wrong this day and I finished up with my back to the opposition and got blindsided by the Harbour captain, Richard Turner. Known to everyone as Pod, he was one of the hardest hitters in the game. Part Samoan, he's as big as me and was always ferocious in the tackle. Well, he hit me in the midriff and the roar from the crowd was massive. Down I went . . . and I couldn't get up. I couldn't feel my legs. I was just rolling around saying, 'My legs. I can't feel my legs.' I swear that to this day I have never been hit that hard. Next thing, Rushie's standing over me, shouting, 'Get up. You're okay. Just get up!' But I wasn't okay. I had no feeling at all in my legs. Rushie showed no sympathy. It was his way of telling me that I couldn't show I was hurt. How's that? He's playing for the bloody opposition. Eventually I got to my feet, but didn't take much more part in the game.

At that stage of my career, I don't think players were particularly targeting me – that was to come later. With Pod, I think it may have had a bit to do with that old Samoan–Tongan thing. The Samoans are the biggest hitters in the game. Outside of Richard, I'd say hooker Trevor Leota, and wing Brian The Practor Lima would be the biggest hitters I've come across (Practor is short for chiropractor . . . say no more). I got to know Richard pretty well after that game and these days, when we run into each other off the field, he always reminds me of the tackle; reckons it was pre-planned. We still joke about it. I tell him it didn't really hurt. He just smiles. My manager, Phil Kingsley Jones, has never let me forget it, either. He takes great delight in winding me up about it.

Despite losing three of our last four matches in the NPC, we proved we were more than competitive against the big boys. The only match we got hammered in was against Canterbury in our Ranfurly Shield challenge. In our last game of the season, against Auckland, we bounced back to run the eventual national champions very close. In the end, we finished up mid-table.

My first season of first-class rugby had come to an end. There had been many highlights, but, perhaps most importantly, there were a couple of failed tests to reflect on. There was a World Cup coming up in South Africa and I wondered if I was going to be part of it. I'd had a taste of the All Blacks set-up and I wanted more. Complicating my thoughts, though, was another issue — rugby league. Lingering doubts and lurking scouts, you might say. Yeah, I had more than enough to think about over the summer months.

CHAPTER FIVE

BEAM ME UP, LAURIE

Phil Kingsley Jones and I are tight. The arrangement we have is not just a player–manager thing. It goes way beyond that. When I first asked him to help me out, back when I was a youngster, little did I know the relationship would develop into an unbreakable bond — a bond that would tie us together through even the most difficult times. In the ten years we have been together, Phil has been all things to me: a mate and a manager, a brother and, at times, the father I never really had.

Phil and I have been through so much together. I talk to him about my problems and, likewise, if he has any problems, he discusses them with me. I've seen all the crap he's had to put up with over the years. You know, 'Mr Twenty Per Cent' and all that. People look at some of the deals he's done and say he's money-hungry. It just couldn't be further from the truth. Hell, he's my manager. He's just trying to do the best for me and sometimes he has to be tough about protecting my interests. I didn't just become Jonah Lomu the rugby player, I became Jonah Lomu the product. I know that's hard for some people to understand, but that's the way it is. My image is my image. At times, over the years, there have been attempts to hijack that image and make money from it. Some companies think it's their right to use photos of me to try and promote their own products. It's not fair and Phil always seems to cop it for just doing his job. I don't care what people think. Neither of us does. Phil knows only too well how short a player's career really is, and he understands the sacrifices a player must make during that time. It's not just about rugby today. It's also about trying to make sure your future is secure.

One thing that really bugs me is the belief in some quarters that we'll do anything if the money is right. Wrong. I couldn't begin to count the number of times we've turned down good money to endorse a product or make a public appearance because it simply wasn't the image we've wanted to portray. If it's not something I believe in, I won't put my name to it. Phil's the same. Occasionally he'll put up a proposal knowing that I'll probably say no. We don't argue about it. Sure, he will sometimes question my decisions and that's cool. He is, after all, my manager and it's his job to put everything in front of me. Basically, though, he respects my beliefs and he knows that when I say no, I mean no.

Money has never been the first consideration or the driving force in my career. If it had been, then I'd probably have left New Zealand years ago. Phil and I started off with nothing. We've worked hard for everything we've got and there have been no free rides. Along the way we've turned down plenty. When Phil first agreed to be my manager we had no idea it would one day turn into a business of its own – Number 11 Management – employing staff and operating out of its own offices.

After I was dropped following the French series in 1994, everything seemed to come crashing down. One minute I was an All Black who everyone wanted to know. The next I was nothing. Even the car I was given, which was part of the All Blacks 'package', got taken off me. 'You're not in the team, Mr Lomu. Please return the sponsor's car.' I was pretty down and it all came to a head one day when I told Phil – not for the first time – that I wanted to switch to rugby league. I'd enjoyed the game when I was younger and it seemed like a good option with the doors seemingly closed on the All Blacks.

Things got serious when I was approached with an offer by the Canterbury Bankstown rugby league club in Sydney and, while Phil and my great mate Rushie were dead against me changing codes, Phil actually helped set up a visit to the Bulldogs' head-quarters in Sydney. Now, Phil's a rugby man to the core and I don't think he seriously thought I'd actually make a move to the other code. I think he just figured it might be a good way for me to get this 'league stuff' out of my system. The offer from the Canterbury Bulldogs was huge – around Aus$300,000 per season. Remember, there were no rugby union professionals back then and, for a young guy with basically nothing, that sort of money was pretty tempting.

I arranged to meet Phil for lunch at a restaurant close to where I was working at the bank in Pakuranga to talk things over. I was nervous, but eventually managed to get the words out. 'I've made up my mind,' I told him. 'I'm off to Sydney to play rugby league.' 'Oh, is that right, is it?' was all he said. This was never going to be very easy for me. It was obvious from Phil's tone that he wasn't exactly over the moon. 'Yeah, I'm going to play for the Bulldogs, but I'd like you to manage me.' Phil was playing it pretty casual, but was sure making things uncomfortable for me. 'Why would you want me to manage you, Jonah? Sounds like you've got every-thing sorted out.' 'Well, I'm still going to need a manager,' I said. 'You're the man I need.' Phil looked me straight in the eye. 'I'll tell you what, I'll manage you, but it'll be under my terms, and this is what it'll cost . . . ' 'Name your price, Phil,' I said. 'How much do you want – twenty, thirty per cent?' 'No. What I want, Jonah, is your first Test jersey after you make it back into the All Blacks. Give me that jersey. That's all I want.' I was amazed. I knew there and then that Phil was desperate to see me fulfil my dream of playing for the All Blacks in the World Cup. His remarks pretty much convinced me that I should stick with rugby. 'Okay, Phil, it's a deal.' There was no further discussion. For the moment, anyway, rugby league could wait.

The contract was drawn up that night. It didn't run to any great length. In fact, it contained just one paragraph. It said that in return for acting as manager, Phil Kingsley Jones would be paid, 'Jonah Lomu's first Test jersey at the 1995 World Cup'. To this day we still don't have a formal manager–player contract. Everything has been done on a handshake. Our word has always been our bond. I never ever forgot about our first 'deal'. In fact, for the next few months I thought about it constantly. I wanted so much to 'pay' Phil. I wanted that All Blacks jersey so I could give it to him and say thanks.

As much as Phil and I are close, we've had our share of disagreements over the years. It's only to be expected, I guess. We're both strong individuals and we both hate backing down. Once our minds are made up, that's usually it. Probably the worst tantrum I've ever thrown with him was at the end of 2002. I had been invited to be a guest on the British comedy show, *So Graham Norton*. I hate being late for any event, least of all a television show. That night, Phil was holding things up. I was getting sick of waiting for him in the lobby of the hotel while he was up in his room, probably doing his hair for the tenth time. I was bloody annoyed. I rang through to his room and told him to get a move on. He told me not to worry. 'It's all right, mate,' he said. 'We've got plenty of time.' I got even angrier. 'No, mate,' I replied. 'I want to get there early. If you don't hurry up I'm leaving without you.' 'Okay, leave without me if that's what you want to do,' he answered. I did.

When Phil eventually turned up at the studios he was pissed off big-time. He completely lost his nut with me. For quite a while we just sat there fuming at each other, two raging bulls. It's funny looking back at it now, but at the time it wasn't pretty. Like all our arguments, though, it was forgotten by the end of the night. Interestingly, Phil has a different take on this story and actually blames me for being late. Tough luck. It's my book.

Another classic bust-up happened in a car one day, while we were on the way to a golf game in Auckland. I had picked up Phil and we were just shooting the breeze when the conversation turned to a mutual acquaintance. We started off arguing about this guy and eventually we began shouting. Bugger this, I thought. So I just stopped the car in the middle of a busy road. I told Phil to get out and find his own way to the golf course. After he got out of the car I threw his golf clubs out as well. He laughs about this story now. He wasn't laughing at the time, though. He had a fair walk with those clubs on his back.

Phil's got a real quick wit. It obviously comes from his time as a comedian on the club and pub circuit in Britain. One night after he'd appeared on the *Holmes* show I rang him to tell him I wasn't very impressed with his performance. 'Yeah, well sometimes I'm not that impressed with your efforts on the field,' he replied as quick as a flash.

Taupo is many things to many people in New Zealand. Lake Taupo is famous for its boating and its trout fishing and is set among some of the most beautiful scenery in the North Island. Taupo is a great place for a holiday. For me, though, I will always remember the big lake for the three days of sheer hell I endured there in early February 1995. You see, I wasn't in Taupo to catch a trout or laze around on the lakeshore. I was there to prove myself; to prove to the All Blacks selectors that I wasn't some flash in the pan; to let everyone know that I was worthy of the All Blacks jersey; that I was a genuine contender for the World Cup. Lake Taupo 95 – it was sink or swim for Jonah Lomu.

The training camp at Taupo was the third in a series of five the All Blacks selectors were using to help settle on the squad to go to the 1995 World Cup in South Africa. Taupo also happened to be the first camp they had invited me to attend. They had picked a squad of thirty-odd players to attend the first two camps in Queenstown and Auckland in late 1994, but I had only been named in a back-up squad. Finally, it seemed, I was back in the selectors' sights.

Initially I hadn't been too disappointed when I'd missed out on the A squad and I tried not to dwell on it too much over Christmas. Instead, I looked at the positives and took on board the words of encouragement I was getting from Phil and Rushie. 'You're good enough,' they'd both say. 'Just stick at it.' Sevens was also proving a useful distraction and Rushie was always around to give me some added inspiration.

The World Cup, though, was the real carrot and the call for me to join the training camp in Taupo was my All Blacks lifeline. Not wanted in Queenstown or Auckland, this, it seemed, was my last chance. The thing that would keep me going through this camp was the thought of the two losing Tests I'd played in against France. Two Tests. Two losses. That wasn't supposed to be how an All Black started his career and it sure as hell wasn't the way I wanted it to finish. The French series had become a recurring nightmare that I was desperate to get rid of. I was haunted by the first-Test loss, but worst of all was the memory of that missed tackle in the second Test. What did a win in the black jersey feel like? I needed to know. Taupo did not mean an All Blacks jersey, but I looked at it as my third Test.

From the moment we assembled in Taupo, the warning signs were there for all to see. We were called to a team meeting at which Laurie Mains set the tone for the camp. The message came through loud and clear. 'This camp is where we separate the men from the boys,' he said. 'This is where we find out just how much you want the jersey – just how much you want to be in this team. I want to see how much you can give, how much you want to give,' he continued. 'At times you'll feel like giving up – and that's when I'm going to find out who the real men are. At the end of the sessions I don't care if you're walking or you're crawling, just as long as you've showed you want to finish.' The scene was set for the camp from hell.

We trained twice a day and we trained like never before. Even the senior members of the squad, some of whom had been All Blacks since the mid-1980s, were amazed at Laurie's regime. This was basic training at its most brutal. Two three-hour sessions a day. Drills repeated and repeated again. Straight, hard running. Down and ups. Tackling. Hard, no-nonsense tackling. Rucks. Clean-outs. Kicking and retrieving. Over and over. And at the end of the day, when you were gasping for breath and your lungs were screaming, Laurie would yell, 'On the line!' That's when heads would start to drop. We knew what was coming: a series of twenty-two sprints over 150m and after each one the same routine – turn around and walk back to the 22m line and then jog back to the start again. One minute and twenty seconds per set.

The first five sprints are relatively easy. Guys are still talking and there's even the odd joke. After seven the joking stops. After ten no one is talking. You're just concentrating on trying to breathe. At my first session I entered a zone I'd never been near. I was lagging behind and as I was jogging back for the restarts I looked into the eyes of the other players who had already turned and were ready for the next sprint. And all the while I was aware of Laurie watching me . . . watching me with that damned stopwatch in his hand.

The first day was certainly the hardest and along the way I learned a lesson I would never forget. We were coming to the end of the sprints session and, from memory, we had just a couple left. I was running about second to last in my group and I thought I'd hold back for a final push. Big mistake, Jonah. As the last sprint came up, Laurie yelled, 'This is it, boys. Let's all dig it in!' No sweat, Laurie. I charged out of the gates and wiped the field out. I must have won that last sprint by 20m. Laurie was at boiling point when he called me out. 'You were holding back. You couldn't possibly sprint like that if you'd been giving it every-thing. Give me ten down and ups!' The dreaded down and ups. Press-ups, effectively, with 20m sprints in between. As if that wasn't enough, the whole squad was ordered to do two further 150s. I wasn't popular at the end of the session. When I had finished, Laurie fixed me with a cold stare: 'Don't ever do that again.' I didn't.

After Laurie's tough sessions, many of us were like complete zombies. I was so exhausted at night that I could hardly eat my dinner. I've always had a reputation as a big eater, but in Taupo I had no energy left for food. I'd just grab something light and take it to my room. Sleep came as a blessed relief. Safe for another day. Let's see what happens in the morning. When I hit the pillow it was like I'd died and gone to heaven.

Frank Bunce (All Blacks centre 1992–97): Let's get one thing straight. There's not a player or a coach around who would ever tell you Frank Bunce was one of the world's great trainers. What I had in Taupo, though, was a fair bit of savvy — and by God, I needed it. I'd been told by a few of the Otago players back in 1992, when I first came into the All Blacks, that Laurie had mellowed in his approach. Shit, I'd hate to have been involved when he was in his heyday. Taupo remains the most brutal camp I've ever endured. At one point I seriously thought Jonah was going to die — and I also had grave reservations about the amount of time I had left on the planet myself.

What made it harder for Jonah, though, was that he was inexperienced in this sort of environment, an environment that can be hugely intimidating. Basically he was still a shy young Island boy. He kept to himself and never asked questions. The key to a training camp like Taupo, where there are heaps of sprint repetitions, is to find a groove or a rhythm that you are comfortable with. What Jonah failed to understand early on was that the coaches didn't want to see you running at the back for fifteen or twenty of the 150s, and then going on to win the last sprint. I used to tell him to stay with someone like Norm Hewitt. Norm would just guts it out – guts it out at his own pace. Norm never came last and he damned sure never won one.

In the end, though, Jonah came through it, and for that he deserves a lot of credit. I was one who believed from day one he wouldn't last the distance. You've got to remember, there were some very experienced players at the camp who couldn't hack it and were discarded by the selectors. The fact the big boy came out the other end intact is remarkable. It wasn't flash and it sure wasn't pretty, but good on him.

It wasn't just the backs like Frank and Rushie who helped me survive Taupo. I also received encouragement from the forwards. Sean Fitzpatrick and Zinzan Brooke set the standards at that camp. They have always had an amazing attitude to training and a great strength of will. They will never give up, never be beaten. They drove themselves to near breaking point at Taupo and they expected the other players to follow them. As senior players, I sensed they also needed to know which players wanted to be there.

Richard Loe has a reputation as a tough, no-nonsense prop and it's fair to say he's been involved in a few controversial incidents. At Taupo, though, the unlikely Mr Loe was another source of inspiration. Time and again he'd turn to me and say, 'Come on, it ain't far to go.' My mind would start drifting and then he'd be there talking to me and helping me to switch back on. I can still hear him saying, 'Keep going, bud, keep going . . . '

I owe so many players for the support they gave me at Taupo. I've never forgotten their help. It was largely thanks to them that I got the nod for the next camp at Christchurch. I had passed my personal Test. As for Laurie, I always tell anyone who asks that if you've got him on your side he's just the greatest bloke around. If you've won his respect, you've won a major battle. If you don't win that respect, look out. I had high hopes for the next camp. I knew it would be tough, but at least I could mentally prepare myself.

It was a huge disappointment for me that at Christchurch I was unable to perform anywhere near as well as I had at Taupo. Early on in the piece I got a cut on my leg, which quickly became infected, and one morning I woke up and could barely stand on it. This was something I had been used to for most of my life. Whereas other kids would get cuts and scrapes that cleared up in no time, mine would always take ages to come right. Growing up, though, I never gave it much thought. I didn't know any better. I believed it was normal. So my energy levels were down at Christchurch and I knew that a lot of the good work I'd achieved at Taupo was being undone. Laurie spoke to me after the camp and laid it on the line. I had to work on my fitness – and I had to work on it smartly.

Laurie Mains: Jonah showed real courage at Taupo and all of us, including some senior players, felt we had seen something special. Some other players never made it past that camp, because they didn't show that sort of courage. At

Christchurch, which was only a few weeks after the Taupo camp, things changed dramatically for Jonah. We were concerned about his fitness. One thing we noticed early on were some sores on his legs — ugly sores that looked like boils. We obviously didn't know anything about his kidney condition at that stage and we put it down to some bad food we thought he might have eaten.

Brian Lochore, who had been appointed All Blacks World Cup campaign manager, and myself spoke to Jonah before we left Christchurch and said that if we had been selecting the final trial teams for the World Cup to play the following week, he would not have been included. He just wasn't fit enough. We were all worried about him. Meanwhile, Sean Fitzpatrick came to me after the camp and said he believed we needed Jonah to help give us an edge at the World Cup. He said he wanted Jonah to remain on the programme. Other senior players shared the same view. From memory, Olo Brown, Eric Rush and Sean all volunteered to help Jonah out with extra training. That's how much we all believed in him.

The leg infection was a real blow and it prevented me from attending the next training camp at Greymouth, but I was fit enough to turn out for Counties a week or so later at the National Sevens in Palmerston North. I had already been to South America in January for two tournaments with the New Zealand side and I was eager to get among the action again. Counties repeated their success of 1994 in the Nationals and I was rapt to be given special dispensation to tour with the New Zealand side for two further tournaments, one in Fiji and then the big one in Hong Kong. The All Blacks selectors knew I loved sevens and I think they figured it would help with my fitness.

We got knocked out at the quarter-finals stage in Fiji, but we knew we had a classy combination and were still confident of putting on a good show in Hong Kong. Rushie captained a side that included, among a heap of stars, Adrian Cashmore, Joeli Vidiri, Dallas Seymour and a young Christian Cullen. Cully got just one game in Hong Kong that year – his time would come – but it's fair to say that I had a pretty good tournament. I played all five games and picked up five tries, along with the player of the tournament award. We crushed Fiji in the final, giving us back-to-back victories. That was sweet. To this day that victory at Hong Kong remains one of my fondest memories in sevens.

Gordon Tietjens (New Zealand Sevens coach 1994–2003): Jonah had showed enough at Hong Kong in 1994 to suggest he was going to be a great player, particularly in the semi-final against Fiji when he stepped the great Waisale Serevi off his left foot to score New Zealand's first try. That's something I'll never forget. In 1995, though, he went one better in the final when he single-handedly attacked the Fijians. He was totally dominant in that match. Strength, pace and the ability to step – that's just so hard for any opposition to counter. In contested field situations he could take out three or four tacklers, which would free things up for the rest of the side. In all my time as New Zealand sevens coach, Jonah remains one of the quickest players off the mark we ever tested – remarkable for a man of his size.

As far as his fitness was concerned, I never expected him to reach the levels of some of the players I had, but he always worked very hard – to his peak, really. In the sevens environment, the New Zealand team is very close. If Jonah lagged behind, whether it was in shuttles or any other tests, players would always get in behind him. He always responded to that sort of support.

Despite all the hype after the Hong Kong sevens, the old self-doubt was beginning to resurface. I hadn't heard anything from the selectors and I was beginning to think they didn't want me around. I got selected for a NZRU President's XV to play a match against Ross Cooper's New Zealand Divisional XV at Wanganui. Ross's team had just returned from a tour of Canada and Fiji and we were no match for them. It was a fairly low-key game, but I suppose it gave the selectors a chance to look at a few more players. I picked up a couple of tries, but not having had any contact with the selectors made me believe time was running out.

Even after I was selected for the inter-island match at Dunedin in early April, I was still having second thoughts about my career in union and was considering making myself unavailable for the game. I'd just had no vibes at all from the selectors that I was even close to making it back into the 'big' team. Phil and Rushie both knew I was unhappy and that I was again thinking of leaving union – jumping ship and going off to play rugby league. They were still against me making any move, but I'd virtually made up my mind. The two of them are totally different people, but both are equally forceful. Rushie said, 'Hold up. Just come and play with the brothers one more time. Give it a last shot. Play the match and see how you feel afterwards.' At the same time, Phil was working hard behind the scenes to try and find out exactly where I stood.

The league offers were still rolling in. I hadn't yet turned twenty and the money on offer was proving a real draw. Eventually, though, Rushie and Phil won me over. The back line was a sweet temptation. Frank Bunce would be at centre, Oz at fullback and Rushie was named on the other wing. I'd play with the bros one more time, but after that I was outta there. Or so I thought . . .

It's amazing what a difference one game can make. The North Island team was full of first-choice All Blacks and we scored a big win over the South. I picked up two more tries and felt satisfied with my effort. After the inter-island game, the selectors chose two more teams, but again I was disappointed to be named in what was effectively a New Zealand B team for a match in Palmerston North against the touring Canadians. The first-string side, under the Harlequins banner, would go to Hamilton to meet Waikato. Decision time again. In the end I thought, 'Hell, what can it hurt?' I'd scored four tries in two matches and I'd been given another chance to impress the selectors. Palmerston North here I come.

To anyone reading this, I suppose it must seem that I was a very mixed up kid. It's just that I was young and not very worldly. When I wasn't selected for this team or that, I took it as a rejection of me as both a player and a person. It didn't help, either, when a television channel reported that I wasn't in the frame for the World Cup team. I really took that one to heart, even when the story was later retracted. That All Blacks jersey, though, is a powerful magnet – the closer I thought I was getting, the more I wanted it. Rugby league could wait. Well, for a week or two, anyway.

Almost as soon as I'd arrived in Palmerston North, I got the news that Rushie had strained his groin in Hamilton before the A team's first training and that the selectors wanted me to replace him. I couldn't wait for a flight so I jumped in a car and drove the five hours north. The trip gave me a good chance to think things over. Naturally my thoughts turned to Rushie, who to this day remains one of my closest mates in the game. I thought about all the help he'd given me so unselfishly since I'd arrived on the first-class scene. He, too, was desperate to make the World Cup team and he was also going for one of the two left wing spots in the squad. Now I was going to replace him in an important match that could well decide my future in the game. I hoped it wasn't the end of his dream.

Laurie Mains: After Rushie got injured we rang Earle Kirton, who was looking after the New Zealand XV in Palmerston North, and told him we wanted Jonah in Hamilton. Earle said that Jonah's face just lit up when he gave him the news. His smile, apparently, was a mile wide. The management team still had an issue with Jonah about his diet and this surfaced just after he arrived. He must have been super-hungry and when he sat down to lunch his plate was just piled high with chicken wings — an absolute mountain of them. I didn't want to upset Jonah, so I had a quiet word with Rushie and asked him if he'd speak to him.

At that stage my relationship with Jonah wasn't all that I wanted. I was still finding him shy and difficult to communicate with. On the way to the ground for our first training run, I deliberately walked with him and gave him some words of encouragement. I told him to try and be one of the guys, to just get stuck in and not hang back. He needed to prove himself to the other players and I told him the best way he could do that was on the training field.

Jonah obviously took my words seriously. At our first session on the tackle bags he was awesome. He hit Paul Henderson so hard he was sent flying, doing two backwards somersaults on the way. Richard Loe saw the funny side of it and reckoned Ginge, a proud Southlander, might be in need of a few more Bluff oysters. Later, I had the backs holding the hit shield for Jonah. By this stage they were genuinely frightened of him, so I put Richard on the shield. When Jonah hit Loey for the first time he lifted him clean off his feet and sat him on his back. Ginge couldn't resist his opportunity. 'Need a bit more Canterbury lamb, Loey?' he chuckled.

The shadow All Blacks Test team dealt to Waikato in Hamilton. We almost posted a century and I had another good day at the office, scoring three tries, but further doubts arose that night after the match. A journalist asked me why I was hanging around when it was obvious that the selectors weren't considering me for their World Cup squad and that made me think, oh no, maybe he's right and I'm only here because Rushie's injured. In a few brief hours I learned just what people mean by the expression 'emotional rollercoaster'.

When I told Rushie what this media bloke had said he brushed the comments off. 'What do they know? You played really well today,' he said. 'Give it another week.' I sat on my own for a while, feeling miserable and with everything swirling around in my head. Then Laurie approached me and asked me what was wrong. 'You should know what's wrong with me,' I said. 'Jonah, I don't know what you mean.' Yeah, Laurie . . . whatever. I just walked off.

Laurie was obviously worried about my mental state and later he spoke to Phil to try and find out what was going on. I knew that Laurie often rang Phil. In 1994 he was always asking Phil if he thought I was ready for the All Blacks – if I could handle Test rugby. Anyway, Phil told Laurie what this journalist had said, that I wasn't in the selectors' plans for the World Cup. Laurie made it clear to Phil that it was plain bullshit and that they were considering me. He said the selectors were keen for me to play in the final trial at Whangarei, the Probables against the Possibles, and told Phil he had to try and 'get Jonah right in the head'.

Another lesson learned: don't listen to the media. Until you get the word from the coach himself, don't believe anything. Things haven't changed in the whole time I've been in the All Blacks. Players are always laughing about media rumours. I mean, where do they get some of their stuff from? I think half of these so-called 'sources' are simply imaginary friends. Once Phil gave me the nod it didn't take me long to 'get right in the head' again. I was named in the Probables and Rushie was picked for the Possibles, but he was again forced to withdraw because his groin injury hadn't healed. How cruel was that? My dream, it seemed, was getting closer by the day, while the door seemed to be closing on Rushie. 'Just worry about your own game,' he told me, 'I'll look after myself.' That's Rushie to a T.

The trial went well for me and my try-scoring run continued. The two I picked up for the Probables at Whangarei gave me a haul of nine in four outings in 1995. After the match, the two teams gathered for the big announcement. I was nervous right up to the moment I heard my name read out. Then it came: JT Lomu, Counties. The relief and sheer joy was like nothing I'd ever experienced. It meant more to me, in fact, than when I was named to play my first Test. The dream had begun. When I heard Eric Rush's name read out as well, I was doubly excited. Much later I was sitting on my own with Rushie and I still hadn't come down from the selection 'high'. I was just like a kid at Christmas. 'Man, I've made it, Rushie. I've made it.' 'No you haven't,' he replied. 'The job has just started. Now you're going to have to get out there and finish it.' The night before we left for the World Cup, I had No. 11 shaved into my eyebrows. I decided then that it was going to be my number. One way or another it has been with me ever since.

CHAPTER SIX

BIG GAME HUNTING

The trip from New Zealand to South Africa is, to put it mildly, a pain. At best, and with all flights and schedules in sync, it's a good twenty-four hours. At worst, it can take up to thirty hours. The trip to South Africa for the 1995 World Cup was one of the worst. It seemed to take forever. I never sleep on a plane, so the trip gave me plenty of time to think about the World Cup and what it meant to the team and to me. Unlike my thinking of the previous twelve months, all my thoughts were now positive. I kept telling myself that I'd done all the work and I'd prepared as well as I could. I was ready this time, really ready to test myself against the best in the world. I looked around the cabin at all the great players in the side and couldn't help but think we had the guys to do the job. The overwhelming feeling I had as we were coming in to land was that this side was something special. This side was capable of anything.

The buzz when we arrived at Jan Smuts airport in Johannesburg was amazing. You could feel the excitement. The All Blacks had arrived and the country immediately went into overdrive. Former players have told me it was the same in their day. The respect among the white population for the All Blacks has always been there and, since 1970, when the All Blacks first took Maori and

Polynesian players to the Republic, the blacks and coloureds have also been huge supporters. Of course, I was aware of the great rivalry between the two countries on the rugby field, but this time around there was even more at stake. South Africa was a new nation, the Rainbow Nation, and I got the impression that a World Cup title would help set the country off to a great start.

Even before the tournament kicked off we felt the heat from the South African public. There were always heaps of people at our training sessions and plenty more milling about at the hotel. It seemed every South African had a story to tell or a programme to show us from a previous All Blacks tour. 'Here, can you sign your sign name next to Bryan Williams's?' It actually got quite scary. We couldn't go out without getting mobbed. I didn't know it at that stage, but for me, things were going to get worse — much worse.

As our first pool match approached I was on edge. From the moment I was named in the team to meet Ireland, my focus was solely on playing well and not making any mistakes. The vibes from within the team were always the same. We've come here to do a job — win the World Cup. Come match day, I was itching to get on to the field and, by the time kick-off arrived for the evening game at Ellis Park, I was more than ready. Mostly, it was the realisation that I was finally back in black, but there were also a couple of events that occurred in the lead-up to the game that got me really fired up.

Eric Rush: There was an absolutely classic fax that arrived at our hotel a couple of days before the Irish match. It was 'signed' by Richard Wallace, the Irish winger who was to mark Jonah. The message basically said he was going to 'waste' Jonah in the match and that he might as well not even turn up. Well, when the big boy read this I thought his eyes were going to pop out of his head. He was so wound up it was frightening. It was only after the match that we all discovered the note was, indeed, a wind-up. Apparently, some of this guy Wallace's mates had concocted the whole thing. It was beautiful.

I have always suffered badly from pre-match nerves and I'm often physically ill. Against Ireland that night it was even worse – my body gave it the whole nine yards. I began vomiting and I continued to vomit, and when I thought it was over I began retching. Violent, dry retching. I remember Earle Kirton, our assistant coach, coming over and asking me if I was okay. I told him I was fine, and promptly threw up in the corner. Earle was really concerned. 'Jonah, are you sure you're all right?' 'No problem, Earle,' and away I went again. I know of other players who suffer similarly before games. In that All Blacks group, though, I think I was the only one. I generally start to come right once I hear the referee's voice call 'Time, boys.' By the opening whistle I've usually got things under control.

The Irish have a habit of lifting themselves against the All Blacks and in this match it was no different. They went at us hard from the kick-off and actually scored first. Andrew Mehrtens kicked a couple of penalty goals to keep us in touch at 7–6 and after thirty minutes the moment I had dreamed of for so long finally arrived. Mehrts put up a high kick, which the Irish full-back couldn't handle. From the scrum I got a pass from Graeme Bachop and crashed over. Nothing spectacular, but it was my first try in the black jersey and for that reason it will always be special.

We led 20–12 at half-time and, while it had been a struggle, I sensed that we were starting to wear the Irish down. I picked up another try early in the second spell and my confidence really grew. I thought about what Laurie had told me before the game.

I thought about the 'licence' he had given me. 'Don't take any prisoners, Jonah. If you feel it's on, just go for it. Have a crack from anywhere . . .'

Walter Little is a special player with an eye for the main chance. When he threw me a monster pass on our own 22m line the time was right. The Irish defence was up flat. 'If you feel it's on, just go for it.' I had about 70m to the line . . . and I went for it. To be honest, I can't remember much about how the try unfolded. It's the same with all those big runs. It's such an instinctive thing. What I do remember, though, is being hauled down just short of the line and having Josh Kronfeld at my shoulder. I managed to flick the ball up to him and he carried on the movement to score. That piece of play must have made a big impression on someone, because at the end of the World Cup it was voted the best try of the tournament. I was rapt for Josh. Sure, he didn't have to do much, but the thing was, he was there at my shoulder. Josh was always there.

I played a lot of footie with Crusher and at times I couldn't believe how he got around the pitch. He always used to say he was just doing his job. That job was to be the link man – and sometimes a finisher; to always be in support of whoever was carrying the ball. And, believe me, he was the best in the business. I've never seen another player like Josh. Others have got close, but to me he was in a league of his own. He just understood the game so well. Great instincts. Great nose for the ball. He seemed to know exactly where to be and at exactly the right time. I was devastated when he left the game in New Zealand. He still had so much to offer.

After the match, Josh and I joked about the try and he said to me that the only time he could ever get the ball off me was when he stuck so closely that I had to pass when I was finally tackled. We actually joked a fair bit about some of the tries on that tour

— the Double J team we used to call ourselves. The Irish match wouldn't be the last time at the World Cup he'd be at my side to score a try.

Even after we'd gone out to a good lead, the Irish never gave up. In the finish we outscored them five tries to three for a 43–19 win. Later, Laurie made it clear he wasn't altogether happy about our performance, particularly in the first half. There were a lot of mistakes and our accuracy wasn't quite there. The thing was, we'd been in Africa for about ten days. We'd done all the work and were raring to get out on the field. Laurie knew this and he could sense we were a bit jittery to start and that we just wanted to get on with the tournament. He never came down on us hard. We all knew we had room for improvement, but most importantly we had secured that first-up win.

After the final whistle I was vaguely aware of the media and some cameras pointed in my direction, but really I was concerned with only one thing. I had a debt to pay. It was a debt that for months I'd prayed I could make good. With my test jersey slung over my shoulder, I went looking for Phil Kingsley Jones. When I found him I looked him in the eye and gave him a strong handshake. Phil has always been big on handshakes. 'Look people in the eye, Jonah,' he used to say in the early days, 'and always give them a strong handshake.' I was very emotional as I handed over my precious black jersey: 'Debt repaid, Phil. Will you still be my manager?'

In the days leading up to the Irish match there had been a few requests from the world's rugby media for interviews with me. I did bits and pieces and didn't think too much about it. After Ireland, though, everything changed. It wasn't quite a frenzy, but it was starting to get, well, let's say, busy. I wasn't the only one with his hands full during the early stages of the World Cup. Phil, who was leading an All Blacks supporters tour to the World Cup, was starting to field heaps of calls and inquiries about me after the Ireland game. Neither of us ever imagined the sort of pressure I'd come under in South Africa. I had never run into anything like it. As the tournament went on I was sheltered from much of the media attention by the team management, and for that I'll always be grateful. All I wanted to do was concentrate on playing the game, but it seemed everyone kept on wanting to know more and more about me.

Sir Brian Lochore (1970 All Blacks captain to South Africa and 1995 World Cup campaign manager): There were many similarities between the fuss made over Jonah at the World Cup and the adulation Bryan Williams received back in 1970. The difference, of course, was that in 1970 South Africa still had apartheid and Bryan was seen as a hero to the black population. They saw him as someone who had achieved in what they saw as a white-dominated world. In 1995 it was no longer a white-dominated South Africa, but Jonah still received a huge amount of attention.

We were fortunate in 1995 that we didn't move around as much as we did in 1970 and it was easier to manage Jonah. The press were always wanting a piece of Jonah and we were conscious of the fact he was a young guy and that there was a limit to how much any one player could do. The media got access to him, but when we thought he'd done his bit we told them, 'Enough!' We didn't stand outside Jonah's door or anything like that, but sure, we sheltered him. Even with all the attention, he was a wonderful member of the squad. He never regarded himself as anyone special – not like some sort of idol. Nothing went to his head. He was a valuable member of the team both on and off the field. Always did what he was asked to do and just enjoyed being one of the guys.

Phil and I have a sort of unwritten law that we never mix rugby with business. He doesn't approach me on anything to do with my career while I'm in the team environment. In South Africa we hardly saw each other, but we kept in regular phone contact and talked about everything except my future. Before we left for South Africa, we'd mapped out a few things and made some loose, short-term decisions. Phil, in fact, had made the decision to leave New Zealand and return to Wales with his wife Sue after the Cup was over. He'd been in New Zealand since the early 1980s and had this ambition to one day coach in Wales, so when he got the offer to coach Wrexham, he jumped at it. At the time, his mother wasn't well and his son was on the verge of being selected for the Welsh national team, so the moment was right. I was happy for him. He'd worked hard for me and this was a great opportunity for him.

Before the World Cup, Phil and I met with Debbie Tawse, the head of a company called Celebrity Speakers. Debbie is an honest, straight-up-and-down person, who I was immediately comfortable with. It was agreed that she would handle all of my day-to-day stuff in New Zealand and Phil would be on call to help out. On major issues, though, Phil would still make the final decision. We had this grand plan that after the World Cup – after I had fulfilled my dream – I could look at the rugby league option in Britain and maybe even go and live with Phil and Sue in Wales.

Phil Kingsley Jones: After Jonah was selected in the World Cup squad the league offers came flooding in. Leading the charge were the British giants, Leeds and Wigan. Also after his signature were Sydney's Canterbury Bulldogs and the Auckland Warriors, who'd just started up. The most persistent chasers, though, were the Bulldogs, led by club supremo, Peter Bullfrog Moore.

The Bullfrog was a real character – a chain-smoking chatterer with a great personality and an enormous passion for his club. I liked him a lot and when he asked for a meeting prior to the World Cup, I agreed. We met in a suite at the Centra Hotel in Auckland and I made it plain from the outset that Jonah's immediate focus was the All Blacks, but that we'd be willing to talk after the campaign was over. Bullfrog wouldn't be denied. 'Yeah, that's fine Phil, but we just want to make sure we've got him after the World Cup.' The spiel went on . . . 'We'll love him like a son; he'll be part of the family.' Bullfrog always talked about the club as his 'family', and I have no doubts he was sincere.

It was obvious from the outset of the meeting that Bullfrog meant business, so I thought, what the hell. I just plucked a figure out of the air. 'Before we even start talking, Peter, we'd want a million dollars a season – that's a million Australian.' Well, Bullfrog coughed and spluttered and just about lost it. 'Oh, hmm, yeah, hmm . . . Well, meat's not cheap,' he finally said. 'We've never paid that sort of money, but it doesn't mean we couldn't . . . Yeah, I think I could get that sort of money for the boy . . . if he has a good tournament . . . yeah, he's got to be worth it to us.' I just about cracked up. 'Meat's not cheap.' That's a line I've never forgotten. I've got to say, the meeting was one of the funniest I've ever attended. All the time we were talking, I was aware of this noise in the background . . . squeak, squeak, squeak. Finally, I said to Bullfrog, 'What the hell's that noise?'

'Oh, shit!' he said. 'The wife.' He'd been on the phone when I'd arrived at his room and in his excitement he'd forgotten to hang up.

When the meeting was over I told Bullfrog that under no circumstances did I want to talk any further about rugby league until after the World Cup. I made the same comment to the other clubs chasing Jonah. The focus was the All Blacks. I hoped they would respect our wishes.

I never received any 'mail' from the Welsh camp prior to our second pool match, but their coach was pretty staunch in the press. He tried the mental game with us, talking up his players to anyone who would listen and saying his forwards would be too good for our pack. It's not uncommon for this sort of thing to go on at international level, but it certainly never affected our build-up to the match. In fact, if anything, it probably fired up our forwards. I've grown to love the Welsh over the years, but their coach that year, Alec Evans, was actually an Australian . . . so I guess I can forgive them.

Being Welsh, Phil is extremely proud of his heritage. Through him I have met some wonderful people and visited the country on numerous occasions. It's probably not surprising to learn, then, that he wasn't the only Welshman to get hold of some of my kit after the Ireland test. The great Welsh winger, Gerald Davies, finished up with my boots from that game and they've found a home at his Carmarthen Athletic club.

I find the Welsh warm, hospitable people with a passion for rugby that is just as strong in their country as it is in New Zealand. It's terribly sad that in recent years their national side has been nowhere near the force it once was. I think I'm right in saying that most real rugby people in New Zealand feel the same way. We've all felt for them when they've been on the end of a few hidings. I'd hate to think what the public of New Zealand would do if the All Blacks got hammered by fifty or sixty points. To their credit, though, the Welsh haven't got their heads down about it and the passion for the game has still been very much in evidence whenever I've played in Cardiff.

Despite the patchy performance we put on against Ireland, Laurie made only one change for the game against Wales. Jeff Wilson hadn't sufficiently recovered from the injury he'd picked up against Ireland, so Marc Ellis got the starting spot on the right wing. So often the All Blacks are criticised for being slow starters. What many critics tend to forget, though, is that every time New Zealand goes out on to the field, the opposition always seem to lift a notch. Wales were no different. They might not have had the skills of old, but all that passion was there and they started with a hiss and a roar. Our forwards, though, pretty quickly got on top. Sean Fitzpatrick and some of the other older heads in the pack hadn't taken kindly to the Welsh coach's pre-match comments.

I never scored in the game, but the Double J team was back in action in the second half. I made a big break from inside our half and managed to fend off a few Welsh defenders as I headed towards the try line. Again, I got dragged down with the line in sight and again Josh was right there to wrench the ball from me and score. This time, however, there wasn't the same joy. I'd landed awkwardly in the tackle and knew straightaway that I was in trouble. I couldn't get up and when the doctor got on to the field I told him I'd 'done' my shoulder. I was pumped after the run, though, and, despite a fair bit of pain, I decided to carry on. I didn't know at that stage I'd popped my AC joint, but as I turned to head back for the kick-off I caught sight of Rushie out of the corner of my eye. Rushie, who had been an All Black since 1992; who had been my greatest supporter in the All Blacks; who had never played a Test match . . . He had already stripped and was actually on the playing field. I looked over at him and he gave me the wink. 'Off you go,' he said. I was happy for my great friend as I left the field.

Even with a pool game against Japan still to play, the 34–9 win over Wales was enough to ensure the All Blacks a spot in the quarter-finals. Of more concern to me, though, was the shoulder injury. This particular injury is quite common among rugby players. Basically, the AC joint is where the collarbone joins the shoulder and the injuries are usually graded from one to three. Mine was diagnosed as the most severe – a grade 3. It's quite a painful injury and they can be tricky things to get right. Doc told me it could be a couple of weeks before I was right to play again. In that respect I was lucky, because I don't think it was ever Laurie's intention that I would play against Japan. In fact, he made a heap of changes to the team for that last pool game.

Doc told me before the next training run that he didn't want me involved in any contact situations. I thought, sweet. I was going to get out of one of Laurie's hard-arse trainings and would have a chance to rest my shoulder. Not likely. Laurie pulled me aside and told me that while the boys were training he wanted me to do twenty-four 150s. I couldn't believe it. I was running on one arm and I was expected to go full-out. That's Laurie, though. I don't think it had anything to do with the fact it was Jonah Lomu. It's simply that with Laurie in charge, no one misses out on the hard work. Like I've said, he was always a hard-arse.

At Bloemfontein, the boys really turned it on against Japan. The game was a bit of a wake-up call for all the team members and reminded us just how much talent we had in the squad. There were no free rides in this All Blacks team. Records went flying as we hammered the Japanese 145–17. Marc Ellis got six tries from centre and Simon Culhane's kicking was amazing – twenty conversions from twenty-one shots at goal was an unbelievable achievement.

Thankfully, the media pressure on me, which had been steadily building since the opening game, was relieved enormously at Bloemfontein. It was at a party in the city that, quite by accident,

I met Tanya Rutter, who would later become my wife. We'd both been invited to the same place and we hit it off immediately. I found she was a person I could talk to – about things other than rugby. Tanya was never really a fan of the game and, don't get me wrong, I didn't have a problem with that. It was just nice to have someone there to discuss things with, to help me escape from some of the pressure. At that stage our relationship was based on friendship. That friendship grew as the World Cup went on.

The build-up to our quarter-final match against Scotland up on the High Veldt at Pretoria was intense. The All Blacks had never lost to the Scots – still haven't – and we used this as a key motivating factor. The same thing applied against Ireland. None of us wanted to be part of the first All Blacks team to lose to either of these countries. There's a lot of awareness among the players about the All Blacks heritage. It's always been the same. We know what teams before us have done and we're always motivated by their achievements.

Laurie made a number of changes for the game against Scotland from the team that played the opening pool matches. Some of them were enforced because of injury. Thankfully, though, I wasn't one of them. The ten-day break since the Welsh match had given my shoulder enough time to recover and I was dead keen to get back on the field. Although we drew the short straw and had to play in white jerseys to avoid clashing with Scotland's dark blue, nothing was going to stop us from making this a special match. Not only was the game our ticket into the semi-finals, it was also Sean Fitzpatrick's hundredth appearance for New Zealand. Fitzy was a great player and a great captain. There was no way we were going to let him down that day.

The All Blacks had a very definite plan at the World Cup. As well as being a tough taskmaster, Laurie was also a great technician, who thought a lot about strategy and game plans. His aim

Proof that I was small once. With Mum in Auckland before I was sent to live with my aunt and uncle in Tonga.

Me with my brother John. He was born exactly one year to the day after me.

At 14, I was big enough to turn out as a lock for the Wesley College First XV. That's me in the centre of the line-out, waiting for the call against Pukekohe High School.

Me and Fiona on our wedding day in 2003.

Moving ahead with Phil Kingsley Jones in 1994. This piece of paper – containing just one paragraph – is the only manager-player 'contract' we ever signed.

Ready for judging the 1998 Miss World pageant in the Seychelles. Phil's looking a bit pale after an eventful and exhausting flight from Rome.

My two main passions outside of rugby are cars and music. Big motors, big sounds —
I love them.

Going up to receive the Investec Special Merit Award in Sydney during the 2003
World Cup.

I've been lucky enough to meet some of the most famous people in the world. Here I am with actor Robin Williams who's togged up in All Blacks gear.

Former Manchester United goalkeeper Peter Schmeichel and I bring jockey Frankie Dettori up to our size.

With world heavyweight boxing champion Lennox Lewis.

Dead heat —
Linford Christie
and I race for
charity.

I signed up with
adidas in 1999.
They've got a
great stable of
top athletes and
I've become
friends with
many of them.
Here I am with
Anna Kournikova.

Scooting in for one of two tries against Australia in the final of the 1994 Hong Kong Sevens. I had a good tournament but that year Hong Kong belonged to Glen Osborne. On the deck is George Gregan — with hair!

Monstered by the Fijian defence, I look for support in the final of the 1995 Hong Kong Sevens.

Doing my bit for New Zealand against Fiji in the final of the sevens competition at the Commonwealth Games.

Rushie, Dallas Seymour and me at the medal ceremony after the final. There were a few tears from the boys on the occasion.

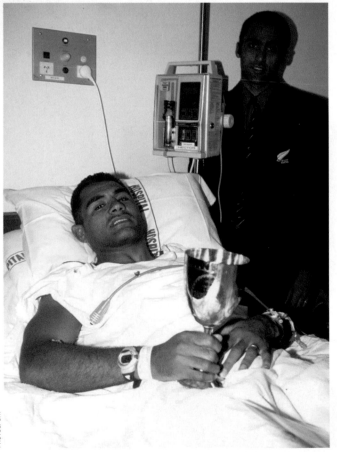

When Rushie was injured only a few minutes into our match against England at the 2001 World Cup sevens in Mar del Plata we were determined to win the tournament for him. This was more than just the traditional huddle…

Back in Auckland and Rushie's got hold of the trophy. Brad Fleming is in the background.

was always to win phase ball close in and try and tie up the opposition's loose forwards. Then it was simple: to get the ball as quickly as possible to the wingers. Laurie always believed that in Jeff Wilson, Marc Ellis, Eric Rush and myself, we had the best strike power out wide of any team at the tournament. Laurie's plan was never better executed than early on in the match against Scotland. I got the ball after a couple of quick rucks just inside our half and I set off down the touchline. I managed to beat a few players along the way and when I was stopped just short of the try line I had Walter Little at my side to receive the pass and score.

It was a good day out against Scotland. For the most part, the forwards delivered great ball and I had quite a few cracks at the defence and scored a try after a nice set-up by Jeff Wilson. Before the match, Tanya had dared me to 'sign' her name if I scored a try. I didn't forget and after I dotted down I was quick to spell out her name in the air.

One player I had huge admiration for in the Scottish side was fullback and captain, Gavin Hastings, a real rock in their defensive line. It seemed like he had been around forever and I certainly remembered his booming boot from the 1987 World Cup. I managed to get through him on one occasion, which caused a bit of humour after the match. Some guy told me he had placed £200 on me running through Hastings. Sorry about that, Gav.

Gavin Hastings (Scotland captain 1995): After our pool games in 1995 we had a day or two's relaxation planned at the Mala Mala game reserve on the outskirts of Kruger Park. After seeing Jonah on television, though, we spent our time practising our tackling on elephants and rhinoceroses. Seriously, though, he was incredible. If I remember rightly in that match, from his first touch of the ball he ran around our winger Craig Joiner and then my brother Scott missed a tackle on him. When I lined him up he just ran right over the top of me. Hell, I'd been around international rugby for nine years. I was 6ft 2 and 15 stone – not exactly small for a fullback – but it was such a totally different proposition to play against him rather than simply watching him on television. Until you actually faced him and witnessed first-hand that power and explosiveness, that strength and size, you just had no idea what you were up against. After that game I loved watching him play. I mean, you literally laughed when he got the ball in his hands. It was the excitement and the anticipation — like, 'What's he going to do next?'

I was on top of the world after the quarter-final. While we again conceded more tries than we would have liked, the forty-eight points we put on against the Scots at Pretoria was a real morale booster and gave us huge confidence for the big one against England coming up a week later in Cape Town. I was just loving it. I was even starting to enjoy the training runs and could hardly wait for the next game. I had the taste – the taste of the All Blacks, the taste for the jersey. Every day I got up, I just thought, I want more. All the things I'd thought about on the trip over to South Africa were coming true. This side had something special. This side had the X factor.

It wasn't just the great players we had in the squad, either. The management team included Brian Lochore and Colin Pinetree Meads, two of the greatest players ever to wear the black jersey and two of the most genuine people you'll ever meet. I was in awe of both men in South Africa. In fact, one of the most nervous moments I've ever had in my life occurred early on at the World Cup when I found myself sandwiched between both of them in a lift in our Johannesburg hotel. Just the mere fact that I was alone in the presence of these two greats was, like, far out – scary! I couldn't wait for the doors to open so I could get away – a boy amongst legends.

Actually, there was a story doing the rounds a few years back that I never even knew who Pinetree was when I came into the All Blacks. Like so many of those sorts of stories there was only a small element of truth in it. I had actually met Colin a couple of times as a youngster. The first time was when I was billeted with his son Glynn while I was playing for Counties at an Under-16 tournament in Te Kuiti. As much as I love rugby now, back then I was anything but a 'rugby head'. Anyway, the Counties guys were all standing around talking before the tournament kicked off and the name Pinetree kept popping up. We were, after all, in the heart of the King Country. I listened for a while and eventually piped up, 'Who's Pinetree?' The whole place went quiet. Of course I'd heard of Colin Meads. I just wasn't aware that he was nick-named Pinetree. Later, the guys were telling stories about Colin and how he used to run up the hills on his farm with a sheep under each arm. I was a bit of smart-arse back then and yelled out, 'Why? Were they tired?' I didn't feel quite so good when Glynn, who had overheard the remark, told me that Colin was his father.

One incident that happened just after the quarter-final has stuck with me right through the years. I was summoned to the back of the team bus by none other than the All Blacks hard man, and a 'back-seat boy' of some standing, Richard Loe. Anyone who knows anything about All Blacks rugby will tell you that the back of the bus is sacred territory, reserved for the most senior players. To get called to the 'back' can often mean trouble. Loey, it seemed, just wanted a chat and I was happy to oblige. As a young player you might not necessarily feel comfortable about having to face the back-seat boys, but you certainly never declined the invitation.

I sat down among some of the legends of All Blacks rugby and Loey put a question to me: 'What were you doing this time back in 1976?' 'I had just had my first birthday,' I replied. He looked at me for a moment and said, 'Mmm. Well, I think I'd just played my first game of senior club rugby.' Loey just shook his head, smiled and told me to return to my seat. At last I was starting to feel that I was being accepted by the players, accepted into that special club which is the All Blacks. It was like I was gaining some respect. The self-doubt of 1994 was becoming a distant memory.

In the week leading up to the semi-final against England, the management team was working overtime to keep the press and supporters at bay. Laurie had put a ban on phone calls through to the players' rooms and no newspapers were allowed on to our floor. Our focus was solely on the rugby. Laurie wanted no distractions. Although I was unaware of it at the time, Phil was also facing his share of pressure. I knew there were rugby league scouts in town. I just didn't know how much of a squeeze they were putting on Phil.

Phil Kingsley Jones: So much for my 'stay away' message to the rugby league clubs. As if the constant phone calls weren't enough, who should turn up in Cape Town a few days before the semi-final, but Bullfrog. He had another of the Bulldogs bigwigs in tow and together they cornered me at the hotel. It was a distraction I certainly did not need. The All Blacks were on fire and our tour group was having a ball – rugby league was the last thing on my mind.

'Bullfrog, I told you I wasn't talking league until after the World Cup.' I said. 'Come on, come on,' says Bullfrog, 'you know we've got a deal.'

'What do you mean a deal? All I gave you was a figure we would want before we even started talking and, besides, I've told you we're not doing anything until we've got this tournament over with.'

Bullfrog couldn't contain himself and he went for his trump card. 'Phil, just hear us out. We'll give you what you want. A million dollars a season for Jonah Lomu. We want to do it right now and we're prepared to put it in writing.'

My tour group was staying at the old Tulbagh Hotel in downtown Cape Town. I decided to have a quiet talk with Bullfrog and his mate away from public view and asked the hotel management if they had a room we could use. I was firm in my resolve, though, that the World Cup was the number one priority. I had no intention of agreeing to anything until after the final, when I would have a proper chance to sit down and talk things through with Jonah.

What followed was hilarious. The hotel staff told me we could use a boardroom on the third floor. We made our way to the lift, which was one of those ancient contraptions with a sort of cage arrangement as the door. After travelling about two floors, the lift just stopped – stopped dead

'Jeez,' I said, 'this bloody old thing's gonna fall to the ground.'

Well, Bullfrog's mate went completely white and started to shake and sweat. 'Oh, shit, not again,' he said. 'I can't handle this. I was stuck in a lift in Sydney once for five hours and I've never got over it. Get us out of here, Phil.'

Bullfrog was also decidedly agitated. 'Come on, Phil. Use the bloody phone. Do something.'

I was pissed off with Bullfrog for arriving at the hotel when he'd been specifically instructed to stay away. Now it was time for a bit of fun. 'Right,' I said, 'We're not going anywhere. What's he worth, fellas? How much are you really willing to pay for Jonah Lomu?'

They both looked at me. 'Name your price - anything you want, Phil. Just stop acting the bloody goat and get us out of here.' Well, just as they said that the rickety old lift kicked back into action. Divine bloody intervention! It was the funniest thing I've ever seen.

I didn't see much more of Bullfrog and his mate after that incident, but the Poms kept ringing me and I kept telling them to bugger off until after the final.

I had another interesting meeting in the week leading up to the semi-final, this time with Richie Guy, the chairman of the New Zealand Rugby Union. We met at his hotel, where we talked about Jonah's future in the game and the threat that Super League was posing to rugby union. At that stage the news hadn't broken about Kerry Packer's proposed rugby circus, the World Rugby Corporation, although there were lots of rumours doing the rounds. Richie is a man I've always respected and he filled me in on the details about what the NZRU was doing to counter Super League and the likelihood of a threat from a rugby circus similar to the one which tore cricket apart in the 1970s. Rugby union was going professional and Richie was adamant when it came to Jonah: 'Phil, we've got to keep him with New Zealand rugby. We don't want Jonah Lomu signing for rugby league or with any rebel group.' He handed me a piece of paper: 'This is what we are offering you.' The rugby wars had begun in earnest.

Phil and I spoke on the phone a few days before the semi-final against England. The South African papers were apparently having a field day about my new South African 'girlfriend'. I explained to Phil — not that it bothered him — that Tanya and I were just friends and we had a good chat about things in general. I told him I had never been so happy. The team was going great and I was loving being an All Black again. It was at this point that

I said to Phil I wanted to stick with rugby union. I wanted that silver fern. Little did I know that professional offers were coming in from all over the place, including the New Zealand Rugby Union.

CHAPTER SEVEN

HIGH IN THE CAPE, LOW ON THE VELDT

I never slept a wink the night before the 1995 World Cup semi-final against England. I don't just mean I couldn't sleep. I never even went to bed. I paced the corridors of the Cape Town hotel and I wandered the car park. I sat in the foyer and I went over and over the game strategy. I played the game through in my mind and as the hours passed by I worked myself into such a state that, come early morning, I was crying out for kick-off. I didn't want to sleep. Every time I thought of what the England winger had said about me in the week leading up to the game I got more worked up. I have never been a great sleeper. For as long as I can remember I've only ever needed about four or five hours' sleep. I generally get to bed around 11p.m. or midnight, but I'm always up or awake by 4 or 5a.m. This night it was different. I was angry. I was the angriest man on earth.

When I finally got back to my room at about 8a.m., I felt I was ready for anything. I was rooming with Frank Bunce – Buncey, the hardest man in the All Blacks back line; Buncey, who didn't just care about the All Blacks jersey, who would be quite prepared to die for it. 'Where the hell have you been?' he asked me. 'Couldn't sleep, Frank,' I replied. He never said anything more.

By this stage of the World Cup campaign, Frank had become

used to some of my more unusual habits – television going all night, 'sounds' blaring constantly from an assortment of music machines, and the telephone . . . Frank reckoned if I wasn't listening to music or watching television, I was always on the phone. Team management had deliberately paired us up in South Africa. Frank has always said it was an inspired decision and still jokes that it was because coach Laurie Mains believed he'd be a good influence on me. Both of us with Polynesian blood. Both of us from the 'other' world that is the hard 'hoods of South Auckland. Frank Bunce: street-wise All Black; midfield veteran; hard player; hard party man. Jonah Lomu: new boy; non-drinker; non-worldly. Yeah, it was a good decision.

I took a shower and made Frank his coffee. I always made his coffee. Rooming with Buncey gave me the best education you could ever get about the workings of the All Blacks hierarchy – the more experienced the player, the more perks he got. Like when we'd get to our hotel room, Frank would always get the double bed. Didn't matter that the other one would be too short and skinny for me and my legs would be hanging out the end. That's the way it was. Frank, I'm sure, played on the fact that I was very much the junior in the room. I forget how many cups of tea and coffee I made him in 1995 or how many times I ran his bath or dashed down the road to get him his favourite biscuits. I didn't mind being Frank's gofer, though, because he paid it back a hundred times over on the field: 'Stay close to me, Jonah . . . Come inside, Jonah . . . Move up, Jonah.' Frank was the king and Jonah Lomu liked serving the king.

Apart from the fact I hadn't slept all night, I pretty much stuck to my normal pre-match routine for the rest of the day. Frank and I went downstairs and had breakfast. Cereal, yoghurt and toast. No fried foods and no eggs – well, at least not as many as I was eating at the time. Laurie Mains was big on diet. When it came to me, Laurie was very big on diet. As I ate my breakfast, I wondered then what Laurie would have thought if he'd known I hadn't been to bed. Afterwards, I went back to my room to chill out. I like to relax before a game. In that way I'm no different to the other guys in the team. I like to listen to music, but sometimes I just stare into space. Here, I stood by the window for a long time and looked out into the distance at the beautiful Table Mountain. I looked down at the streets below and all the people going about their business and I thought more about the game. They've had their fun. Now it's my turn . . .

As each game passed at that World Cup it seemed everyone had a theory about how to stop Jonah Lomu. Early on, it didn't bother me. Sure, there had been that fake note from some Irish supporters about what my opposite would do to me in the opening game. And, yes, that had got me worked up. The Welsh coach had had a go and the Scots had this 'plan' to stop me. Against England, though, it was different. It was somehow personal. Rory Underwood had made it personal: 'I'm sure that Lomu will have been thinking about Tony [Underwood] running at him and, in a one-on-one, I'd put my money on Tony.' Rory's comment was only part of it. His brother Tony was quoted in a newspaper as saying he thought he could run around me. In the days leading up to the match I would be constantly reminded of that remark. I stuck the clipping on the mirror in my room and every morning it was there, staring at me. On match morning it was my greatest focus.

Lunch on game day can often be a fairly tense time. Different guys have their own way of getting themselves 'up' for a game. Sure, some will joke around, while others will keep to themselves and soak up the energy of the day. Often you need a bit of light relief to help get rid of the tension as you build up to kick-off. At lunch this particular day, I sat next to Zinzan Brooke. Now,

Zinny would be the most competitive person I have ever met in my life. Whether it's on the rugby field, the golf course or just in everyday life, Zinny likes competition. Placed right in front of us at lunch was a large basket of muffins. Zinny looked at me and I looked back and thought, oh no, Zinny – not today. 'How many do you reckon you can eat, Jonah?' He'd laid down the challenge. Kick-off was still a few hours away . . . and we went for it. Bite for bite. Muffin for muffin. I think I was onto my seventh when I surrendered. I knew Zinny wouldn't give up. He would have eaten the whole basket if he'd had to. He would have eaten them until he exploded. Zinzan Brooke does not like being beaten. There was no way I was going to try and stay with him.

During the course of lunch, another odd thing happened as I talked to Zinny. He had been an All Black since 1987 and he'd done just about everything there was to do in rugby. So I asked him what the one thing was he'd like to do in a game that he'd never done before. 'I want to kick a dropped goal in a Test match.' Yeah, right, Zinny. Dream on.

On the trip to the famous Newlands ground I looked around the faces on the bus, much the same as I had on the flight to South Africa. There was so much talent in this side. So much belief. All week we'd had it drummed into us about how bad we'd feel if we lost to England. There was still a solid core of players who had been in the All Blacks side that lost to England in 1993. The front row of Sean Fitzpatrick, Craig Dowd and Olo Brown had all tasted defeat at Twickenham. Zinny, too, was playing that day. So were Ian Jones and Jeff Wilson. All of them had horror stories of what it was like. How bad the feeling was after the match. Losing to England was not an option. I vividly recall watching that game in the middle of the night; watching the faces of the All Blacks as they left the field. To a man they were gutted. No way did I want to feel like that after this match.

As the teams lined up before kick-off, I looked over at Tony Underwood. Nothing was said, but at the end of our haka he gave me a little wink. I was furious. When I'm doing the haka I'm issuing a challenge. At the time, I thought Tony was being disrespectful in the way he took it up. I didn't say anything, but I was thinking plenty. I'm gonna wipe that wink off your face, I thought.

Tony Underwood (England wing 1992–1998): In hindsight, I'm not really sure that I made any comments to the press directly about Jonah before the game. He had put on a couple of big performances, particularly against Scotland in the quarter-final, but I approached marking him the same way as I did with anyone at that level of rugby – I gave him the utmost respect. When asked prior to the game by coach Jack Rowell and Will Carling how I felt about marking him and whether I was up to the challenge, well, what do you say? I said that I was comfortable and would give it my best shot. After the All Blacks performed the haka I did wink at Jonah, but it certainly wasn't meant as any sort of disrespect. I'd marked All Blacks winger Va'aiga Tuigamala on a few occasions before that and I used to do the same thing to him. It was simply my way of accepting the challenge. There was certainly no offence intended.

I never set out thinking, I'm going to smash 'em today, I'm going to score heaps of tries and bust them all over the place. I don't think any player does. Rugby's a team game. Sometimes play doesn't go your way. Other times, everything clicks. There's no doubt I was 'up' for the semi-final, but no matter how wired you are for a game, if play doesn't go your way, there's nothing you can do. Against England we had a plan to get me into the game as soon as possible. Andrew Mehrtens and I had been practising a 'reverse' kick-off since before we left for the World Cup. At Newlands we used the move, which we had called Mahurangi, after the school north of Auckland where it was devised, from the very first whistle. Instead of kicking to where the forwards were lined up on the right, Mehrts would kick to the left – out towards my wing.

That opening move set the tone for the whole day. We caught the English off guard. Mehrts's kick-off dropped into a hole between Will Carling and Tony Underwood and the ball was knocked forward. At that point, just seconds into the match, I had no idea that this movement, this little fumble, would signal the beginning of one of the most talked about tries in All Blacks history. From the scrum, Mehrts sent Jeff Wilson away on the right before the ball was switched back to the left. I knew we had their defence stretched and play was moving back in my direction. I could sense it was on: Ready, Jonah, here it comes . . . here it comes. Oh no, the pass is behind me. No, got it. Look out, here's Underwood coming in for the hit. Misses. Spins. Goal line ahead. Not far now. Around the outside of Carling. Damn, he's clipped me. Stumbling. Keep your balance, Jonah. Get your balance. Look up. Mike Catt. Two strides. No option. Shoulder in my vision. Get your knee up, Jonah. Bang. Into him. Over him. Through him . . . Sorry, Mike.

I suppose the try will always go down as my try, the one people will always remember me for, and while it's true I had a bit of work to do to make the try line, it was really, like so much of that World Cup, the product of some good planning and execution by the whole team. After I scored, it was like a huge release of emotions. It's hard to describe, but everything just seemed to fall into place. My body had been in overload all week and suddenly I had this amazing amount of energy – a huge surge like I was buzzing on twenty shots of coffee. Everything just poured out. I was running on pure adrenaline for the whole match. The game was only a couple of minutes old, but already I could sense something special happening.

Virtually straight after the kick-off we scored again and from then on we were in the zone. Right up until the final quarter, when England fought back really bravely, we were untouchable. I know people find it difficult to believe, but the fact is that I can recall very little of my other tries. It's been widely reported that I was in 'fairyland' when I came off the field — and that's the truth, such was the rush that afternoon in Cape Town. The final score of 45–29 looked good on paper, but we had let England in for four tries. We knew we'd have to do better against the Boks.

After that game Tony Underwood approached me and asked if I'd like to have his England shirt. It didn't seem to bother him that I was never going to trade mine. My first impressions of Tony were wrong. It was a hell of a gesture.

Sean Fitzpatrick (All Blacks captain 1995): There was a lot of motivation to perform well against England with so many of our players having been on the losing side back in 1993. We put a huge amount of effort into our preparation for the game because it's fair to say we did have some doubts before the match as to whether we could actually beat the English — especially in the forwards. What we did know, though, was that if we could win our share of the ball, Jonah would score the tries. His efforts in the previous matches told us that. Our first 40 minutes against England was outstanding. The rugby we played was quite sublime.

Apart from that first try, the most vivid memories I have of the match are of Zinzan Brooke and Frank Bunce. Zinzan for the dropped goal he banged over to fulfil the dream he had shared with me at lunch, and Buncey — Buncey for just being Buncey. In the first half, Will Carling made a break down the right-hand side of the field and fed Tony Underwood. Just after he passed to Tony — well, maybe a second or so after he passed — Frank castled him, caught Will side-on and buried him. And just for good measure, Frank gave Will's head a little rub in the Newlands turf. Frank always said Will was his favourite late-tackle target.

Despite all the hype and a bit of aggro during the game, I hold no grudges towards any of the English players. I've met Tony Underwood on a couple of occasions and I find him a good bloke. We even made a famous pizza advertisement together, although the truth is we never actually met during the making of it. The filming was done in separate countries. It's the same thing with Will Carling. I get on with him just fine. As far as Mike Catt goes, I still feel a bit sorry for him, because we both have to live with that try. I get sick of seeing it replayed year after year, but I can't imagine how he feels.

The boys were on a real high as we headed back to Johannesburg for the final showdown. For me, though, things started to get crazy. I've always enjoyed sightseeing around foreign cities, but after the semi-final it became a nightmare. It seemed everywhere I went I was recognised. I remember once getting a lift to a mall in Jo'burg in one of the team vans. The security guy reckoned I'd be fine as he dropped a few of us off to do a bit of shopping. I walked into one particular shop and tried something on. I couldn't have been in the changing room more than a couple of minutes, but when I came out I couldn't see the entrance for all the people. I was mobbed — and it was just frightening. The owner initially seemed happy enough to have all those people in his shop — until, that is, he realised they weren't buying anything. In the end, the security people had to sneak me out through the fire escape.

I wasn't the only 'target' in our build-up to the final. The whole team was subjected to all sorts of distractions as we tried to focus on the big game at Ellis Park. Fire alarms were set off in our hotel, cars blasted their horns and, despite management's best efforts, the phone rang in players' rooms at all hours of the day. In that respect it probably didn't help our preparation for the big game. Generally, though, it was business as usual. Despite the pressure on the team, inwardly I was fairly relaxed. The World Cup was proving to be a turning point in my career. I couldn't wait for the final.

Laurie did his best to keep things as normal as possible as we built up to the Springboks. He knew we'd all been on a high after the semi-final and he did his best to try and keep the players' feet on the ground. No one, though, could have predicted what would happen to the team a couple of days out from the final of the World Cup. Injuries can happen in the build-up to a match. It's never great, but you accept them. You can't, however, make plans for sickness within the team — sickness which strikes down almost an entire squad.

In hindsight, there was one omen that wasn't good for the All Blacks. While our routine remained pretty much the same as in previous weeks, one thing that did change in Johannesburg was our eating arrangements. Instead of eating with the rest of the hotel guests, we were allocated our own dining room. The question most asked is: Did this in some way contribute to the food poisoning which hit the team? I don't know. Yeah, it's true that a few players didn't eat at the hotel and weren't affected in any way, but who can tell? There have just been so many theories over the years about what happened with our food in Johannesburg that I don't think we'll ever get to the bottom of it. Was it the tea? Was it the chicken? Who ate in? Who ate out? Was it deliberate? What about 'Suzie'? What about the bookies?

All I know is that many of us were as crook as dogs. I wasn't as bad as a lot of the other guys, but I wasn't great, that's for sure. People are free to make their own assumptions about what happened before that game. The fact is that we suffered badly from food poisoning, but no one has ever proved conclusively it was deliberate. Should the game have been postponed? I don't know. There's no sense in beating yourself up about it. I've moved on. At the end of the day, the result on the scoreboard is the only thing that counts.

I was still feeling ill right up until kick-off, but one thing that really lifted me was meeting Nelson Mandela. It's something I'll never forget. Just before I was introduced to him he turned to me and said, 'Hi Jonah, nice to meet you.' You're kidding me . . . Hi Jonah? He almost floored me – this great man, this hero to so many people. Even in those few moments I could tell he had more than just charisma. This man had an aura about him. Since that time he has never ceased to amaze me with his calmness. This man who has been through so much. This man who is so gentle and seems to hold no grudges. We can all learn a lot from Nelson Mandela.

But you can never underestimate New Zealand when it comes to matches against South Africa. Food poisoning or not, this was the Blacks versus the Boks. For decades this contest has always been a heavyweight affair. It's one of world rugby's greatest rivalries. What do they say? *In sickness and in health* . . . The haka always gets me going and I put plenty into this effort in front of 60,000 screaming supporters. By the end of it I was just about eyeball to eyeball with South African lock, Kobus Wiese, and I was ready to get on with it.

Whereas we had tried – and succeeded – in playing a wide-ranging game in the previous five matches of the tournament, in the final we weren't given the same sort of space. The Springboks had done their homework on the All Blacks, no doubt about that.

The game was an old-fashioned slog. The forwards just belted hell out of each other. Gladiatorial. I got one of my few chances early in the first spell and made some good metres, but I was eventually dragged down by half-back, Joost van der Westhuizen, and prop, Os du Randt. Mehrts kicked a penalty goal from the ruck that followed my run, but Joel Stransky soon replied. The pattern continued throughout the match. Mehrts – poor Mehrts who was one of the players most affected by the food poisoning – would kick a goal and Stransky would reply. By half-time, Stranksy had the Boks in front 9–6 through two penalty goals and a dropped goal to Mehrts's two penalties.

The second half was much the same – two hungry sides slugging it out and not prepared to give anything. Mehrts brought the scores level with a dropped goal after fifteen minutes and that's the way it remained until full-time. The Boks did a good job of shutting our backs down. They did the job on me, no question. Sometimes they just used a smothering sort of defence, making sure they got to me just as I got the ball. Other times they employed a blind spot defence. It's a dangerous tactic that can often leave a gap between the centre and the wing. If you're able to hit that hole 'short' it can expose the defence. We didn't do it that day. Their tackling was rock-solid and I suppose we didn't adapt quickly enough. I marked James Small. He's a guy who's pretty controversial in South Africa, a real tough nut. He also happens to be one of the best players I've marked. He defended against me really well. I admired him for his grit – never-say-die James Small.

You can't ever underestimate the commitment of a South African side, especially on home soil. Don't forget they were playing in their first World Cup after years of being isolated. They were written off by many people before the tournament started and I think this strengthened their will. On the way to making the final, they had caused a major upset when they beat Australia first up at Cape Town, and their win over France in the semi-final was gutsy to say the least. At Ellis Park this day they were pumped.

We had a couple of opportunities to win the game in the second half. With the scores locked at 9–9 and only a couple of minutes left, Mehrts shaved the uprights with a dropped goal attempt. My chance came when Walter Little put me into space inside our own half. The goal line was begging. It would have been a long, but pretty much uninterrupted run, with only full-back Andre Joubert between me and the line. I reckon I might have made it. Referee Ed Morrison saw it differently. He whistled for a forward pass. I disagreed. Walter was furious. He swears to this day it never went forward. Tough on us, but, like they say, the ref's decision is final.

Extra time was something none of us expected before the final kicked off. We were all aware the new World Cup rules allowed for ten minutes each way if the scores were level at full-time. World rugby's first hundred-minute test – it was like the whole game had been pre-written. In the end, extra-time was just a repeat of the first eighty minutes. In the first minute, Mehrts goaled. At 12–9 we had the winning of the World Cup. Against the odds, I thought we had it. The dream was within our grasp. Stransky, though, had other ideas and he brought the Boks back to level-pegging with a penalty goal just before the end of the first period of extra-time. The winning blow was struck early in the second period, when Stransky kicked his second dropped goal of the match. We couldn't reply – 15–12. All Blacks don't cry. This was the end, though . . . and All Blacks cried.

I don't begrudge the Boks their victory. They were just as desperate as we were. They beat some great teams at the World Cup. Good on them. Given our circumstances, I think we fought brilliantly. Obviously there wasn't the same sharpness about our play that we'd shown in our earlier matches, but in the end fifteen players pulled on their black jerseys that day and in the end we came up short. Would we have won if we'd been fully fit? Who can say? I've accepted the loss. You can't go through life making excuses. Winning is sweet and winning in the All Blacks jersey is the sweetest thing in life. All Blacks pride and guts got us as close to glory as is possible. All Blacks are good winners. Sometimes, as much as it hurts, All Blacks have got to be good losers.

Dressing rooms are funny places. They can be the greatest places on earth and they can be miserable and lonely. After that match, I looked around that dressing room at some of the faces of the great soldiers of All Blacks rugby. There was such pain – pain for Fitzy who had won a World Cup in 1987, but who desperately wanted another one. Zinny, too, had been in that 1987 squad, but he hadn't played in the final. Buncey was into his thirties. He had played for Western Samoa in 1991 and switched to New Zealand, the country of his birth, a year later. His chance had gone. I looked at Jeff Wilson and Mehrts. Like me, they were young. If we wanted it badly enough then maybe we would be lucky enough to get another shot. You couldn't help but quietly ask yourself the question: How many players would get another chance at rugby's big prize?

Laurie Mains is seen by the public as a tough taskmaster and a man not afraid to say what he thinks. He upsets people. His attitude has always been that if it's good for the All Blacks, then he doesn't care what people think. Be honest with Laurie. That's the easiest way. Be honest and he'll be dead straight with you. Sometimes our paths got kind of clogged up. I didn't understand him when I came into the All Blacks. Simply, we were from completely different worlds. It took a long while for us to get on the same wavelength. Whatever, Laurie wanted that World Cup as much as any of the players – some might say more. When he came into the dressing room he was fantastic. He wanted to make sure that all the boys got their frustrations out, while at the same time reassuring us that we'd done our best; that we'd done New Zealand proud. Hard man on the training track is Laurie Mains. Loved his players. Loved the All Blacks.

My life changed forever after the World Cup. I would never again be just plain Jonah Lomu. I didn't want to be recognised everywhere I went. Whether it was autograph hunters or the media, I wasn't prepared for life under the spotlight. There's only so much you can take of people always wanting a piece of you. I had come from a life which I basically had under control and then all of a sudden it was just ripped away from me. Fame, if that's what you want to call it, has huge benefits. There are great rewards and amazing recognition. I was almost speechless when I was given the news at the end of 1995 that I had been named BBC Overseas Sports Personality of the Year. I mean, the award is just huge and it was a very humbling experience. You only have to look down the list of past winners — Borg, Sobers, Nicklaus, Ali, Pele . . . Lomu. It was too much. However, there is, of course, a downside that comes with fame, especially in a country of New Zealand's size. When I came back from the World Cup I was still only twenty, but my private life was gone — forever.

CHAPTER EIGHT

SILVER CUPS AND GOLDEN CONTRACTS

I don't drink alcohol all that often. An occasional glass of wine these days is about my limit, but after we lost the World Cup final to the Boks I didn't get drunk, I got trashed – and I wasn't on my own. Phil reckons it's the only time he's ever seen me really drunk. I think he's probably right. The Sunday morning after the final we had our usual team meeting. It started as a bit of a happy hour and developed into, let's say, a happy day. The evening before had been big, too, for a lot of the players. I remember bringing my tape deck down to the bar. I think it was still playing the next morning. I got next to no sleep and it was all on again on the Sunday. With the way flight schedules were back then, we weren't due to head out of South Africa until the Tuesday after the final. Let me tell you, there were a couple of players still going strong on the Monday.

The thing was, we had worked so hard to win the tournament. We had got so close, yet we had come away from South Africa empty-handed. The big 'sessions' were a release for the team. I know that sort of carry-on is probably frowned upon these days, but it was a way for the players to let off a bit of steam. Bonding. For all our hard work and exciting play, we'd come up short. The World Cup final also signalled the end of my close association with Phil. He was leaving for Wrexham and, although we both knew I was going to be in good hands with Debbie Tawse at Celebrity Speakers, I still somehow felt I was going to be on my own.

Just before we left South Africa, rumours about professional rugby started to get stronger. I know now some of the senior All Blacks in the 1995 side had been aware of the possibility of a professional group starting up, but the younger guys, myself included, were pretty much in the dark as we headed back to New Zealand. I tried to keep my focus on the home-and-away series against Australia, which was to kick off in Auckland just over three weeks after we returned from the World Cup. There were no trophies to bring home from South Africa, so the Tests against Australia at least gave us a chance of regaining the Bledisloe Cup, which had been lost to the Aussies in a close one at the Sydney Football Stadium in 1994.

The build-up to the first Test against Australia was interesting to say the least. The New Zealand Rugby Union, along with the Aussies and the South Africans, had scored a big television deal with Rupert Murdoch's News outfit, so it had plenty of cash and was looking to sign up the players. The NZRU had been worried about the Super League threat and now they also knew about the threat from Kerry Packer's World Rugby Corporation. There was a lot to think about. Rugby was definitely going professional and it was going to happen in a short space of time. The NZRU was keen to get signatures as quickly as possible. The All Blacks, though, the senior players especially, made it plain to the NZRU that we didn't want to discuss contracts until after the Bledisloe Cup.

Although Australia hadn't made the semi-finals at the World Cup, we still saw them as a tough side and we didn't need any distractions in the lead-up to the series. We knew they'd be hurting after South Africa and in the first Test at Eden Park it proved that way. Their forwards took it to us and for long periods they managed to shut down our attacks. We eventually got up to beat them 28–16, but it was really only towards the end of the match we made the game safe. We had a lot to thank Andrew Mehrtens for that day – Mehrts, the money man. Twenty-three points from his boot. Pure gold. For me, the match was memorable for my first Test try in New Zealand. It was a spectacular team effort, which I really only had to finish off after Jeff Wilson got nailed just short of the try line.

We were one game away from regaining the Bledisloe Cup, with silverware in our sights, and we were definitely up for the match in Sydney the following week. We trained hard, with the Cup as our spur, and while I hadn't been all that happy with my game at Auckland, I was confident I'd be able to put in a better effort in the showdown at the Sydney Football Stadium. There had been a bit of talk after the first Test about how the Aussies had closed me down and how they could do it again in their own backyard. That sort of thing always motivates me. As it turned out, the game in Sydney would be remembered for a number of interesting things other than just the result. It was the hundredth Test between New Zealand and Australia and, although none of us really knew it at the time, it would also be the last 'amateur' Test the two sides would ever play.

On the morning of the match, I was super-relaxed. By this stage my relationship with Laurie Mains had really improved. I'd always respected him as a coach. By now, though, I'd actually got to like him and I found we were communicating much better. Laurie had a Test match routine which he always followed. Before team meetings on the day of a match he waited for all the players to get seated before removing his jacket. He'd then carefully put it over his seat and place his hands on the table. His next move was to look around the room at the players and fix each of us with a stare. It seemed that more often than not he'd finish up in a staring competition with me. In Sydney, I thought, I'll fix you, Laurie; I can play this game, too. So I arrived at the meeting with my Walkman on and, after taking my seat, I put on this outrageous pair of sunglasses, the mirrored sort where the person looking at you gets their own reflection back. When Laurie finally got to me with that famous stare, hell, did he get a fright. He looked even more stern than usual and I thought I was going to get an earful. Eventually, though, he moved on. Not bad, I thought. Not everyone gets a win over Laurie.

Whereas we'd struggled up front against Australia in Auckland, the forwards were fantastic in Sydney. Despite the Aussies being narrowly ahead at half-time, I never thought we were in danger of losing this match. The second half, we were in complete charge. I got a try and had a few big runs. The Aussies had double-teamed me in the first Test and they tried it again in Sydney. With the sort of back line we had back then it was a dangerous thing to do. We knew that if they put two players on me there would always be a hole somewhere else. If you can't address this situation in your defence, then you're in trouble. In Sydney, the Aussies got into trouble and we punished them. The 34–23 win did not really do us justice. We outscored them five tries to two.

David Campese, one of my childhood heroes, was named in the reserves for this match. I had hoped one day to be able to mark him. My chance came in the second half when he replaced Damien Smith on the right wing. Too much. After the match I raced straight up to him in the tunnel and asked if I could swap jerseys with him. Up until then I had only ever swapped one All Blacks jersey. Campo, though, was special. He was happy to trade. What I don't think he realised at first was that he was giving me his reserves jersey – No. 16. Campo always started the match. Campo always wore No. 11.

He realised later what he'd done when I asked him to sign it: 'You've just got yourself a special jersey. I don't think I've got another No. 16.' Rugby memorabilia has never really been my bag, but I've still got that jersey. It's one of my prized possessions. Campo was one of the greats. We've become good mates since and whenever I'm in Sydney I always enjoy catching up with him.

After the match I was over the moon and so proud to have been part of an All Blacks side which had won the Bledisloe Cup. The Australians have become such a good side over recent years and the trophy has become so much more important to rugby people on both sides of the Tasman. With the way the two matches are set up each year, on a home-and-away basis, it's become difficult to win the Cup from the holder. We had at last brought home our piece of silverware. We were rapt. When I caught up with Laurie later, he got in the last word on the events of earlier in the day: 'You played well today, Jonah. Lucky for you. Otherwise we'd have been having a few words about that Walkman and those bloody sunglasses of yours . . . '

We didn't have much time for celebrations after the match. The All Blacks bus was on a mission — a professional mission. We headed out into the Sydney suburbs, the upmarket suburbs, to the home of one of Kerry Packer's top employees to talk about the World Rugby Corporation. At the meeting I just sat and listened as this guy outlined the details about the WRC. Some of the other All Blacks talked as well. As I've said, a few of the senior guys had known about the deal for a while and they were keen — real keen. Still, I just listened. The money they were talking, even by today's standards, was mind-blowing. One hundred thousand dollars as a signing-on fee and hundreds of thousands of dollars per season. You could basically play a season or two and retire comfortably. It was much more money than the NZRU was offering. Most of the players signed up. I didn't.

In the week or so leading up to the Sydney Test I had spoken to Phil in Wrexham and his message to me could not have been clearer: he didn't want me signing with any rebel organisation. Maybe we could look at the rugby league option again, but the Packer group was out of bounds. Phil knew at that time my heart was with New Zealand and the All Blacks, but if everything fell apart, then both of us agreed that instead of joining any rebel group, we'd go the league way.

Phil Kingsley Jones: I told Jonah I had a real problem with the WRC and there was no way I was going to let him join any rugby circus. I said I didn't think it was any good for rugby and it was certainly no good for him. No way. I could never have agreed to him signing up with any Mickey Mouse outfit. I didn't want Jonah Lomu playing rugby for a team with no soul. We agreed that I'd have another look at the rugby league option. Leeds were still chasing him big-time and they were talking huge money. In one conversation I had with their CEO, Alf Davis – an old-school Yorkshireman and a decent bloke – he said to me, 'Just be honest, Phil. Tell us what you want for your boy.' I said what Jonah and I really wanted was for him to keep playing for the All Blacks. I added that if the circus took off and world rugby looked in jeopardy, we'd sign for Leeds. In those days most of the top league players in Britain were earning around £200,000 per season. If I recall correctly, the figure they were talking about for Jonah was around £500,000 per season.

I know people reading this are going to think, 'Oh, yeah, Jonah was holding out for the big bucks,' but that's not true. The Packer people asked me a lot of questions as to why I wouldn't sign. I just said to them I wanted to play for the All Blacks. Sell the deal to me so I can still wear the black jersey, then I'll sign. No problem. Their answer was that if I signed on the dotted line then thousands of people would turn out to see me play. Not good enough. In the end they couldn't deliver the one thing that I wanted out of rugby union. They couldn't deliver the black jersey.

It's history now that the WRC threat collapsed. Jeff Wilson and Josh Kronfeld broke ranks with the other players and negotiated separate deals with the NZRU. I know some team members felt betrayed by Jeff and Josh, because they'd been part of that original group who'd signed up with the WRC. I've heard some people say one of the reasons the WRC thing fell over was because I didn't sign. I know at one stage Phil met with one of the WRC big shots in Australia, who told him that if I didn't sign the whole thing would probably fall over. I'm not so sure about that. I think in the end it had more to do with the WRC not being as well organised, at least moneywise, as a lot of players thought. As far as I was concerned, the players knew exactly where I stood from the start. They never put any pressure on me to sign and they never gave me any grief when I refused. I was grateful for that.

As much as anyone, Phil was responsible for keeping me in rugby union. He knew how much I wanted to stay in the game and he was under as much pressure, probably more, than I was. As well as rugby league and the WRC business, there were serious offers for me to try out American Football. Phil was approached by NFL people representing various teams, including the Dallas Cowboys and the San Francisco 49ers. The London Monarchs from the European League were also interested in me and at one stage wanted me to go over to England for a sort of superstars of sport competition. Phil copped a bit of flak around that time from people who didn't believe the American football talk, but, while I was never really tempted, there were certainly offers floating around.

I got impatient as negotiations went on between Phil and the New Zealand Rugby Union. I wanted a contract that said, 'Jonah Lomu will continue to play for New Zealand.' I needed to know that I could carry on playing for the All Blacks. In the end, Phil was able to put together a good deal with the NZRU. Four years. Another crack at the World Cup. It was the result I'd wanted. Financially we were happy, but like I've said, it wasn't just about the money. I've always left the financial side of things to Phil, but he's like me in that money is not the be-all and end-all. I know what it's like not to have money and in that respect it has taught me something about values. I've been at both ends of the money tree. Even into the professional age I continued to work at my job in the bank – and I always appreciated my pay cheque. As far as professional rugby goes, all I've ever wanted is to be comfortable. To be comfortable in New Zealand – at home in the country I love – is the ultimate reward for me.

Eric Rush: It's always amazed me how people sling off about Jonah and the money he's made and the contracts he's signed. A lot of it just comes down to jealousy. I'm convinced of that. He's got to be the most generous player I've ever toured with. I can't begin to recall the number of times he's done things for other players; helped them out. He never stops giving. As an example, I remember in South Africa in 1995 he bought a portable stereo system on his way into the country. Jonah bought one on every tour. Loves his sounds. We were packing up at the end of the tour and he just turned around to this black woman who was cleaning our room and said, 'Here, you have this.' She was stunned. Remember, the All Blacks weren't professionals then, but that's just Jonah. His generosity is legendary.

You're always going to get a few problems arising when money is involved in sport, but one thing has never changed in the whole history of the All Blacks: money or no money, the players still want to play for New Zealand. From where I sit, that's why I believe we've got it over so many other countries. Even since professionalism came in, the players' attitudes haven't changed. Sure, there was an issue over win bonuses for the All Blacks at the World Cup in 2003 — you're always going to get that — but the jersey is still the greatest draw for all of us. You ask most players who have been All Blacks and they'll tell you that they'd much rather stay in New Zealand than go offshore. You get very few who go overseas while they're still in the All Blacks frame. When your time is done, why not look at the big contracts in Europe or Japan? I don't care what anyone says, loyalty still counts in the All Blacks — you bet it counts.

They called them the rugby wars and, in the end, professionalism won. The battles had been tough and, sadly, they sometimes had All Black going up against All Black. Thankfully, the whole business was over by late August when the players signed with the NZRU. I was eager to get back involved with Counties and their NPC campaign. We started out promisingly. I missed the first game against Waikato, but was back for the King Country match and played a further five games as we secured a spot in the semi-finals.

This was Counties' first year under Mac McCallion, the tough-as former SAS soldier. Like Ross Cooper before him, Mac encouraged an attacking style of rugby. And he had the players to do the job. The back line was loaded with gas men. There were great steppers and real power players. Towards the end of the season we were able to field a back line which included Pita Alatini at full-back, Joey Vidiri and me on the wings, George Leaupepe at centre, Tony Marsh at inside-centre, Danny Love at fly-half and

Michael Scott at half-back. Just the thought of that back line makes me shudder. Counties won five NPC matches on the trot and finished the round robin in second place behind Auckland, to guarantee ourselves a home semi-final. In the end, we were disappointed not to be able to get the job done against Otago, but it was still a heck of a season and one that really dragged the crowds back to the Pukekohe Stadium.

One downer during the NPC was the attempted assault on me during the Canterbury match at Pukekohe. A spectator threw a punch at me and another guy tried to tackle me after the game. I'm still not sure what it was all about, but it shook me up at the time. Up until then I'd never really feared for my safety, especially not at home. The result was that I was given an 'escort' off the field for the rest of the season. These sorts of things are always on, I suppose, when you're in the public eye. Everyone wants a piece of you. The fans and the autograph hunters I could handle just fine. Physical assaults, though, give you a bit more to think about.

Life as rugby professionals began for the All Blacks on their end-of-year tour to Italy and France. The first stop was Sicily and we were certainly glad when we finally arrived. From memory, the route went something like this: Auckland–Sydney–Los Angeles–London–Rome–Sicily. The boys had each been given new watches before we left New Zealand. The whole trip became an exercise in timing each of the legs and working out how long we'd spent in the air. In the end it seemed like weeks.

The few days in Sicily were a fabulous experience. I'll always remember my time there – the long, long lunches that the locals enjoyed, the amazing old buildings and the history associated with them and, of course, the Mafia. The boys joked about the Mafia on the trip over and we joked – quietly – about them when we arrived. The only time I saw anything out of the ordinary was on the morning of the match against Italy A at Catania. Before the game, two big black cars turned up and out hopped these big guys wearing trench coats. They walked into the ground with this little fellow in between them. They looked around at the grandstand and when they got to a certain point the crowd just parted and they took their seats. Quite freaky. Even though we beat the A side, they still seemed to enjoy the match. Lucky, eh?

We lost Andrew Mehrtens in the Catania game with a severe knee injury. We discovered later he'd ruptured cruciate ligaments and he was out for the rest of the tour. It was a huge blow to the team. Mehrts isn't just a great player, he's also a top guy to have around. I roomed with him on our first night in Sicily and what an experience that was. It was hot, stifling, so I made a grab for the bed by the window and left it open all night. The mozzies had a field day. In the morning he looked like he had chickenpox. Sorry, Mehrts.

Mehrts is one of the great All Blacks characters and also a guy who, I think, often hides his emotions. I know that after the World Cup final he just took the whole thing in his stride. Late in the game, he had a couple of cracks at goal that just missed. Of course, no one blamed him. How could you? It's just an unfortunate part of rugby. The person who takes the kicks always gets the heat from the fans and the media if the team loses. I know deep down Mehrts probably thought, if only, but, like I said, he's good at hiding his emotions.

Rooming with Mehrts is like living with a walking encyclopaedia. The man is worldly. Highly intelligent. Ask him anything and he's got the answer. One of his pet hobbies is the laws of the game. I don't know how many times he's read 'the book', but he knows it backwards. There have been a few referees who've come off second best to Mehrts. It's simple. Never argue with Mehrts, especially about the laws. On the field he's always the same — a move ahead of everyone else. So many players need to get the ball in their hands before they work out what they're going to do next. Mehrts is like a chess player and is sometimes thinking a couple of moves ahead. So much time as well – that's the mark of a good player.

Over the years, rugby has taken me to many interesting and, I suppose, unlikely places. Sicily was certainly one of them. I didn't play against Italy A, but the game was memorable for three players who would go on to become top-class All Blacks. Justin Marshall, Todd Blackadder and Taine Randell all debuted for the Blacks in Catania and they all went on to captain New Zealand in Test matches. On top of that, Laurie made Frank Bunce captain for the day – the first and only time he ever led New Zealand. It was a huge honour for Buncey, who still brags about his record of never having captained a losing All Blacks side. Like I said, unlikely places . . .

After we left Sicily we moved on to Bologna for a Test against Italy and this is where the hard training really began. Laurie Mains and I had discussed my diet before the tour began. In fairness, I may have been carrying a few more pounds than at the World Cup and I did mention this to Laurie before we left New Zealand. I told him I'd try my best to get into top shape and he didn't forget that conversation. Laurie always remembers things like that.

Laurie Mains: Jonah was overweight before the tour began. I'm sure it had something to do with his kidney condition, as it has done throughout so much of his career. Anyway, he volunteered to me at the start of the tour that he'd put himself on a dinner diet of soup and bread. That really impressed me. For good measure, I mentioned this to Frank Bunce and asked him to keep an eye on Jonah. After two or three days Frank said to me, 'Did you tell him how much soup and bread he could have?' I asked why and Frank replied, 'Well, last night he had five bowls of soup and two loaves of bread . . .'

After that we got him on to a more sensible diet and his weight started to come down. A few days later, I again asked Frank how the diet was coming along.

'It seems to be going just fine, Laurie,' was the answer. Now I knew Buncey and Jonah were good mates, so I asked the question again. 'Well,' said Frank, 'there's just been one small lapse. He had a bit of Kentucky Fried Chicken last night.'

'And how much did he have, Frank?" I asked.

'Well, Laurie, he did give me a piece.'

'How much, Frank?'

'Mmm . . . I think it was a fifteen-piece pack.'

I played my first game of rugby for money in Bologna. In fact, the Test against Italy was the first in the world to be played under the new professional rules. I earned my money, too. The Italians were a fiery mob and for one of the few times in my career I actually threw a few punches. There was niggle throughout the game and I lost it when a couple of their players put a bit of dirt in when they tried to tackle me. The ref wasn't impressed and I got a bit of a serve. Another time I remember one of their wings shaping up to Buncey. Lucky for him it only got to the pushing and shoving stage.

Apart from the off-the-ball stuff, the Italians actually played well, at least in the opening stages. We only managed a couple of tries in the first half, but the forwards took over in the second spell and we clocked up seventy points. Towards the end of the game I got my second try from a move deep inside our half. I yelled out to our half-back, Stu Forster, to pass me the ball after noticing my marker was caught in a maul. Ninety metres later I was knackered. Good lesson. When you're ahead by fifty or sixty points, keep your mouth shut.

The Italian section of the tour was really only the warm-up for the main event — a tour of France, which included two Tests and, for me, a chance to get some revenge for the nightmares of 1994. I was also keen to ram home my views on French nuclear testing, which had only recently resumed in the Pacific. I was one of five members of the touring squad who wrote open letters to the French president, Jacques Chirac. I told him that I had seriously considered not touring France because of his country's policy on nuclear testing — in my backyard. I told him I was proud of being a New Zealander and also proud of my Pacific Islands heritage; that I was angry the French scientists and military men had decided to conduct their experiments in a part of the world that was very important to me. I finished my letter by saying that the nuclear testing had helped me with my motivation and that hopefully the All Blacks would be able to show the French a few explosions of their own — in their backyard.

Laurie gave me plenty of work early on in France. I started in two of the three lead-up games to the first Test in Toulouse and came on at half-time in the third. I'm the first to admit I wasn't at my best early on in the tour. The touring life was interesting enough, but I was homesick and struggled with the language. 'Merci' and 'bonjour' were about my limit out on the streets. I spent a lot of time talking to people back home.

From the time we arrived in Toulouse to virtually the day we left, it never stopped blowing. On Test day the wind swirled around and around the stadium — and we got blown away. We just never fronted. We got outplayed. Outmuscled and outplayed. Before the game I thought we could win. I knew what this side was capable of, but the more we tried the worse it got. It was like quicksand, that day. The deeper we tried to dig, the further we sank. Sure, they pushed the offside laws to the limit and a couple of their tries were a bit doubtful, but in the finish they scored three tries to none. That's hard to argue with. If it wasn't for Simon Culhane's boot and his five penalty goals, the scoreline could have been a whole lot worse. We got done. I was gutted. Three Tests against the French and three losses. Someone said to me later that the Toulouse Test was the thousandth match by a New Zealand side. Oh, great. That really made me feel better.

Two games to go and just one chance to get that elusive win against the French. I got the midweek game at Nancy against a French Selection which, looking back, was probably the turning point of the tour. When we arrived in Nancy we were all feeling pretty bad. It had been a long season and we were all tired and, in my case, homesick. Just after lunch we had a team meeting. After Laurie finished his bit, Colin Meads got up. The room went quiet. When Pinetree speaks, you listen. He asked for the rest of the management team to leave the room. He wanted to talk to the team alone. Give or take the odd naughty word, his speech went something like this: 'French teams don't beat the All Blacks. The performance you jokers put on in the Test was a disgrace. I should have come out at half-time and put pink ribbons in your hair. I don't care what the hell you have to do, but you won't lose to this side again.' He got into quite a few players and when it came to me he didn't hold back. He talked about the three black wingers playing international rugby – me, Chester Williams and Émile N'tamack. He said I now ranked three and that I wasn't performing well enough. I got the message. All of us got the message.

You've never seen anything like the effort the boys put into the training that followed Tree's talk. Our anger levels were up and we just ripped into it. At the end of the session we were battered and bruised and some players even required the odd stitch. The speech had done the job. I don't think anyone else could have talked to the All Blacks the way Colin did that day. Colin Meads is our greatest All Black. That day he made us angry. He made us remember who we were and what we represented.

Not surprisingly, we gave the French Selection a hiding at Nancy. It was my sixth game on tour and I hadn't scored a try since the Italian Test. I was ready to change that. However, I remember the game especially for the antics of Glen Osborne. Oz had been one of our stars at the World Cup but, like me, he'd been struggling for a bit of form in France. He had lost his position at full-back for the first Test against France and the Nancy game was a final chance for him to push for a starting spot in the second Test in Paris. One of Oz's biggest problems was that he just couldn't sleep on tour. On the evening of the match at Nancy he asked the doctor for a sleeping pill. The doctor gave him a couple with instructions to take only one. Oz woke at 10a.m., still feeling tired, and decided to take the other one. The game was scheduled to start at 2p.m.

When there was no sign of him at the start of the team meeting a few of us went to get him. He was in la-la land. We got him up, walked him around and eventually got him on to the bus. He was still drowsy when we got him into the changing rooms and we knew he was in real trouble when he walked smack into a mirror. The All Blacks full-back was out of it. As we ran onto the field I asked him if he'd be okay. 'Yeah, yeah. No sweat,' he said.

Eric Rush was on the right wing, Frank was at centre and Walter Little at inside-centre, all of us mates. We'd have to cover for him. Sure enough, from the kick-off they put a 'bomb' up. I looked at Rushie and we both legged it back to Oz. We needn't have bothered. He took the kick – yeah, no sweat – with three Frenchmen bearing down on him. He stepped the first, swerved around the second and outsprinted the third to score a brilliant try. He finished up having one of the best games I've ever seen him play. He couldn't do a thing wrong. 'Man, you play better when you're half asleep,' I said to him later. 'Keep poppin' those pills.' Oz's performance that day saw him get the nod for the second Test. Jeff Wilson, who'd played full-back in the first Test, was ruled out with injury, but I'm sure Laurie would have reinstated Oz anyway.

We moved on to Paris knowing that anything other than a win would be a disaster for the team. The disappointment of the World Cup was still fresh in our minds and, while we'd done the business against Australia, two losses to France would not make for a happy ending to the season. This was to be Laurie Mains's last Test in charge of the All Blacks. He'd been through a lot. He was absolutely wrecked after the World Cup final. We wanted this win for ourselves, but we desperately wanted it for Laurie. Motivation would not be a problem.

It all came together in Paris. We were focused. There were no missed tackles. We weren't taking any prisoners. We were a completely different team from the week before and we served it up to France. They actually scored the first try, but after that it was one-way traffic. Rushie scored a great try in reply to the French effort and Simon Culhane kicked the goals to give us a 20–5 half-time lead. I got a taste of the action in the first half and in the second I finally broke my duck against the French. We called a move which had me coming into the line from inside-centre – it was one of my favourite cuts – and I gave it plenty. The defence seemed to come from everywhere, but I wasn't stopping. I don't know how many players I got through. It didn't matter. I smashed towards the line and got the ball down. Man, what a feeling.

We cleared out in the second half and won comfortably. The boys were stoked. For me, the feeling was extra special. I had broken my hoodoo against the French. My fourth Test and my first win.

It couldn't have been any better. As we left the field, Zinny and Robin Brooke hoisted Laurie onto their shoulders. Thanks, Laurie. Thanks on behalf of all the boys.

After the game I had a heart-to-heart talk with Laurie. It wasn't planned. It was just one of those spur-of-the-moment things. For the first time ever, I let my guard down with him. I told Laurie how my life had been. I told him how different my world was to his and that when I first came into the side I had struggled to understand him; struggled as well with the team culture. I told him that right from my introduction into the All Blacks all I wanted was to be wanted. I told that if he didn't understand how I ticked, then he just had to ask. It sounds easy, I suppose. Really, though, Laurie knew nothing of my background and, quite rightly, he just tried to treat me like he would any young All Black. In fact, sometimes I think he went the extra yard for me. It's just I didn't know it at the time.

It was an emotional conversation. I was close to tears. He understood where I was coming from and I saw a side of Laurie I'd never seen before. We had finally talked and we had finally clicked. It was very sad for both of us – the end had come just as I had begun to understand him and appreciate what he was about and how much he had given me. He taught me about the jersey. He taught me never to accept second best. Laurie Mains taught me to believe in myself.

The tour had been a great way to end the season. Homesick or not, the bonds between the players had become tight. We had gone through the highs and the lows of a tough season together. If we had been doing it for ourselves we wouldn't have survived. The 1995 team never won the World Cup, but along the way we played some fantastic rugby. The team were special.

CHAPTER NINE

TWO WEDDINGS
AND A FINAL

March 1996 was mad. I got married in March and I cried on television and apologised to my parents. I lost my driver's licence in March and I apologised to the whole country. I got close to assaulting a photographer in March and I apologised again. In March 1996 there was also some rugby – the Super 12 kicked off. So, where do I start?

My relationship with Tanya moved quickly during the World Cup. We got very close. After that first meeting in Bloemfontein, and as the tournament went on, we talked all the time. By the time the Cup was all over we were hitting it off really well and we both decided we wanted to see more of each other. I only had a few weeks between the end of the World Cup and the start of the Bledisloe Cup. I was twenty years old, she was nineteen, and I thought, yeah, this is the real thing! I decided to head back to South Africa to spend more time with her. We picked up exactly where we had left off. It was around then, during that visit to South Africa, that we made the decision we'd really like to be together. She came to live in New Zealand just before Christmas in 1995 and we were talking about marriage by early 1996.

It's easy to look back now and say we didn't really know what we were doing or that we were both too young to get married.

Whatever. We took the decision and we took the decision to go it alone. Not asking our parents to the wedding was something that would continue to haunt us for months, even years, after the event. As Tanya said at the time, 'We stuck by what we did. It will stay with us for the rest of our lives. It mightn't have been the right thing in the eyes of everyone, but it's the way we wanted it.'

At the time, Tanya was everything to me. The one person I had been able to put all my trust in over the previous few years had gone to Wales. Without Phil around, I only had Tanya. She was the only person I felt I had a connection with. Everything was moving so quickly for me back in those days. I had become a celebrity after the World Cup and everything just seemed to go crazy. There was nothing in my life that was stable any longer.

Tanya and I got married on the banks of the Manukau Harbour on 17 March 1996. It was a Sunday wedding and it was small. It was also supposed to be a private affair. The service was performed by a court registry celebrant. In the bridal party were my best man, Michael Jones, and his wife, Maliena, and groomsmen, Junior Tonu'u and Eroni Clarke. Within a couple of days the whole country and, it seemed, half the world knew about the marriage. The fact we hadn't invited our parents was the focus for the media. One thing I quickly found out was that once you're an All Black nothing you do in New Zealand is private for very long. No one could have cared a damn if I hadn't been Jonah Lomu, the All Black.

I had always meant to tell my mother as soon after the wedding as possible and it was the same with Tanya. What can I say? The media beat us to it. We jumped into this thing very quickly. Not inviting my mother was the hardest thing, but I just don't think she would have approved. I don't know about my father and, frankly, I don't care. We told virtually no one. Not Debbie Tawse.

Not even Phil. He got a call from Debbie in the middle of the night in Wrexham telling him of the news. Apparently she was crying her eyes out. I hate to think what Phil said from 12,000 miles away, but I bet it wasn't too nice. Looking back now I really feel bad for Debbie. She worked so hard for me while Phil was away and I'll always respect her for that. She must have felt really let down.

Once the media were on to the story they didn't let up. They spoke to my mother and father and to Tanya's mum and dad in South Africa. The two sets of parents handled it differently. Tanya's were obviously disappointed and surprised by the announcement. Mine were shocked. It didn't surprise me. Ever since that time, I have consistently said that I regretted the decision not to invite my parents. Well, it's not true. I regretted not having my mother there, but for reasons that are pretty obvious to everyone now, I did not want my father present.

The news of the secret wedding was, of course, huge and the pressure got to both of us. Without Phil around I wasn't sure what I should do in response to all the media requests for interviews. Eventually, I decided to go on the *Holmes* show. I had been interviewed by Paul Holmes once before, but back in those days I didn't know him all that well. What I did know, though, was that his television show was massive in New Zealand and that probably half the country would be watching him that night. Tanya and I both fronted up for *Holmes*. So, too, did new All Blacks coach, John Hart. Paul, who is New Zealand's leading broadcaster, immediately made us feel at ease and at first the questions were straightforward. He was happy for us and I was relieved. When he got onto the part about us not having our parents at the wedding, I was struggling to contain my emotions. I told him how much I loved my mother. Then I cracked up. The tears came and they wouldn't stop. Paul was great. Sure, he knew it was fantastic television, but I could tell he was respectful and sympathetic.

Paul Holmes (New Zealand's leading broadcaster): When the news of his secret wedding broke, the story was always going to be massive and my instructions from Television New Zealand were clear: you have to get Jonah. I had established a very good relationship back then with John Hart, who had just been appointed All Blacks coach. I rang John and told him I had to get Jonah on the programme. John said he thought he knew where to get hold of him and that he'd do his best for me.

As the day went on we heard nothing. At 4p.m. I rang John again. He was with Jonah by this stage, but couldn't say any more. My people were agitated. It seemed the whole world was looking for Jonah Lomu. Just after 5p.m. John rang: 'I have Jonah and Tanya with me. What time would you like them?' I walked out of my office and quite calmly said to the team, 'Jonah Lomu and his wife will be here at 6.45 p.m. and will go on live.' I've never been such a hero.

Jonah and Tanya duly arrived and I can honestly say I have never seen a bigger man in my life. I had met him before but until that day I really wasn't conscious of his enormous size. Staggering. As I introduced the programme, Jonah and Tanya were holding hands. They were tender to each other and very shy of the world. They were young. On the one hand you had Jonah, who had suddenly become infinitely more famous than he had been the day before and, on the other, you had Tanya, who was new to the country and new to the idea of speaking on television.

I started the interview and everything seemed to be going fine. Then I asked Jonah about not inviting his mum and dad. Jonah was close to his mum. He said something about her being the one who had brought him into the world. Tears started falling. Tanya held his hand more tightly. I never spoke. People later suggested it was a long, calculated pause on my part. The truth is, I had no idea what to do. I just sat there thinking, 'The world's most famous rugby player is in tears and he's live on New Zealand television.'

The big man finally recovered and the interview finished quite cheerfully. I firmly believe, though, that in those fifteen to twenty minutes Jonah Lomu sealed himself inside the hearts of all New Zealand. The interview was a sensation. Within half an hour we were receiving calls from Australia and the United Kingdom. The story was played all over the world. I think that one interview helped forge a bond between us. Since then, whenever the big moments have arrived in his life, and he's chosen to speak out, he's always come on *Holmes*. I'm proud of that. People sometimes ask, 'How big is Jonah Lomu in terms of New Zealand stars?' Well, the answer is simple: how big can you get in New Zealand? I love interviewing Jonah.

Thinking back now, I'm not sure that doing the *Holmes* show was the greatest decision I've ever made. The advice I got back then was to go on with Paul. I was young and very mixed up and I went along with it. It was such a difficult thing to do and for a long time afterwards it was hard to live with. As I said, I didn't know Paul that well and here I was trying to explain to someone – to the whole country, in fact – the reasons why Tanya and I wanted a secret wedding and why we didn't invite our parents. I can't think of anyone else in New Zealand who has had to do that and now I think why did I have to explain myself to anyone? Paul later said that as I cried on his show, the nation cried with me. I don't know about that. I still wish I could have done it differently, but I don't have any bad feelings towards Paul. He was doing his job and he treated Tanya and me well. In fact, these days I get on with him great. He's a nice guy and I'm always comfortable around him. We see each other out and about a bit socially and we always stop to chat. It's never about rugby. He's always interested in what I'm doing but he doesn't bug me about rugby. I like that.

The whole wedding thing was made even more embarrassing because of an incident that had occurred a few weeks earlier. I was in Taranaki with Michael Jones, doing some promotional work at country schools. We had finished doing our stuff and were heading to the airport at New Plymouth to catch a flight back to Auckland. I was at the wheel of a Jaguar XJS and I was pulled over for speeding. From memory, I was doing 127km/h. That was bad, but what was worse was that I didn't have a driver's licence.

The irony about the whole thing is that I was racing to catch a flight to Auckland to attend a police function. We never made it. We ended up having to charter a small plane home. Michael had a good giggle about the whole thing and couldn't wait to tell the boys at training the next day. I didn't mind. I was just worried about what the media was going to say. When the story hit the newspapers I didn't handle it very well. I should have just come out and said what I'd done was wrong. Instead, I panicked and said I thought I was okay with an international licence. I regret the whole incident. In the finish, I paid the price — a fine for speeding and a fine for not having a licence. Worst of all, I had paid the price in public — again.

The third thing that contributed to my mad March was a bit of a dust-up I had with a photographer, Kenny Rodger, at Eden Park. It was just after the wedding and, I suppose, I was still hot news. I had just finished training with the Blues and was on my way to the car when he started taking some photos. Sweet. I didn't mind to start with, but then he got the camera right in my face and I just said, 'Nah'. As I was getting in the car he just kept clickin' away. I'd had enough and I lashed out and broke the flash unit on Kenny's camera. Not only that, but the whole thing had been caught on camera by a television crew. Before the story had even hit the six o'clock news, though, I'd made up the damage and Kenny had a cheque for NZ$700 for the broken flash unit, plus the CEO of Auckland rugby had also apologised on my behalf. I think Kenny and I both learned from the incident. I try to be more tolerant and he always asks when he wants a pic. We both get on pretty well now.

Coming to terms with being famous is not that easy. It's something I struggled with a lot early on in my career. Now, though, I'm pretty comfortable with being recognised every time I'm out in public. I can live with people asking for autographs as long they're polite. The only time it really upsets me is when I'm at a restaurant and someone plonks a piece of paper under my nose and expects me to just sign it.

Of course, you're always going to get the odd smart-arse. I've been deliberately bumped in restaurants and bars by people who want to take a shot at me. Usually they're full of drink. The worst incident happened in Auckland one night. I was on my way back from the bar with some drinks for my friends when this guy nudged me. I dropped the lot. At first I thought it was an accident, so I just cleaned up the mess and went back for some more. On my way back he did the same thing. Again, I dropped the lot. Still, I resisted the urge to have a poke at him. As I walked past him for a third time I just turned to him and said, 'You try that again and I'll kick your arse.' He just looked at me and said, 'What did I do?' I couldn't believe it. He was pissed and he thought he was bulletproof. 'Oh, you're the big man now, aren't you?' he sneered. I thought about teaching him a lesson. I was seriously unhappy. In the end he was lucky I managed to keep my cool.

The thing is, along the way I've had to weigh up all those annoying little things that happen in public life against what rugby in the professional age has done for me. It's allowed me to do things that I would never have dreamed possible while I was growing up in South Auckland. I've met some of the most famous people in the world. Actors like Will Smith and Robin Williams, who are really super guys. I've partied with Lennox Lewis and talked fast cars with Martina Hingis. I've had tea with the Queen and even fed her corgis a couple of sandwiches. I've raced against the great Linford Christie for charity and I've shaken the hand of the greatest of them all, Muhammad Ali. What a moment that was. The makers of the James Bond movies have even asked me to play small roles, twice, which was tempting.

I've been recognised in some of the most unlikely places, too. The funniest moment I can recall is when I stepped off the plane in Kuala Lumpur for the 1998 Commonwealth Games. Rugby wasn't big in Malaysia and I thought I'd be able to relax with the rest of the sevens guys. I genuinely believed I'd be pretty much anonymous. Wrong. As I got off the plane the first person I saw was a Malaysian airline worker. 'Hi Jonah,' he said casually. I couldn't believe it. 'How did you know my name?' I asked. 'Oh, I watch you play rugby all the time,' he replied. The same sort of thing has happened all over the world. Most of the time it's cool. In Britain I have become very well known over the years and have always been treated with kindness and respect by the public and the media. I remember doing some shopping once at Selfridges, just before Christmas. As I jumped on the escalator it seemed half the store followed me. They were all whispering and pointing. I guess they were just trying to find out if it really was me – nice, but a bit freaky.

The thing I can't handle in New Zealand are the media stalkers. Of course, I accept that I'm always going to be a target for the media and, in fairness, I've done my share of interviews with magazines about certain aspects of my private life. That's cool. I could easily have turned them down. Most of the time, though, I've done those sorts of interviews to stop rumours and to put across my side of the story. I have always trusted those writers. The stalkers, though, are different. I've had photographers and journos literally camping outside my home — up in trees, hidden behind cars — and it's bloody awful. At other times I've had photographers on my tail the whole day, photographing me at restaurants, at the airport, moving house. It gets to me. I've never got used to that invasion of space and it's tough on my wife, Fiona. It upsets her and that makes it even harder for me.

Fame and the money that goes with it as a professional rugby player are sweet as long as you keep your head screwed on. I've had good people around me the whole time. People like Phil and my accountant, Ian Duff. They've given me good advice. That's what I tell any of the young guys who ask me about professionalism. Some of these kids are fresh out of school. Many of them think it's just about signing on the dotted line. 'Get good people on your side,' I tell them. 'Get good advice.' There are lots of traps for young players and I've certainly fallen into a few along the way.

March 1996 also saw the start of the Super 12 competition, with teams from New Zealand, Australia and South Africa competing in a new professional provincial tournament. It should have been a great time for me. Instead, there was so much going on off the field I hardly had time to think about it. My life was being turned upside down. I needed Phil. The wedding had brought everything to a head. He was criticised for going off to Wrexham when some people thought he should have been here looking after Jonah Lomu, but that's bull. Phil was finally doing something for himself. He loves coaching and I was pleased when he got the opportunity to go back home. I had no idea when he left that everything would get so tough, but I didn't know where else to turn, so I rang him and asked to him to get on a plane and come back.

Phil Kingsley Jones: When I first made the decision to go to Wrexham, I never envisaged Jonah would become so big. Neither of us did. Debbie did a fantastic job in my absence, but there were things Jonah found difficult to talk to her about. She would often ring me and say, 'Your boy needs you. He's a bit depressed.' So I'd jump on a plane and come down to New Zealand. This happened about half a dozen times from the end of 1995 and through into the following year. I'd wait for Wrexham's Saturday game, then fly to New Zealand and spend a couple of days with Jonah. Then, on the Thursday, it was back to the UK.

Finally, though, everything came to a head. Jonah rang me one night very upset. Things were getting him down and he told me he needed me back in New Zealand permanently. That was it. He sounded like he was ready to pack it all in. I told the club that I would have to cut short my contract. They were obviously disappointed, but at the same time they were hugely supportive. Wrexham were having a very successful season, though – we had won the North Wales Cup for the first time in years – so it was a tough call all round.

Super 12 began on 1 March 1996. It kicked off in Palmerston North, where the Hurricanes hosted the Auckland Blues. In those days Auckland were the most powerful provincial team in New

Zealand. Under Graham Henry, they were the holders of the Ranfurly Shield and at the end of the 1995 season they had won their third successive NPC first division title. I was one of only a handful of Counties players included in the combined Super 12 squad and the experience I had that year is something I'll never forget. The game had only gone professional at the end of 1995, but right from the outset with the Blues I knew I was in the middle of a really professional outfit.

The Blues were able to field a team made up almost entirely of All Blacks. For that first game against the Hurricanes, I think there was maybe only one player who never went on to wear the black jersey. The Hurricanes, too, had a team of stars. Their forward pack was more than useful and in the backs they had Christian Cullen, Tana Umaga, Roger Randle and Alama Ieremia. There had been a big media build-up to the match and there was a huge amount of hype before the game. Two hours of pre-game entertainment was put on in front of a capacity crowd.

We had the heat put on us right from the kick-off. Alama Ieremia scored the Hurricanes' opening try after only a couple of minutes and we never got the lead until just a few minutes before the end of the match. In the end, our forwards managed to get on top and we came out with a 36–28 win. I didn't see much ball, but I was happy with the win, happy to be involved in this special match. We had been the favourites and we'd been taken to the wire. Bonus points had only just been introduced into the game. Our five tries gave us an extra point to go with the four we got for winning. The Hurricanes, though, came away with nothing. They were unable to score another try after Alama had put them in front early on and they just failed to finish within seven points of us, which would also have got them a point. I felt they deserved at least one from the match.

Life under Blues coach, Graham Henry, was, I guess you could say, a little different. I went into the Auckland-based setup with an open mind, but I was soon in no doubt about who the boss was. Graham was direct with his players and ran a strict, disciplined ship. It wasn't hard to work out why this side, like so many previous Auckland sides, was a winning outfit. Graham Henry knew what he wanted from his team and generally he got it. He could also be very persuasive, especially when it came to attracting players to Auckland.

Early on in my career, Graham had actually rung Phil and tried to get me to switch provincial sides for the NPC. Phil told Graham that he doubted I would want to move, but he would get me to call him anyway. I did call and I listened to Graham as he put his case for me moving up the motorway. Really, though, my mind was made up even before I rang him. I just said, 'No'. I don't think Graham was all that pleased, but at that stage of my career I was loving it in Counties. I was a South Auckland boy and I wasn't moving north for anything or anyone. You've got to give it to Graham, though. In terms of professionalism he was way ahead of his time and he was never scared to go hunting.

The Blues followed up their success in the Super 12 opener with a big win over the Crusaders in Christchurch, but in the third match we got one of those rugby reality checks when we travelled to Canberra to meet the ACT Brumbies. Back then, the Brumbies had been written off by everyone as the 'third' Australian side in the competition. All the talk was that they were made up of players not wanted by Queensland and New South Wales. We didn't think so after they beat us 40–34. Their team of young 'nobodies' included the names Gregan, Larkham, Roff, Finegan, Giffin and Noriega.

With the Super 12 in full swing, I got a break when I was named in the New Zealand team to play at the Hong Kong sevens. When the NZRU drew up my contract the previous season, Phil had got them to put in a clause saying I was free to play sevens for my country. Only All Blacks duty could prevent me from playing sevens. I know that caused a bit of discussion and a few raised eyebrows at the time, but for me it was a great result. The clause has been part of my contract ever since then. I love the game and, over the years, I've found it's been a great launching pad for fifteens.

Hong Kong was the number one event on the sevens circuit back in the 1990s. It was also my favourite destination and the only tournament I played in 1996. Two years earlier Glen Osborne had been the superstar in New Zealand's win and in 1995 I'd been named player of the tournament. In 1996, Christian Cullen came along and just blew everyone away. I'd known Cully from our school days and knew what a real talent he was. He'd been a part of the Hong Kong team in 1995, but only got the one game. This time he got all six matches and he was phenomenal.

The signs were there from our opening pool game against Sri Lanka. Cully just lit up. He scored seven tries and kicked a conversion to smash the tournament record for most points in a match. After that performance I didn't think it could get much better. I was wrong. He finished the tournament with eighteen tries from six matches, saving his best for last when we met Fiji in the final.

What Cully did to the Fijians in the first half from just behind our goal line was unbelievable. He was cornered right on the dead ball line and somehow managed to find his way around a couple of Fijians, then step a couple more defenders before sprinting upfield and delivering a pass to Waisiki Masirewa for an incredible try. I watched as he bobbed and weaved his way out of trouble like there was no pressure on him at all. After he broke the defensive line he just changed gear, like only Cully could, and hightailed it. I've never seen anything like it in my life. None of the boys could believe what he had done. Although our winning margin in the final was only two points, the Fijians were shell-shocked. I read years later that our coach Gordon Tietjens described Cully's performance in that match as the finest individual effort he'd ever seen in sevens. Damn right.

Christian has always been one of the smoothest runners in the game. Some guys can pull out the power run; others are just flat-out quick. To me, watching Cully open up is like watching running water. He glides – and that glide is deceptive. Make no mistake, he is very quick. There aren't many players around who can step at full pace and still keep traction. Cully is one of them. Because he doesn't say much, Christian is often misunderstood. In many ways he's quite similar to Michael Jones. Off the field they're both really mellow, quiet, shy guys. But on the field? Just superb. Cully was a class act. After Hong Kong, I wasn't the only player thinking that Christian's call-up to the All Blacks wouldn't be far away.

It was straight back to Super 12 action after my return from Hong Kong. We picked up four straight wins before getting a real hiding from the Queensland Reds in Brisbane. We were never in it and got smashed that day. It was one of those games that seem to happen every now and again. The Reds were a great unit, no doubt about that, but to have fifty points stuck on us was hard to take. It was our second loss on the road and it wouldn't be our last. I didn't play the next match, against the NSW Waratahs at Eden Park, but I was in the side that lost to Transvaal in Johannesburg. We went down to Durban to face Natal in our final round-robin match knowing that we had to win to make sure of a home semi-final.

Winning in South Africa is never easy, and after our embarrassing loss to Transvaal – they were near the bottom of the points table – Graham Henry put a massive amount of work into preparation for the Natal match. He was always a coach who prepared well. This time we concentrated on our defence and on shutting down their first-five Henry Honiball. For the whole game we were basically neck and neck with Natal. With only a few minutes left and the scores close we got the message from Zinny Brooke: 'I don't want to lose here,' he said. 'I want to win this match and get a home semi. If we lose we're stuck here for another week. Do you guys want that?'

The boys just looked at each other. Nothing else was said.

We got our ticket home after Eroni Clarke was set up for a brilliant late try by Lee Stensness. The call at the final whistle wasn't exactly, 'We've won', but more like, 'We're going home!'

We came home from South Africa feeling good about our chances in the semi-final. The win against Natal had given us a real lift in confidence. Even with our three losses we still finished up second after round-robin play and were drawn to meet Northern Transvaal in the second semi-final at Eden Park. The Reds topped the ladder and would meet Natal in the first semi at Ballymore. To my mind, the Reds had been the best team throughout the competition and it came as a real surprise when Natal upset them to make the final.

We didn't have too many problems against Northern Transvaal. The boys clicked. The forwards were unbelievable and the Blue Bulls just never got into it. In all, we managed eight tries. I got two and also heaps of opportunities with the ball in hand. The confidence we had found in Durban had not left us. We were into the first ever Super 12 final and we were going to play at home.

The atmosphere for the final at Eden Park was as good as it gets. It seemed that for the whole week leading up to the match, everyone in New Zealand was on our side. We weren't just the Blues. We were New Zealand — and we were playing South Africa. We weren't going to lose. Henry Honiball had been the guy we had targeted two weeks earlier in Durban. This time Graham saw their full-back, Andre Joubert, as a big threat. In this game we made life difficult for him. To keep him guessing, Joeli Vidiri and I swapped wings at different times. It worked perfectly. Joey didn't score that day, but I'll never forget one occasion when he 'stood up' Joubert from a standing start, and that from only about five metres in front of him. Joubert was no slouch, but Joey had wheels. It was classic.

Throughout the game there were a fair few verbals going down. Natal had their share of mouth men and we didn't need much encouragement. A lot of us were still hurting after the World Cup final and we gave as good as we got. At times it was quite funny. Kevin Putt, the former Waikato half-back, was never shy when it came to chipping the opposition and this day he was in great form. It didn't matter. We couldn't be put off our game and in the end we took the final quite comfortably. The game still remains one of my favourite rugby memories and I rate it as one of my best performances for the Blues. I picked up another try and I got space – lots of it. I made the most of it, too.

The last three weeks of Super 12 1996 were an incredible time, and it wasn't just the rugby. We grew so much as a team. We built a great spirit and the environment was one of the happiest I've ever been involved in. As I was to learn as my career went on, that part of the game is vitally important.

Tanya and I only discussed the possibility of a second wedding ceremony in South Africa after all the bad publicity we got from the first one. Of course, that's not what we said at the time. For years, I stuck to the story that Tanya and I had always planned a second wedding. It's easy to say now that perhaps I should have come clean and said exactly why I hadn't invited my parents to the first one. What's done is done. The second wedding was held because Phil actually talked us into it. I don't blame him. He thought he was doing the right thing at the time and felt it was a good idea to try and clear the air between the families.

The wedding was held in Tanya's home town of Kimberley in late 1996. As much as our first wedding had been private, this one was public — very public. There were three or four hundred guests, including about forty from New Zealand. My whole family came over. Phil was there. So, too, were a couple of my team-mates, Michael Jones and Charlie Riechelmann. It was a media show as well. Paul Holmes fronted up with a film crew and *New Idea* was there doing its thing. Phil suggested we sell the wedding story and photos to the women's magazine. Tanya and I weren't actually that happy about it, but Phil was thinking about the cost of the wedding. On top of that, we had to pay for so many people to get to South Africa. Our families were not wealthy. In the end, the wedding went off okay. We partied late into the night and the band finally left as the sun came up.

If we had our time again, maybe Tanya and I would have done things a bit differently. Who knows? Do I have any regrets about the second wedding? A few. I suppose to outsiders it looked like we had finally done the right thing. It certainly helped heal a few wounds on Tanya's side of the family. The ones between my father and me, though, ran too deep. Those few days in South Africa were full-on and we did have some fun, but deep down I was never really that comfortable.

After we got back from our honeymoon in the Virgin Islands, we were looking for some peace and quiet. The home we bought in Karaka in South Auckland was ideal. It was big and it was private. We could be happy there. Country living. A pond. Some ducks. Not quite what we were used to, but perfect, we thought, for newly-weds . . .

CHAPTER TEN

A GOOD HART AND A BAD KNEE

Harty arrived in 1996. He was my second All Blacks coach and over the next four years we would share some great highs and a fair number of lows. John Hart was different to Laurie Mains. Very different. Harty was from Auckland. Laurie Mains was from Dunedin. John came from the world of big business and the media always said he was a 'corporate man' (whatever that means). Laurie ran a small building company. Laurie had been an All Black. John had not. The one thing they had in common, though, was that they both loved the All Blacks with a passion. The way I saw it was that everything they did was always in the interests of the team. They were both New Zealanders. They were both rugby men. It's just that they went about things differently.

My first contact with John came when I was still at school. He had a big job for Fletcher Challenge back then and his company was sponsoring a sevens tournament which Wesley College was playing in. It must have been around 1992. I don't remember much about first meeting him, but I was certainly aware of his reputation and how he had turned Auckland into one of the best sides in the world in the early 1980s. In late 1994 he picked me in the New Zealand Barbarians side to play the Australian Barbarians at Mount Smart Stadium in Auckland. It was a few months after the nightmare Tests against the French and I will always be grateful to John for selecting me.

The game was staged as a farewell to John Kirwan, who had announced his retirement from rugby. I didn't partner JK on the wing, though. Harty included me in the side as a flanker – he always thought I'd make a good loose forward. The game was played in typical Barbarians fashion. Heaps of tries, including three for me and a couple for JK. One of my best memories of the match came towards the end when former All Black, Joe Stanley, and his son, Jeremy, came on to the field as replacements. They were together for about seven minutes and the crowd loved it. That sort of thing doesn't happen too often.

It was no surprise when Harty was finally appointed as All Blacks coach in 1996. He had been co-coach with Alex Wyllie at the 1991 World Cup and had been around the scene for a long time. Some people were surprised he didn't get the big job after Alex stepped down at the end of 1991. Anyway, he was the logical choice after Laurie finished in 1995 and I decided, just as I had with Graham Henry at the Blues, to treat his appointment as All Blacks coach with an open mind. I had heard a few stories of how he liked to play mind games with players. I wasn't quite sure what that meant, but if I had to put up with a different style, then that was fine by me. At the end of the day it was still about wearing the black jersey.

John Hart (All Blacks coach 1996–1999): Jonah was still very shy when I first took over the All Blacks. He seemed a little ill at ease talking to people in official roles. I understood that. He was still a kid, really. He had been thrust into the limelight at a very early age and I always believed he'd never been given the same chance to grow through his teenage years like most other young people. Communication with him was not easy in the early days but, casting that aside, I enjoyed Jonah from the outset. He was quite obviously a special player.

For the opening Test of 1996, the All Blacks met Western Samoa at Napier, a brand-new Test venue. The Test was played under lights, which was also a first in New Zealand. Any match for the All Blacks against the Samoans is always going to be tough. Because of the Samoan influence in the All Blacks side – Frank Bunce and Michael Jones of that 1996 side, for instance, had both played for Samoa early on in their careers – there is always that extra edge. The games are physical and the tackling is ferocious. Right from the haka it's game-on. The Samoans have their own 'war chant' and it's become the custom for them to perform their challenge, the manu, at the same time as the All Blacks. It was no different in Napier. The big crowd loved it.

As we expected, the Samoans came at us hard. Christian Cullen made his All Blacks debut in this match and showed with his three tries just why those of us who had been involved with him in sevens couldn't wait for him to get his chance at the top level. He copped a couple of decent shots from the Samoans, but even back then Cully was a tough nut and he just jumped up and got straight back to work. He wasn't the only player that night to feel the heat of the Samoans. I was stomped in the head by Brian Lima and at the time I was pretty upset. Harty was furious after the game. He has always been big on self-control and discipline. It was all I could do to restrain myself in Napier. The thing about some of those incidents is that they often look much worse than they really are. I'm not saying what Brian did wasn't bad and I'm not making excuses for dirty play. It shouldn't have happened. Sometimes, though, in the heat of the moment, players can lose it. Brian has always played his rugby hard. That night, unfortunately, he just lost it. I don't hold a grudge.

On the subject of 'boots', there were a few hassles prior to the match concerning the players' choice of footwear. At that stage the All Blacks were sponsored by boot manufacturer, Mizuno, and we were all expected to wear their products. A few of us, myself included, had our own personal sponsors. Jeff Wilson, Ian Jones and Josh Kronfeld were sponsored by Nike, while Reebok was my sponsor. I'm not sure exactly what the deal was with the other guys, but it got a bit ugly along the way. I never had a problem wearing Mizuno, thanks to the deal Phil had done with Reebok. They were fantastic sponsors and when we signed with them after the World Cup they said they were happy simply to have me as an individual. They knew the NZRU had their own arrangements with an 'official' sponsor and there was never any pressure on me to wear their boots while I was playing for the All Blacks. In all my personal sponsorships, throughout the years, Phil has always been careful about not rocking the All Blacks boat. He never wanted to put me in a position where it made me look like I was some sort of rebel.

Phil Kingsley Jones: The Reebok deal was ideal for Jonah. I told them right from the outset that if they wanted him they had to be aware he would not be wearing their boots when he played for New Zealand. We did not want to antagonise the Rugby Union. That was the deal, plain and simple. For their part, they couldn't have been more obliging. At no stage did they ever have a problem with him wearing Mizuno. Now, that's pretty fair considering the size of the sponsorship contract we signed. I have never been prepared to talk exact figures with anything that's been negotiated on Jonah's behalf, but let's just say the whole deal was done in US dollars and, for the time and for where rugby was professionally, it was enormous. There were plenty of other sportswear companies chasing Jonah back then, but I'm not sure they could have lived with the conditions we laid down. The association with Reebok continued for a couple of years. It was great at the time and they were marvellous sponsors. We loved Reebok and Reebok loved Jonah.

After clocking up fifty points against Western Samoa in Napier, the next assignment for the All Blacks was a two-Test series against Scotland. I got a try in the first Test at Dunedin. Christian Cullen scored four, which gave him seven in just two Tests, and there's no doubt he's got much happier memories of Dunedin than I have. I wrenched my right knee midway through the second half and, although I didn't know it at the time, the problem would stay with me for most of the international season. It was one of those tricky little injuries – a bit of damage to the lateral cartilage – which the medical staff thought would probably come right reasonably quickly. It wasn't causing too many problems after the match and I thought I'd be fine for the second Test in Auckland. Anyway, it was later decided I should give it a rest for a week or so. In the end, I sat out the Auckland match and Eric Rush was called into the side. We had run up sixty points against the Scots at Carisbrook, but they played much better at Eden Park and only went down 36–12. The most surprising thing, I suppose, is that Cully never scored.

I came back two weeks later for the first ever Tri-Nations game, against Australia, at good old Athletic Park in Wellington. Let me just say that on a good day the facilities at the ground were pretty awful. On a bad day they were hopeless. Wellington on 6 July was a bad day. There was a freezing southerly wind and it never stopped raining. Before the game we couldn't all fit in the main changing area and some of the team were having to put their gear on out in the toilets. This was not the sort of pre-match build-up we would have liked and, to cap it all off, the Wallabies' captain, John Eales, won the toss and took the wind.

Well, as it turned out we could do nothing wrong in Wellington. After just a couple of minutes, Frank Bunce made a break that eventually saw Michael Jones score. From then on we were unstoppable. Our plan in the first half was to crash the ball up and try and keep things tight. Harty was especially keen to use me in this role into the wind. We did this well enough, but it was the other areas of our game where we really came good. I couldn't believe our handling in those conditions. We hardly dropped a ball in the whole match. Everything stuck. It wasn't just our handling, either. The kicking was near perfect, and when Australia attacked us our defence cut them down – every time. By half-time we'd scored four tries and already had a bonus point.

The Aussies pounded us in the second spell, but couldn't get through. The loosies – Zinzan Brooke, Josh Kronfeld and Michael Jones – were awesome. By this stage of his career, Michael Jones was very much a senior member of the All Blacks, but even then he was quiet and always seemed to let his on-field actions do the talking for him. It was a bit of a surprise, then, when he led the defensive call in the second half against the Wallabies. He urged us on and he appealed for pride. 'Pride in the line,' he yelled at us as the Aussies hammered away. It was something I had first experienced in the Super 12 with the Blues – we never wanted to have our goal line crossed. Against Australia this day, Michael was calling for even more from our defence in the second half, even though we had the game in the bag. In the end, the Aussies managed two penalty goals.

Michael Jones was my idol when I was growing up and I still regard it as one of my greatest privileges in rugby that I was able to play with him. The first time I ran out on to the field with

My first All Blacks trial in Gisborne saw me come up against John Kirwan. Here I do my best to contain the great JK, one of my childhood heroes. At right is Marty Berry.

Possibles winger Marc Ellis makes the tackle on me in the final All Blacks trial of 1995 at Whangarei. I got a couple of tries for the Probables, but the best news of the night came after the match.

Me and Rushie training our hardest in 1995. I owe so much to him for all the support he gave me back in the early days.

Swamped by autograph hunters at Pukekohe after my first game back for Counties following the 1995 World Cup.

PHOTOSPORT

March 1996 was a mad month for me. Here I am on the way to my car after Blues training, just moments before I lashed out at photographer Kenny Rodger.

Daryl Gibson goes high to try and stop me in the Blues' match against the Crusaders at Christchurch during Super 12, 1996.

About to 'dot down' against Natal in the 1996 Super 12 final.

In my comeback game for Counties Manukau, against Otago in Pukekohe in September 1997, I ran straight into my All Blacks wing partner Jeff Wilson. Goldie was always happy to see me...

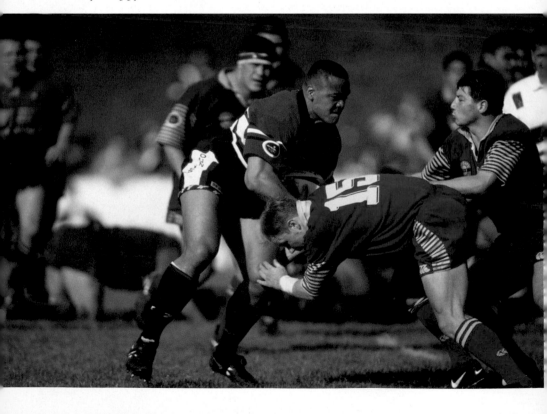

My first outing as a Chief, against the Blues at Hamilton in the 1999 Super 12.
Joey Vidiri is the Blues player on the ground.

The Chiefs had a mixed season in 1999, but one win which remains special was over
the Brumbies in Canberra. Here Brumbies flanker Jim Williams is at full stretch as he
tries to bring me down.

Scoring one of my two tries against the Sharks at Westpac Stadium in my first game as a Hurricanes player in Super 12, 2000.

Marika Vunibaka and I had a running battle down the sideline before I scored the second of my two tries against Canterbury in the 2000 NPC final at Christchurch.

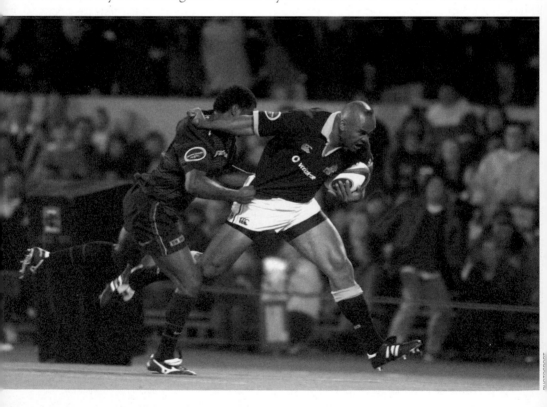

The final whistle has sounded in the 2000 NPC final — it was my proudest moment in provincial rugby. Filo Tiatia (left), Cully, Milton Ngauamo and Jerry Collins are also pretty pleased.

Doc Mayhew carrying the bag for the All Blacks — the medical bag that is.

Overleaf: My last attempt at trying to make the 2003 All Blacks World Cup squad came in an NPC warm-up match against Taranaki at Porirua.

him I had to pinch myself. Here I was, playing alongside the great Iceman. He had all the skills of a great loose forward and could play in all three positions, on the open- or blindside flank or at No. 8. Fast. Strong. Athletic. He was the greatest loose forward I ever saw and he was certainly the greatest I ever played with. On top of all that ability he has a great love for the game. He is a proud New Zealander and he is one of the proudest All Blacks I played with. Michael Jones is also humble. He doesn't have a bad bone in his body. In my early days he looked after me. As a fellow Polynesian, I looked up to him, just as so many Pacific Islanders have done in recent years. He was another person who really helped me believe in myself. I owe Michael Jones.

With about ten minutes to go against Australia, Sean Fitzpatrick did something he'd never done in seventy-odd Test matches. Fitzy left the field. It was a strange sight as he walked off. I'd always thought of Sean as Mr Indestructible. Little did anyone know at the time, but this would be the beginning of the end for Fitzy. His injury was to a similar part of the knee as mine, but his was worse, far worse. Years of wear and tear had apparently worn away part of the bone. From that day on, it seemed that whenever he ran, his knee would puff up. I'm still amazed he was able to carry on at Test level for as long as he did. The injury didn't finally beat him until late the following year. Pain was never a problem for Sean Fitzpatrick.

It's strange, I suppose, that despite the terrible weather in Wellington and the awful facilities, I still rate that game as the most complete performance by the All Blacks that I was a part of. Whether on attack or defence, we were in the zone. The 1995 team had played some great rugby, but in some ways this game signalled the start of another great era in All Blacks rugby. That Australian team of 1996 was a powerful unit. That day, though, they just couldn't foot it with us.

John Hart: To my way of thinking, that match rates as one of the great All Blacks displays, especially given the conditions. We scored some great tries and in some ways Jonah's effort that day typified the whole performance. His running with the ball was tremendous and he never stopped chasing kicks or turning to help defend. He showed everyone at Athletic Park that day his full range of skills and, believe me, he possessed them all.

If you look back over the latter part of his career, where he dropped a few balls and made some mistakes on defence, a lot of it comes down to his chronic kidney condition. If you're lethargic, your concentration just leaves you and, at Test level, that can make things very difficult. To me, Jonah's skills were never in question. He could do it all – run, catch, slip passes. And talking about skills, I've been involved with a fair few players over the years and I never saw anyone throw a ball further than the big man. On his day, Jonah Lomu could literally make the ball talk.

Despite our knee problems, Fitzy and I were both in the starting line-up for the second Tri-Nations match, against South Africa, at Christchurch. It was our first match against the Springboks since the World Cup final. They were the world champions and, while I guess revenge for that loss in Johannesburg was always in the back of our minds, really we were focused on the Tri-Nations and getting a second win at home before our two away matches. Revenge would be a bonus.

Christchurch turned on great weather for the match, but the game was spoiled from the start by the refereeing. The Scottish ref, Ray Megson, started blowing his whistle from the opening minute and he never stopped. I think he dished out something like forty penalties. It's no wonder that people, especially back then, got turned off the game. Whistle like we had that day is no good for the players and it's no good for the spectators.

In the opening stages of the match, the Springboks threw everything at us. They were obviously hurting from the loss they'd suffered against the Wallabies in Sydney the week before and their forwards ripped into us. There was a lot of needle and tempers flared not long after kick-off when Fitzy was headbutted by his opposite, John Allan. I nearly lost the plot at one stage when I got stomped on the shoulder at the bottom of a ruck. It was a cheap shot and I wasn't happy. I grabbed hold of the player's sock and thought, you ain't getting away! I got up and was ready to let a few fly when Walter Little jumped in and restrained me, which was probably just as well.

We got the win — and World Cup revenge — but it was close. South Africa put us under a lot of pressure through their forwards and with hard-hitting, in-your-face defence. We didn't react very well. All of us were guilty of mistakes, but eventually it was Andrew Mehrtens's boot which got us home. The Boks managed the only try through Andre Joubert. I wasn't that happy about that one, because it came after I'd messed up a high kick. Mehrts also made a few mistakes, but he more than made up for those with five penalty goals which saw us sneak in 15–11. While they were disappointed to lose, the South Africans were pretty upbeat about their chances in the return match at Cape Town. They're so much like the All Blacks in that respect. They'll never have themselves beaten before a match. The next Test would be played on their territory and they were confident.

We headed to Brisbane for the second Tri-Nations match against Australia knowing a win would give us the title. It would be a huge challenge. The Wallabies were hurting after the thumping we'd given them in Wellington and we knew them too well to think they'd be a pushover at Suncorp Stadium. They made a whole heap of changes for the match and we sensed from all the talk throughout the week that they'd come out fighting. How right we were. The game will always be remembered for the massive punch-up between the Wallabies No. 8 Michael Brial and Frank Bunce. The fight was a one-way contest. Amazingly, I don't think Buncey threw a single punch. He just covered up as Brial unloaded blow upon blow.

I'm still not exactly sure what got Brial so wound up. He had made a few remarks in the build-up to the Test about how the Aussies wouldn't take a backwards step against us in Brisbane, and it's fair to say Buncey did give him an elbow in a tackle, but what followed wasn't pretty. After the game Frank got plenty of stick for just standing there and taking the punches. He brushed it off by saying they were coming so quickly he thought it was best to keep his head down. He also enquired of a few players as to why they hadn't jumped in to help. That shut everyone up. We all knew Buncey was a man who could handle himself. By that stage we were also very aware of where Harty sat on the discipline issue. Every one of us had been warned about retaliation. Frank would live to fight another day.

The match itself was every bit as hard as we thought it would be. In fact, I'd have to say we got out of it by the skin of our teeth. It was all Australia in the first forty minutes and again it was only Mehrts's kicking which kept us in the game up until half-time. We turned behind at 16–9 and were soon down 22–9 after Matt Burke kicked a couple of penalties. Mehrts's boot again got us back to within striking distance and the turning point came not long after with the score at 25–15. I got an opportunity down the left-hand side. It had been a quiet after-noon for me, but I was determined to make the most of this chance. I made it into the Wallabies' 22 before I was dragged down. From the ruck that followed, Justin Marshall found space on the blindside and scored. Mehrts converted to bring us to within three points.

We got to 25-all a few minutes from full-time when Mehrts kicked his sixth penalty, but then came a movement I'll never forget. Even after all the games I've played it's still one of my clearest memories. It came from a 22m restart after David Campese had missed with a dropped goal attempt. Mehrts plugged the ball into Aussie territory. We chased – and we chased hard. We were desperate and the whole All Blacks back line zoomed in on the ball. Their winger, Ben Tune, was on his own when he fielded the kick and we expected him to kick for touch. Instead, he tried to run the ball back at us. Bad move, Ben. We couldn't believe it. I think I got to him first, but I wasn't on my own for long. There was no way the ball was going back on the Wallabies' side. From the scrum we called a double-round move and, after having a go on his own, Christian Cullen was a bit lucky in being able to lay the ball back for Buncey to score the winning try. It was the sort of finish you dream about. Mehrts converted, of course: 32–25. We were lucky. The Bledisloe Cup was already ours and, with one match still to go, the Tri-Nations tournament also belonged to us.

John Hart: Even with an injured knee, Jonah played a vital role in the Brisbane Test. He created the try that got us back into the game after we'd been in trouble at 25–15. He must have taken out about five defenders in a damaging run, before we won a quick ruck for Justin Marshall to get across.

There was some criticism back then that we weren't using Jonah with the ball out wide, giving him space. That run was a classic example of the damage he could do from close in. I never saw him solely as a finisher. Sure, he was fantastic with what he achieved out wide – and, of course, we tried to use him that way as much as possible – but he was also a player who relished physical contact and, as a consequence, he was able to take out so many defenders. The thing that's often forgotten is that, by 1996, defence had become a key element of the game and it was very important to have players who could take out a number of defenders. Jonah was a master.

Despite making it through the Brisbane game, my knee was still causing me problems. As well, I had a slight ligament tear in my heel that had happened in the Test against Australia in Wellington. I was getting frustrated. I was also unsure about where I stood with the new coach. Harty's approach was just so different to Laurie's. He liked to tinker a bit with the guys' minds. I didn't realise it then, but it was just his way of trying to make us mentally tougher. In those early days with John, I never felt I knew exactly what his intentions were when it came to me. He would constantly challenge you mentally. This sort of approach was new to me – and it was all a little bit strange. As I said, though, Harty's first priority was always the team. As much as Laurie Mains was the ultimate technical coach, John was the ultimate professional in the way he organised things. Looking back, I would have to say both men had equally positive influences on me.

I tried to put the injuries to the back of my mind and focus on the upcoming tour of South Africa. It was something I was really looking forward to. We were eager to finish off the Tri-Nations undefeated, but there was also a three-Test series against the Springboks to follow. The All Blacks hadn't met South Africa in a full-scale Test series in South Africa since 1976. The All Blacks had never won a Test series in South Africa. I desperately wanted to be part of it.

For me, South Africa has been a bit of a love-hate destination.

I have always had wonderful support from the black and coloured people; I've also had my share of support from the white population. It's fair to say, though, that there have been times when I've not felt so welcome and I've copped my share of abuse. I think, in general, the abuse has been light-hearted. For instance, on the way to the World Cup final in 1995 there were people banging on the sides of the bus and yelling out all sorts of rubbish, a fair bit of it directed at me. Other people had poles with little Jonah Lomu figures on the top with nooses around their necks. Most of the time it doesn't worry me. It's headphones territory. I put them on and try and shut everything out of my mind.

Things certainly hadn't changed much when the All Blacks arrived in 1996. My first taste of the country's rugby fever came at Plettenberg Bay, a resort on South Africa's famous Garden Route. We used Plett as our base for the build-up to the four Test matches. At a function put on by a local rugby club, I was literally mobbed and things started to get out of hand. I signed autographs and tried my best to be polite, but in the end it all got too much. John Hart was beside himself and he decided to get me out of the place. Later that night, Harty told me how impressed he'd been at what I'd done in trying to cater to all the supporters' wishes. I appreciated that. Despite all the attention, the stay at Plettenberg Bay was a worthwhile experience. It helped the team grow closer and we needed to be strong for the challenge that lay ahead.

I sat out the opening match of the tour against a Boland XV, but that day is one I'll never forget. The team bus was mobbed by supporters and we had to stay on board while the police, in some cases using dogs, cleared away all the people. It got quite scary. I saw one guy get his arm badly bitten. We love our rugby in New Zealand, but, thankfully, I've never seen anything like that here. Once we got off the bus I came in for special attention from the supporters. Again, I tried to be patient and polite, but I was beginning to wonder whether I should have heeded Harty's advice and stayed in the hotel. During the game there were people, mainly coloureds, scrambling to get over the barbed wire fences. They loved the All Blacks. Their passion never ceases to amaze me. Crazy. None of us had ever seen anything like it. However, the midweekers shook off all the distractions to come away with a 32–21 win. The business end of the tour was about to begin.

Cape Town was the venue for the first Test. When we arrived, Doc Mayhew arranged for an MRI scan on my knee. It was supposed to have been arranged quietly, but ended up turning into a bit of a circus. There were people everywhere when Doc and I turned up at the clinic and, in the end, I think the South African media and team management knew the results almost before we did. Harty wasn't too pleased about that. The scan confirmed what Doc Mayhew had always believed. There was some minor cartilage damage, but an operation was ruled out and instead it was decided to give the injury some more time to come right. A crook knee and a crook heel. I tried everything to get them right – strapping, acupuncture, massage – but nothing seemed to help. All I could do was give it time.

I don't think Harty ever considered me a serious chance for the Test in Cape Town. Glen Osborne got the nod on the left wing and I didn't even make the bench. I was pleased for Oz. He'd lost his position at full-back to Christian Cullen, but he fought back. The try he got against the Springboks in Cape Town showed he hadn't lost any of his great skills. I watched the Test from the grandstand as the All Blacks finished off the Tri-Nations tournament with a convincing win. Of course, I'd have liked to have been out there, but I wasn't right and I still got a lot of enjoyment out of supporting the guys. After the match, I learned that our eleven-point winning margin in Cape Town was the biggest ever by the All Blacks in South Africa. That sort of statistic brings home to you just how hard the Boks are to beat on their own soil.

Cape Town was the end of phase one of the South African tour. It completed the Tri-Nations, but we all knew the second phase would be an even greater challenge: a three-Test series to decide which of the two teams was the best in the world. I got my chance to push for a Test place in the third match of the tour, against Eastern Province at Port Elizabeth, and I knew I'd have to play well if I wanted to take the left wing spot from Oz. I scored one of our four tries as we narrowly beat Eastern Province, but overall it wasn't a great performance. My biggest surprise came when Harty named me on the reserves bench for the Durban Test. I would be covering not only wing, but also loose forward.

John Hart: Right from the first time I saw Jonah in the All Blacks jersey, back in 1994, I always had this desire to see him play at loose forward. If his health and fitness had been right, I think he could have been a devastating No. 8. I used to imagine him coming off the back of the scrum — so quick, so powerful . . .

For the Durban match we went with the traditional three forwards and three backs in the reserves. Blair Larsen would cover blindside flank and lock, and Mark Allen and Norm Hewitt were our front-row reserves. Jonah was obviously included primarily as a wing replacement, but on the strength of an amazing line-out session prior to the test — his spring was simply unbelievable — Jonah would provide extra cover in the loose forwards. As it turned out, we never used any reserves at Durban. It would have been an interesting call if he'd been required.

Sitting on the reserves bench can be bloody nerve-wracking. All of us were on the edge of our seats as the All Blacks gutsed out a 23–19 win. The Boks were competitive, but it was our fitness in the end that got us home. We would go to Pretoria one-up in the series. Up to the High Veldt. Up to real Springbok land. We knew this All Blacks team was on the verge of greatness.

I was given the game against Western Transvaal at Potchefstroom and, although the midweekers scored their best win of the tour, 31–0, again I didn't have a great game. When the Test team was announced for Pretoria, I wasn't even in the reserves. Harty went for four specialist forwards and two backs on the bench. I was disappointed and I suppose, looking back, I did take the decision a bit tough, but if I am honest with myself I'd have to say I really wasn't surprised. I hadn't been able to stride out properly all tour and the other guys were doing the business. How can you complain?

The Pretoria Test would be the most important of the year for the All Blacks. It certainly didn't start out that way, but after the victory at Durban we were just a win away from creating history. The feeling within the team was that we had to win in Pretoria. It had been a long season and I know that Harty, especially, felt that having to go and win at Johannesburg the following week with the series locked up at one-all would be a huge ask. It wasn't exactly do or die, but Loftus Versfeld, I knew, would be massive.

I couldn't believe the atmosphere when I took my place in the stand with the 'dirty dirties', the guys not on the reserves bench. The buzz was huge. The South African crowd knew, just like us, how big this game was. So often in this type of game, the action never lives up to the hype. No worries about that in Pretoria. Big Hannes Strydom scored for South Africa not long after kick-off and the crowd went berserk. Then a man the South African crowds always loved to hate made his entry. While captain Sean Fitzpatrick was the hard-nosed forward the South African people always singled out for special attention, Jeff Goldie Wilson was equally unpopular on the wing. He was the flashy back who rode the crowds and got up the South African noses. On this tour he was in sensational form. To my way of thinking, he played some of the finest rugby of his career in Africa. Our forwards were superb in Pretoria, no mistake. They matched, and eventually got the better of, the Springboks forwards. That was huge, but to me, watching Goldie at Loftus was a real privilege.

Jeff has always been a bit of a showman. His on-field antics are often mistaken for cockiness. No way. It's just the way he is. He always wears his emotions on his sleeve. He loves to celebrate after scoring a try or making a break. I could tell after the final Tri-Nations match in Cape Town that Jeff was going to enjoy himself on tour. Some time during the night's celebrations he had a number one haircut. When I saw him the following morning, he had a big grin on his face. 'Had to do it, man,' he said. It was typical spur-of-the-moment stuff from Jeff. It looked cool. Goldie has always been his own man.

Jeff scored two tries in Pretoria and the second one was pure class. He has always been able to do things on the field that other players can only dream about. He had the swerve and the side-step. He had great ball skills and he had great pace. But most of all he had vision — all the great players have vision. The kick and chase, too, has always been a deadly part of Jeff's bag of tricks and on this day it worked to perfection when he chipped Andre Joubert and raced round him to score. Jeff Wilson was a true athlete. That try was a Goldie special. The score put the All Blacks in front and it was a lead we never gave up.

We were ten points up at half-time, but definitely not out of sight. The Boks threw everything at us in the second half and actually closed to within a point of us with twenty minutes to go. The final minutes of the match were nail-biting. Up 30–26, and with only a couple of minutes left, Zinzan Brooke dropped a goal. Loose forwards just don't do that, certainly not in Tests. That was Zinny's second in two years against South Africa. The man had all the skills – and he always picked his moments.

The Springboks were as proud of their achievement of never having lost a series against us on home soil as we were committed to rewriting the record books. In those final few minutes they pounded our line. A converted try would have at least given the Boks a draw. What I saw from the grandstand was unbelievable. Desperate, do-or-die attack from the Boks and brutal defence from our forwards. It was a war. I could hardly watch. When the ref finally blew time I was exhausted. Mentally I was gone. God knows what it was like for the players. I could only imagine how they felt. We had all wanted this so badly. The players, the management, the handful of New Zealand supporters at the ground and, of course, the dirty dirties. Rushie turned to the rest of us in the stand and yelled, 'Let's do it!' 'Kamate Kamate . . . ' We performed in honour of the 1996 team, we performed for the jersey and we performed for all those teams who had gone before us. We were proud, man, we were so proud. The South Africans around us were stunned. They had just watched the Boks lose a series to New Zealand and now they had to suffer our haka in their own backyard.

For me, the tour had been difficult. It wasn't just my knee and my heel. I had been diagnosed with a kidney condition way back in 1994. Then it was felt it might come right in time. It didn't. It just caused problem after problem on tour. But in those final moments at Loftus I was able to forget about my problems. I forgot about my kidneys and how they weren't working properly, how the sores on my legs seemed to take forever to heal. I forgot about my knee and my heel. I forgot how everything that went wrong with my body seemed to take so long to come right. The All Blacks had made history and, man, was it sweet.

John Hart: Let me just say that Jonah Lomu remains one of the finest team men I have ever been associated with. He was totally committed whether he was in the side or not. I could never criticise his commitment to the team. He was always prepared to give you something. Always enthusiastic. The big fellow always put the team before himself.

My final match of the South African tour was at Kimberley against Griqualand West. In the days leading up to the match, I trained probably as well as I had all tour. I felt great on game day and Harty said later he was delighted with my effort in the first half. That was the problem, though. I only lasted half the game. I injured my shoulder and I couldn't see out the game. That was my tour over. I knew I couldn't be considered for the final Test.

The All Blacks were beaten at Johannesburg. It was the final test of the 1996 season and it was always going to be difficult. We'd achieved everything we wanted. A clean sweep in South Africa would have been nice, but, like Harty said in his book, it was 'a bridge too far'. In the end the Boks won convincingly. At one stage it was looking like we'd get a hell of a hiding when they led us 32–5, but in the end we got it back to 32–22. Pride turned things around in that last twenty minutes. When we returned from South Africa, they reckon there were more than 250,000 people who turned up for a ticker-tape parade down Queen Street in Auckland. The series win was massive back in New Zealand and it was really quite humbling seeing all those people turn up to congratulate us. I don't think I'll ever forget that day.

The NPC was in full swing by the time we returned to New Zealand in early September. I made it back for three of Counties' matches, including the semi-final against Canterbury at Pukekohe. It's a game I remember for all the wrong reasons. It was a big-scoring match in which we finally got home 46–33, but it wasn't the score and the fact we'd made the final that will stay with me. I was cited for a spear tackle on the Canterbury full-back, Kieran Flynn, and had to appear before a judicial hearing. I went to Wellington confident I wouldn't receive a match suspension. Wrong. They gave me a week, which ruled me out of the NPC final against Auckland.

The thing about spear tackles is that they always look so bad. They are dangerous, I accept that, but I reckon there are very few players who would actually make a tackle like that on purpose. It was late in the match when the incident with Kieran occurred. There were about five minutes to go and Canterbury were attacking just inside our 22. I came up very fast on their line and caught Kieran just a split second after he'd flicked the ball on, one-handed, to a player outside him. I was absolutely committed to the tackle and I think the judicial committee accepted that. Kieran was moving at full tilt. So was I. He was actually off balance and off the ground when I collected him. He was always going to go flying. The impact meant that his feet went up in the air and his head was pointing towards the ground. Let's face it, he was probably a bit over 80kg and I was probably around 118kg – and I hit him hard. As far as I was concerned, it wasn't that bad a tackle. I never deliberately tried to turn him or flip him up. If you catch someone the way I caught Kieran, these things can happen. It was purely accidental.

At the hearing I tried my best to make my point and explained that the spear tackle wasn't intentional. I was on a hiding to nothing, though, when they slowed the videotape down. It looked bad. It always does. My belief is that in circumstances like this one the judicial people have got to get away from slowing the tapes down. You're always going to get a tough deal when they do that. Played at normal speed, I thought the tackle was fine.

I was absolutely gutted with the suspension. An NPC final is not something that comes around all that often. I was so convinced about my innocence that I decided to appeal the decision. I got the same result at the appeal hearing. The New Zealand Barbarians were due to travel to England for two matches at the end of the year and I was told the English had really wanted me on the tour. But I was bloody annoyed and at one point I considered making myself unavailable for the Barbarians. In the end I decided to tour.

My health hadn't improved much by the time we left for England. Doc Mayhew actually considered pulling me out of the tour. My leg injuries were coming right, but I was pretty ill for the whole trip. I ended up with bronchitis and my temperature went through the roof. I also got another leg infection, but I played in both matches, against Northern Counties at Huddersfield and against England at Twickenham.

The weather for the Huddersfield game was terrible. It was snowing on the way to the ground and I was sitting next to Alama Ieremia. We were discussing how great it was that it never snowed in the islands. Christian Cullen was sitting in front of us and turned around at one point and said, 'It does snow, man. There's a mountain in Samoa and it snows up there.' Alama and I couldn't believe it. 'You're kidding, aren't you Cully?' Alama said. 'No, it's true,' he insisted. Whatever, Cully. There was another 'island' crack-up during the match. Joeli Vidiri was in the reserves and at one point Harty told him to warm up before he went on. No problem. He got up and jogged about wearing a big blanket. He was so cold that when he finally got on he just dropped the blanket and ran on still wearing his gloves. Classic. I don't think Joey ever lived that one down.

We put eighty-odd points on the Northern Counties side and then beat England 34–19 at Twickenham. I think we scored something like eighteen tries in total. I didn't manage one in either match. I felt pretty lousy throughout the tour. My kidneys just weren't functioning properly. It was crunch time in my rugby career. The doctors knew it and I knew it.

CHAPTER ELEVEN

HARD PILL(S) TO SWALLOW

My relationship with Doctor John Mayhew started just like any other doctor–patient association. It began in the mid-1990s and it grew. It grew just like my kidney condition grew. Now we are friends and we're tight. If I'm honest, I'd have to say I wish we hadn't had to become so close. Don't get me wrong. All Blacks doctor John Mayhew is a fantastic person. It's just I'd rather his surgery hadn't turned out to be like a second home. In the past ten years he has shared all my problems. He has given me all the good news and he has given me plenty of bad news. Doc Mayhew is honest. He knows Jonah Lomu as well as anyone else in the world. He probably knows my body even better than I do. My kidneys have almost become his kidneys . . .

They call it nephrotic syndrome. That's what I have. What does it mean? To me . . . buggered kidneys. In fact, nephrotic syndrome isn't just one single problem, it's a whole bunch of things. Basically mine just don't function properly. I get swelling in my lower legs. I have low protein in my blood and I have a high cholesterol count. Nephrotic syndrome actually comes on as a result of kidney damage. I don't know how long it has been with me and nor do the medical people. As I've said, even as a young boy growing up in South Auckland the signs were there that all wasn't well with my body: those cuts and scrapes that turned into abscesses; the infections and the coughs and colds that took weeks to get rid of; and, often, just plain tiredness. The signs were there, all right. I just didn't realise at the time that these things weren't normal.

Has the condition got something to do with the fact I'm Polynesian? I'm not even sure that the medical people have any definite answers. Sure, there has been quite a lot of publicity in recent times about the number of Polynesians in New Zealand who suffer kidney failure or who have diabetes. It has become a real problem, especially in South Auckland. Again, the medical people don't know exactly why, but some believe that it's due to our diet.

Doctor John Mayhew (the long-serving All Blacks doctor): There is certainly a high incidence of kidney disease and diabetes amongst Maori and Polynesian people, but I'm not sure it's just a case of saying it's purely socio-economic related. It may be, in certain instances, that the treatment of their childhood illnesses is perhaps not as good as it could be.

In addition, and without wishing to sound racist in any way, diet must also have something to do with the disease rate. Simply, they're often eating the wrong sorts of foods and in many cases the sufferers are overweight. Certainly, across the world the poorer people tend to have greater rates of obesity. It's a fact that convenience foods, if you like, are generally fattier than what we might normally describe as more wholesome food.

I would not like to be critical in any way of Jonah's parents, but it's fair to say that as a child he may well have had an illness that wasn't immediately recognised. I once saw a letter from a doctor Jonah was seeing as a kid in South Auckland. In it he expressed concern about a possible kidney problem.

Really, though, it was fairly tenuous. There is no doubt that by the time Jonah came to the attention of us as an adult it was too late.

I was first made aware I had a kidney disorder back in 1994. The diagnosis, though – Doc Mayhew always described it as the formal diagnosis – was actually made in 1996 and it came quite by accident. When I say by accident, I mean that a lot of people, Doc Mayhew and Phil Kingsley Jones included, had been worried for some time about how long I was taking to recover from small, everyday medical problems. Even as far back as late 1995, I was starting to struggle. Fatigue was the big issue. I was always tired. Things finally came to a head after I cut my shin at rugby training. Days went by and it didn't heal. When the cut got really badly infected, Doc decided to run a series of blood tests. What the tests discovered was quite frightening. The problems were enormous. My blood cells weren't right and my kidneys weren't processing things in the normal way. The list went on.

The next step was a biopsy. That's where they take away a small piece of kidney and look at it under the microscope. The results confirmed the worst. My kidneys were damaged and I would have to go under the care of Auckland specialist, Professor Ian Simpson. Back then it was felt there was a chance that things could improve. Back then there was some hope. Throughout 1996, Doc Mayhew and Professor Simpson monitored my condition closely. Nothing was made public. Instead, there was just constant testing, especially of my urine, and there was always the belief that my disorder might improve or, in fact, disappear altogether. With a kidney disease like mine you actually leak protein – a lot of that goodness in your body – into your urine. The testing regime proved quite a mission.

John Mayhew: I remember one interesting story from 1996. We were in Dunedin for the All Blacks–Scotland Test and we had Jonah on a twenty-four-hour urine collection to measure how much protein he was losing. He has always had a big fluid intake and in a twenty-four-hour period we would collect three or four huge bottles of urine. In Dunedin he was storing them under his bed. Coming back from training one morning with the fourth bottle, I went to collect the other three and found that the hotel cleaner had thrown them out. She must have wondered what the hell Jonah was doing with these bottles under his bed. Everything at that stage was top secret.

I'll never forget the letter that arrived around Christmas of 1996 from Professor Simpson. By now, I had been under his care for some time, but nothing could have prepared me for that note. Professor Simpson is New Zealand's leading kidney man. He is top-dog nephrologist. Professor Simpson is a straight shooter and there's never any bullshit with him. I like Ian Simpson. Both Ian and Doc Mayhew have never tried to hide anything from me. I knew right from the start that I had serious problems. But the letter . . . It came as a real thunderbolt, just such doom and gloom. It basically outlined the full extent of my problems and said that I only had a couple of treatment options. The letter also said the illness could finish my rugby career. My immediate thought was that it was all over.

Tanya and I immediately rang Phil Kingsley Jones. I was confused and, I guess, a bit emotional, but I wasn't bitter. In fact, I've never been bitter about my condition. I've always thought of it as my problem. No one caused it to happen to me. I've always said it's something that I have to manage myself. Of course, there have been odd times when I've asked, why me? How did I get it? I mean, who wouldn't? Phil was on holiday in Whakatane, but when I finally managed to get hold of him, he said he'd call Professor Simpson straightaway. He put the question right on Ian: 'What's all this about — he can't play rugby again?' Professor Simpson said he hadn't said 'never', but that he'd made it clear that it was a possibility and, in the meantime, I'd have to give up rugby for a while to get some special treatment. When Phil told me I was so relieved. If I had to give up rugby for a period, then that was fine. It wasn't like it was the finish or anything.

We were to start on a treatment called the Ponticelli regimen. It's basically a form of chemotherapy and it would be used to try and slow down or reverse the deterioration of my kidney functions. Ponticelli was a famous Italian renal surgeon and I was told that many of his patients had benefited from this particular course of treatment. There was a good chance that the drugs would make me feel better and there was a chance — a much smaller chance — that I would make a full recovery. There was also the possibility that the disorder would get worse. Ian and John never tried to kid me. This treatment would not be easy.

We made the public announcement in January 1997. The New Zealand Rugby Union decided we should call a press conference to announce the formal diagnosis and let the public know exactly where I was at. It was held at the Waipuna Hotel in Mount Wellington. We were all there — me and Tanya, Phil, Doc Mayhew and All Blacks coach John Hart. In the past, I had done plenty of interviews and press conferences. This one was the hardest. I'll never forget walking in. I was probably more nervous than I get even before a Test match. The news was huge. We told the world all about Jonah Lomu's kidneys and that I would be out of rugby for at least six months. Then came the questions.

The journos didn't let up. I don't know how many calls Phil received over the next few weeks, but it seemed that everywhere I turned the media was talking about Jonah Lomu. After the initial fuss died down I concerned myself with just one thing. Professor Simpson had actually said to me I could be out of rugby for a year to eighteen months. In my mind I was ticking off the months and the days. Mmm. There was an All Blacks tour of Britain at the end of the year. It was about nine months off. I wanted to make it.

I knew nothing of the Ponticelli regimen before I started. By the end of it I was an expert. I can clearly recall Professor Simpson talking me through the whole thing. He has always been such a super-cool dude. He just sat there chewing on his glasses as he explained everything to me. I could tell that he was waiting for my reaction to this strange new treatment. It was heavy stuff, that's for sure, and he told me it would be hard going. He must have wondered how I would take it. I just listened and nodded. I mean, hell, it's not as if they hadn't looked at all the other possibilities. I think the doctors had contacted every specialist they could to see if there was any other option. Whatever, Professor Simpson was the man and what he said was good enough for me.

The early treatment started with a heavy course of a drug called prednisone. I would get to know these little pink pills very well over the coming months. They are what the doctors call cortico steroids and for the first month I was chewing up plenty of them. They work in a completely different way to anabolic steroids. These ones actually eat into your muscle, whereas the anabolics build up mass and muscle. Prednisone is an anti-inflammatory drug and one of the main reasons it was given to me was to try and reduce swelling around my kidneys. I was also told the tablets would make me retain fluid. The doctors were right. I ballooned up to 150kg during the treatment – that's over twenty-three stone. I was a very big boy for a while there.

I kept taking the prednisone tablets as the Ponticelli regimen kicked in properly. The beginning of each month was the worst. The treatment was intensive. For the first three days I would go to Doc Mayhew's surgery and he would give me dexamethasone – like prednisone, but more powerful – intravenously. Just the thought of that needle now . . . The size of it – holy cow, it was big. My arm would go numb for about thirty or forty minutes. The injections would make me feel really crook. Doc was shooting this stuff straight into my blood system. After that it was back to the tablets. Then came another drug, called chlorambucil. I guess the best way to describe chlorambucil is that it's designed to eat away at cancer cells. Prednisone, chlorambucil and the intravenous treatment. It was a kind of month on, month off routine.

John Mayhew: Jonah's weight would fluctuate wildly from week to week. I remember seeing him once at the All Blacks hotel in early 1997. He was just huge. Puffed up. He looked awful and, although I was used to seeing him like this, I told him to make himself scarce before any of the press photographers caught him. He wasn't too worried, though. The next week he would be 10kg lighter. Quite staggering. He was on very high doses of a couple of powerful drugs. Chlorambucil is a chemotherapeutic drug, something which is used to treat cancer, so make no mistake, we are talking about heavy-duty stuff here.

The prednisone and the IV treatment not only caused my body to retain fluid, but they also had the effect of speeding up my metabolism. I was constantly eating. For example, I would get so hungry that I would sit down and eat a whole chicken. Then, just a short time later, I would eat another one. People around that time often got the wrong impression about my weight. It was like, 'Oh, he's not training and he's just packing on the weight.' The fact is, the prednisone was making me eat like a horse.

The side effects from the chlorambucil were completely different. Those drugs would heighten my senses of taste and smell – and they could sometimes do my head in. A normally pleasant cologne would, for instance, smell terrible to me. It would be just so intense. Same thing with cigarette smoke. I could smell it from miles away. Who's smoking? I used to wonder. The person could be across the other side of the street. For a while there, everything – and I mean everything – tasted and smelled bad. My diet would change by the month. First, it was four weeks of bland food. Everything I ate had to be boiled. Chicken, potatoes – you name it. Then it was back to normal for the next four weeks. I did this for about eight months. The doctors were right. This was a tough course. For a time I was taking up to sixteen tablets a day.

It wasn't just my body that went haywire during this period, though. There was a mental issue as well. I would have dramatic mood swings. One minute I was up and the next I was really down. No screaming or yelling, nothing like that. It was more about feeling great and being really chatty one moment, then just as quickly not feeling like talking to anyone. All the drugs seemed to affect me in that way. It can't have been easy for people around me at that time, but no matter what my mood, the people close to me continued to give me massive support – Phil, Doc Mayhew, Professor Simpson and my wife Tanya. Along with her cousin, Odette, who had come out from South Africa to live with us in 1997, Tanya was really strong and helped me get through the tough times. I also hung out a lot with Michael Jones. He had ruptured a knee tendon in the first Test of the season and his leg was in plaster for a long time. He is a man of great faith. He encouraged me when I became dejected. Michael wasn't just a great player. Michael is a great person.

John Mayhew: I have nothing but admiration for Jonah in the way he coped that year. The pills, the drips, the whole deal . . . he must have felt like crap, but he never once defaulted on an appointment with me. He always turned up and he never complained. Not once. He was a model patient. I could have understood him saying, 'Bugger this treatment. I'll just put up with the kidney disease.'

After that initial diagnosis there was always a distinct possibility that he would one day need a kidney transplant. Jonah has lived with that thought since 1996. I have no time for ill-informed people who have criticised him for continuing to play all these years. In fact, we've all been criticised – me, Jonah and Phil. The fact is, there is no evidence to suggest his condition worsened or that his career was shortened because he kept playing. It's always been a question of informed consent. Jonah must have got sick of me continually asking the same question of Ian Simpson: 'Are we making him worse by playing him?' I used to ask Professor Simpson that question in Jonah's presence, just to reinforce the point. The answer has always been no. His condition never worsened because he was playing rugby.

Interestingly, I've been criticised by certain people at the New Zealand Rugby Union for being too close to Jonah. Sure, I was the All Blacks doctor, but I also became his general practitioner. Is he a special case? Damn right he is. I make no apology to anyone for the relationship I have had with him over the past ten years.

Training, any sort of training, was difficult while I was receiving treatment. Rugby, though, was never far from my mind. While I tried to distance myself from the team environment, I still kept a close eye on the Blues in their Super 12 campaign. What a year.

To go through the competition unbeaten was an incredible achievement. The final against the ACT Brumbies wasn't one of the great matches, but along the way the Blues played some fantastic rugby. I was rapt for the guys when they made it back-to-back Super 12 titles. I was a bit emotional, too, when All Blacks captain Sean Fitzpatrick lifted the Tri-Nations trophy for the second year running. Too much. I couldn't help thinking about the trophy he'd almost broken his back in trying to lift the year before. That was the one where the makers had got all the measurements wrong — inches instead of centimetres. It was an absolute bloody monster! Classic — the Super 12, the Tri-Nations and the Bledisloe Cup. Yeah, I thought about footie constantly in the winter of 1997.

One thing that helped keep me occupied during the lay-off was the overseas travel I did with Phil. We went all over the world making personal appearances and doing after-dinner speeches. Phil is a legendary speaker and entertainer. He actually did it professionally in Britain and he is still in big demand in New Zealand. He's a born entertainer and can be the funniest person in the world. I was never a great after-dinner speaker, but in those eight or ten months in 1997, Phil taught me so much and I actually started to enjoy it.

I wasn't playing, but at least I was amongst the action, especially early on in the year. The invitations just poured in. At one stage I felt like I was actually on the sevens circuit again. At the Hong Kong tournament, which doubled as the sevens World Cup, I was invited to be a comments man for ITV. Me and Gavin Hastings. It was busy, but it was a blast. Watching New Zealand lose to South Africa in the semi-finals was the hardest part. I went to the Japan sevens as a guest of the Japanese Rugby Union. Great food and fanatical supporters, sushi and signing sessions. Tokyo was full-on. I was invited to Paris for their tournament and got treated incredibly well. I even made it to Roland Garros for the

French Open. That was a special highlight. The tournament organiser arranged a ticket for the president's box. How good was that?

I had a great time in Australia, too. Phil and I did five speeches in three days. We spoke at Brisbane and Sydney and then the big prime minister's luncheon in Melbourne, before the Tri-Nations match against the Wallabies. That was a classic. Me and Phil along with David Campese and Chris Handy, the commentator and former Aussie prop. There was a great crowd in that day and I even managed to take the mickey out of Eric Rush, who was on one of the tables. Speaking in front of big audiences was becoming a lot easier. As Phil said, I was honing my skills. Still, I'd much rather have been out in the middle.

However, one thing that annoyed the hell out of me in 1997 was the stuff-up with my medical insurance. Basically, the forms had not been filled out correctly prior to 1997. Neither Doc Mayhew nor I completed them. Instead, it was left to people who I really felt should have done better. In the end, it hurt me big-time. My medical condition was well known back then, but somehow some of that information never appeared on the pre-insurance forms. I was dark about it at the time. It cost me a heck of a lot of money. I could accept that I was out of the game because I was sick, but it was hard to accept that the insurance company wouldn't pay up through no fault of mine. I remember being told that some insurance companies turn down about seventy per cent of medical claims. I don't know if that's true, but it certainly didn't make me feel any better. After that experience we've always been careful with insurance. I was able to reinsure myself after 1997, but the premiums were obviously much higher than those of most other players.

I remember the date — it was 6 August. My kidney condition was finally beginning to settle down. The disease hadn't gone away, but Doc Mayhew and Professor Simpson seemed pleased with my tests and my general progress. I was about to swallow my last serious bunch of tablets. I had done virtually no physical exercise for six months or so and, when Doc decided I could start going for a few runs, I was over the moon. The hardest part was always going to be the pain. My tolerance levels were way down and while I knew it would be tough going, in the end it simply came down to how much desire I had.

Training started slowly. And I mean slowly. I began with the legendary run through the Auckland Domain – the one the Auckland boys always referred to as the Ho Chi Minh Trail. This run would normally take me around eighteen minutes. The first one I did with All Blacks fitness trainer Martin Toomey took me just under two hours. I stopped to rest more than twenty times. Doc also came on a few of those early runs with Martin and me. Doc isn't the fastest runner in the world and it must have been strange for him to have to stop and wait for me to catch up. I remember outsprinting him once at the finish. He was like, 'Hey, Jonah, I've had to wait ten minutes for you to catch up. Now we're at the business end you just burn me off?' Sorry, Doc.

The National Provincial Championship was in full swing at the same time I returned to training. I was still carrying a lot of weight and I knew that if I wanted to make the All Blacks end-of-year tour I would have to play some NPC matches. I know a lot of people at the time thought I was mad trying to come back so soon. It didn't worry me. I had committed to making myself available for that tour. I ran and I cycled. By mid-September I was down to just a couple of stops on the Ho Chi Minh Trail. I ate all the right foods and I followed the doctors' instructions to the letter. I was still just over the 140kg mark when I resumed training. In four and a half weeks I weighed in at just under 130kg. I wasn't one hundred per cent fit – far from it – but I was down to eight pills a day and I was hungry for some game time.

I made my comeback to first-class rugby on 21 September 1997. It had been almost eight months to the day since it had been announced publicly that I was suffering from nephrotic syndrome and that my whole rugby future was in doubt. The experience had changed my life. In a funny way I had become a much stronger person. I had learned so much about myself. I had learned about things I'd hardly ever thought of before. Willpower was one of them. If you want something badly enough, then anything is possible.

I loved playing for Counties Manukau at Pukekohe. For my comeback game against Otago I was only on the bench, but the people of South Auckland turned out in force. I was so excited I nearly ended up on my backside as I came down the tunnel. I'd forgotten how steep the run down to the ground was. Fitting, I suppose, because the road back to rugby had been just as crazy. I came off the subs bench that day against Otago with my emotions running wild. I thought of all the people who had helped me. Phil later told me he had a tear in his eye when he saw me run onto the field. I had dreamed of this day. It was my first step back towards the ultimate goal – the black jersey.

The match itself was one Counties had to win. The team had lost their previous two matches and if we were to have any chance of making the NPC semis then we had to get the points against Otago. In the end it didn't matter that it was only a two-point victory. I was stoked for the team. For myself . . . what can I say? Joy. Relief. Jeff Wilson was at full-back for Otago that day. I probably wasn't fit enough to take on Goldie in a head-to-head clash, but gee, it was great to be back out there.

Jeff Wilson (All Black 1993–1999, 2001): When he came on it was like, oh no, here we go again. I was just thankful I wasn't on the wing. The truth is that nothing ever changed when it came to the big fella. Whenever he was on the field it always felt like there were sixteen or seventeen players in the opposition. Really, though, in 1997 I was just rapt that he had come back. I was delighted for him and delighted for New Zealand and the All Blacks. The fact that he went on to again become a major force in world rugby is a great tribute to the man. He hung on to his All Blacks dream during what must have been such a tough year. He never gave up. That says so much about his desire. World rugby was lucky to get him back. There will never be another Jonah Lomu. Never.

Counties made a bit of a habit of winning the close games in 1997. We got another narrow one against Taranaki in my second game back. It was a one-point nail-biter at the Bull Ring in New Plymouth. Again I came off the bench. Although I was nowhere near match-fit, it was another small step. My first starting spot came against Southland in our final round-robin game of the NPC. It was a match we had to win to secure a spot in the semi-finals and I came in at the expense of David Wood. He and Jona Qio had both done a good job for Counties while I'd been out. It's always a tough call when you've been there most of the year and a player comes back to regain his spot at the end of the season.

We absolutely wasted Southland at Pukekohe. I got two of our twelve tries in our 85–17 win, but the real star that day was Tony Marsh, who scored four. Tony was a wonderful player for Counties and a real loss to New Zealand rugby after he left to play in France. I've followed with interest not only his progress on the field since he became eligible to play for France in 2001, but also his battle with cancer. I was thrilled to see him named in the 2003 French World Cup squad.

After the Southland match my confidence received a boost when

I spoke to John Hart at the after-match function. He had kept in touch with me during the year and I'm sure he received regular updates on my condition from Doc Mayhew and Martin Toomey, but I hadn't had much personal contact with him. Harty told me at the after-match that he had come out to Pukekohe specifically to look at me. He told me I should keep working hard and that I was in the frame for the end-of-year tour to the UK. There would be thirty-six All Blacks chosen for the nine-match tour. I was pumped.

The big win against Southland gave us the fourth qualifying spot for the NPC semi-finals and a date with Waikato at Hamilton. What a game it turned out to be. We got monstered from the start and by half-time we were down 28–8. Things didn't improve much in the second half until, at 37–15 and with about twenty minutes to go, the ground announcer, former All Black Buck Anderson, made a big mistake. He started telling the local fans how they could buy tickets to the final. Screw that. Who the hell do they think they are? Errol Brain was the Counties captain that day. Always an inspirational leader, he'd already given us the 'speech' at half-time, but it was the ground announcer's message that really did the damage. We just climbed into Waikato. The forwards started winning us great ball and Joey Vidiri, on the right wing, was on fire. He scored three tries, including a beauty with only a couple of minutes to go when he burned off half the Waikato back line. Final score: Counties Manukau 43, Waikato 40. Sensational.

The Waikato crowd was stunned as we left the field. The boys kept pretty quiet until the after-match function when Errol got up to make his captain's speech. 'I guess you'll be the only person at the Waikato final,' he said to Buck Anderson. We all broke up laughing. Against all predictions we had made the NPC first division final.

We went to Christchurch in late October confident we'd give Canterbury a good run in the final. In the end we got done. Although we didn't know it at the time, this was the start of a great new era in Canterbury rugby. Their defence that day was awesome. Joey and I weren't given any space out wide. At the end of the day the red and blacks had managed six tries. We got one – 44–13 is a hiding in anyone's language. The result was a real disappointment to me, but the 'work hard' message I'd got from Harty after the Southland game kept me going. My weight, though, was the hardest thing to get under control. Those extra kilos I'd packed on were proving hard to shift. I was doing plenty of training outside of the Counties trainings. I needed to be as fit as possible. I needed to give myself every chance. The black jersey was just so close – like 1995 all over again. I wanted it so badly.

The day John Hart rang to tell me I was back in the All Blacks side was one of the happiest of my life. The whole year had been such a rollercoaster ride. Getting back on the field for Counties was a rush. Harty's call, though, was the best news of all: 'Congratulations, Jonah, you're in. Well done.' That was the thing about Harty. He always communicated with his players before a team was officially announced. I'm a firm believer that players should always be kept informed – given the good news or the bad before the team is announced publicly. I jumped around the place like a madman after his call. Back in black! Yeah, it doesn't get any better.

John Hart: Jonah went through hell in 1997 but we – the All Blacks selectors – were impressed by the way he handled things and the way he fought to get himself right. We were prepared to give him this chance. Sure, the fact we were taking a thirty-six-man squad to Britain gave us a lot of scope, but we would never have considered him if he hadn't done the work. He was nowhere near peak fitness before we left for the UK and he was carrying too much weight, but we were confident that we'd be able to get him right on tour. He deserved this chance.

It was a cold night at Pontypridd in Wales in mid-November 1997. It had been about fifteen months since I had last played for the All Blacks. It didn't matter. I was excited and I was nervous. So nervous, in fact, that I rolled my ankle in the dressing room before kick-off. It wasn't serious. Nothing was going to stop me from running out against Wales A. I had sat out the first match of the tour against Llanelli, but in the grandstand that day, at the legendary Stradey Park ground, it hit home to me how much the Welsh loved their rugby and how much they cherish their history. Their most famous victory came against the All Blacks in 1972. The old scoreboard was still there: Llanelli 9, New Zealand 3. Far out. That's real passion.

I didn't set the world alight against Wales A. I scored a try, which is always a thrill in the black jersey, but really I was just happy to be part of the win. After the match I spent ages signing autographs. Those Welsh supporters — talk about keen. There were a number of players making their All Blacks debuts at Pontypridd and it was exciting to share that time with them. One of the new boys was Aaron Hopa. He was so nervous before we left for the ground that he forgot to pack his boots and had to borrow a pair for the match. Hops was a great guy who was so proud of becoming an All Black. All of us were really shaken when he died so tragically in a diving accident in New Zealand just a year later.

The first Test of the tour was against Ireland at Lansdowne Road. I never expected to be picked and I think Harty made a fair call when he named Jeff Wilson and Glen Osborne on the wings. He went with form and all the players who had done the business for him throughout the season – all that is, except Sean Fitzpatrick. His knee was stuffed. He didn't play in either of the first two matches and he certainly wasn't right for the Ireland match. Justin Marshall was made captain for the Test, but it was the news that Fitzy would not be starting that got everyone talking. Hell, he'd missed only one Test since 1987 and that was when he was rested against Japan in the World Cup. A Test without Fitzy was all a bit strange.

As a dirty dirty I watched on as Ireland and their inspirational captain, Keith Wood, came out firing. The crowd went off when he scored an early try. They were just wild with excitement when he got his second after about twenty-five minutes. From then on, though, it was the All Blacks in control. We had a reasonable lead at half-time and in the second half we gassed it. Mehrts was having one of those days and the thirty-three points he scored was his best ever haul in a Test. Not being in the Test side gave me a chance to enjoy the Dublin experience. It was fantastic. It seemed that every pub we passed was chock-full of Kiwi supporters. On game day it was massive. I walked through the crowd and soaked up the atmosphere. It was totally different to being part of the match side, but being a dirty dirty in Dublin had its upside.

By the time the team got to Huddersfield for the match against Emerging England I was feeling much stronger and fitter. McAlpine Stadium is a great ground with a beautiful surface and the midweekers didn't let anyone down that night against a team that included heaps of full England internationals. Emerging England? That name made us smile. I grabbed a couple of tries in the win and for the first time since my comeback I felt really happy with my performance. John Hart must have felt the same. When he congratulated me after the match I knew I was back in contention for the Test team. Sure enough, I got the word from Harty that I'd be in the starting fifteen to play England before the official team announcement. He was, as always, to the point: 'You've worked hard, Jonah,' he said. 'You deserve your chance.'

The next morning I was so excited I could hardly eat breakfast. I remember just staring out of the window with my mind racing. At one point Grant Fox, the great All Blacks fly-half of the late 1980s and early 1990s, ran by. Foxy had been a fighter. I wondered how he had felt whenever he had been named in a Test team. I hadn't started a Test match since July of 1996. This had made all the hard work worthwhile. This was the ultimate.

The 1997 tour was a weird one for me for a whole lot of reasons. The fact I had made it back to Test rugby was a personal highlight, but there were other unusual things going on. For instance, here the All Blacks were in Manchester to play a Test against England. There was some construction work going on at Twickenham and we were going to face England at a soccer ground. Not just any ground. It was Old Trafford, one of the most famous soccer grounds in the world and the home of Manchester United. Weird all right.

We copped the same old stuff in the British press during the lead-up to the Test. They're always great at talking up England's chances – and not too bad at chopping them down when they lose. The media pressure, though, never really fazes the All Blacks. You get used to it all over the world.

We decided to change our routine slightly for this, the first of two Tests against England. Instead of having our traditional captain's meeting at the hotel, we held it at the ground. Justin Marshall would run it. Fitzy's knee injury again ruled him out of the Test. We got to Old Trafford early, which gave us a chance to walk around the place and get a feel for the atmosphere. It was the little things that got me, like chatting away to one of the security guards before the match. I said to him he must have seen some amazing things over the years. He reckoned one of the funniest had been when the Wimbledon hard man Vinnie Jones put a mini stereo system outside Manchester United's dressing room and turned it up full bore. It was playing the Wimbledon theme song. The security guard was just cracking up as he told me the story. For a while before kick-off I spent a bit of time on my own kicking around a soccer ball, before finally getting my hands on the oval one. My international comeback was at a soccer ground — the Theatre of Dreams. My career was back on track.

During the pre-game haka the atmosphere was tense, to say the least. The English were wired for the game, especially hooker, Richard Cockerill. He must have said something at the start to his opposite, Norm Hewitt, a proud Maori and a man who had waited many years in Sean Fitzpatrick's shadow for his chance to start in the No. 2 jersey. With Fitzy ruled out, he had started against Ireland the week before and this Test was only his third run-on start in about five years. The two players got closer and closer during the haka and by the time we reached 'A upane kaupane whiti te ra!' they were eyeball to eyeball. Cockerill had done more than simply accept the challenge and no way was Norm going to back off. Yeah, let's get it on.

It didn't take long for me to get back into the swing of Test rugby. I'll happily admit that I love the big occasions and I love playing against England. My first real chance came after about ten minutes or so, when I fielded a pretty ordinary kick from Mike Catt. I had space — real space — and I charged down to the English 22m, getting rid of a couple of defenders on the way. From the ruck, Zinzan Brooke got the ball to Jeff Wilson and Goldie got the pass away to Ian Jones for our first try. It was almost certainly at that moment I realised my body was finally on the mend. No strapping. No twinges. No tiredness. No doubts.

Although we led England 15–3 at half-time and eventually pushed on to win 25–8, it wasn't one of the great All Blacks performances. The English played well. Their forwards were experienced and they were tough – Lawrence Dallaglio, Richard Hill, Jason Leonard and, of course, Martin Johnson. I've always respected Johnson, but my view of him changed a bit early in the game when he caught our captain Justin Marshall in the jaw. It was a hell of a blow and it left Marshy pretty groggy for much of the match. Johnson received a one-match suspension for the incident, which took him out of the Poms' match against the Springboks a week later. It was a cheap shot by Martin. He's a lot better than that.

We ground out that win at Old Trafford and in the end we probably had a lot to thank Mike Catt for. Had he not missed a number of penalty opportunities the scores might have been a lot closer at the finish. I wouldn't say I was relieved at the end of the game. Sure, we knew we'd been through a tough one, but I always felt it was a game we had under control. England mightn't have been the reigning Five Nations champions, but to my way of thinking they were still the best team in the Northern Hemisphere at that time. They'd get another shot at us in a couple of weeks.

One memory from Old Trafford will stay with me forever. As I was heading back to the dressing room I became aware of the crowd roaring. I looked across the pitch to see the England players doing a lap of honour. Then I looked up at the scoreboard: New Zealand 25, England 8. I suppose it was just the England boys' way of saying thank you to their supporters. We'd have been rubbished back home if we'd pulled a stunt like that. A lap of honour is a nice thing to do, but I find it works best when you win. I must say that despite all the hype associated with playing England, and the fact it's always great to beat them, I enjoy the English crowds. They are some of the most sporting people in the world, always willing to acknowledge good play. I guess they see the All Blacks as being out there to entertain them. If it happens, then in return they will always applaud. It's quite refreshing.

By the time we arrived in Bristol for our fifth tour match, it was do-or-die time for Sean Fitzpatrick. His crook knee had meant he hadn't had any game time and Harty was finally able to put him on the bench for the match against the English Partnership XV. I think all the boys were just so relieved for Fitzy when he got on the field with about twenty minutes to play. It was a tight match and I'm sure his experience certainly helped Todd Blackadder, who was captaining the midweek side. The boys got home 18–11.

A tradition going back years for touring All Blacks teams is a visit to Buckingham Palace and a cup of tea with the Queen. This time around we met her and Princess Anne. The players felt very privileged and the visit proved to be a real highlight. Phil likes to tell people I was a bit confused when I met the Queen that day. He reckons I'd only ever seen her face on a postage stamp and, when I was introduced, he says I didn't know whether to shake her hand or lick her neck. Good gag, Phil. Not true.

Our first Test of the tour had been at Old Trafford. Our next, against Wales, would be at Wembley Stadium. The old Arms Park in Cardiff was being completely remodelled to make way for the new Millennium Stadium and now we were in London for the Test against Wales. 'This will stop the singing,' someone said during the tour. Yeah, right. I had heard all the stories about the beautiful Welsh voices, but to experience it first-hand was awesome. It didn't matter to the Welsh that they weren't at home. They reckon there were about 50,000 supporters who travelled across the border to watch the match and at Wembley they just went off. I remember being out on the ground with Andrew

Mehrtens at half-time. We were warming up, but the singing made us stop. Far out. It was so powerful. It took a while for us to get things together again. One player, though, who wasn't fazed by the singing was Christian Cullen. Cully owned Wembley Stadium that day. He scored three tries in our win and I think in the finish even the Welsh supporters were in awe of his skills.

Although we didn't know it then, the test against Wales would be Sean Fitzpatrick's last for the All Blacks. He wasn't given the starting spot, but came on for Norm Hewitt with about twenty-five minutes to go. Norm wasn't real happy about being 'dragged' and he showed it. He copped an earful from Harty after the match and was later made to apologise to the whole team. I disagreed with that decision. It was unfair on Norm. He should only have apologised if he wanted to. In saying that, it is a coach's call to pull players. I don't know what John's reasons for subbing Norm were. It might simply have been a tactical decision. In the modern game players have got to be able to accept these things. Fitzy was the tour captain and Fitzy was, well, Fitzy was a legend. It was sad in the end to see him kind of limp out of international rugby.

I'm often asked what made him such a great player and captain. It's not that hard to work out. Apart from the fact he was a fantastic hooker – the best I've ever seen in his position – he was mentally stronger than any other player I've known. He was hard-nosed and he demanded a lot of his players, but he would never ask you to do anything that he wouldn't do himself.

Fitzy's commitment and attitude can be summed up by an incident that occurred against South Africa during one of the Tri-Nations games in New Zealand. He found himself isolated against the Springboks. He was on the deck and they were charging at him – a truckload of big Bok forwards. He just reached over and put his arm on the ball. The South Africans had us on the ropes and they just climbed all over him. Call it rucking, call it trampling, they worked him over good and proper. The thing is, he had saved a probable try. When the ref blew his whistle Fitzy just got up and went on with his business like nothing had happened. Never said a word. Sean Fitzpatrick was fearless.

Fitzy also had a fast mouth and he had the ability to mentally break down opposition players. I've seen him do it heaps of times. He sometimes pushed the laws of the game to the limit. He would use every trick in the book to give the All Blacks an edge. Fitzy pushed the boundaries, no question, but Fitzy only cared about one thing – winning.

There were just two matches left after the Welsh Test. At Leicester, against England A, Todd Blackadder led the midweek side to another win. Four from four. That was a hell of an effort. For the Test team there was a rematch against England and, surprise, surprise, it was going to be played at Twickenham. We weren't complacent going into the game. Sure, we were favourites after beating England in Manchester, but in recent times the English have always proved hard to roll at Twickenham. They must have been hurting, too, after losing to South Africa the week before.

As it turned out, the last Test of the year was a nightmare for us. England did everything at Twickenham that England is never supposed to do. They ran penalties and they played at pace. After forty minutes they had scored three tries to none. A scoreline of 23–9 at half-time is a hard thing for an All Blacks side to swallow. At the break, though, we never panicked. The second half called for guts and pride. We dug deep and we eventually earned the draw. I got a couple of chances in the second spell and from one of them we scored our second try, to Walter Little. The try and Mehrts's conversion gave us the lead for the only time in the match. At 26–23 I thought we'd come away, but the Poms were hungry. Paul Grayson's third penalty goal was the last score of the match: 26–26. We had made a great comeback, but for the All Blacks a draw is as bad as a loss. At the final whistle I didn't bother to look around to see if the English players were doing another lap of honour.

Fitzy watched the final All Blacks Test of 1997 from the grandstand. He wouldn't be back. Zinzan Brooke retired from international rugby after the Twickenham Test. There would be other great players missing from the big team in the coming months and 1998 would be a challenge.

CHAPTER TWELVE

MOURNING GLORY, COURTING GOLD

Following the All Blacks end-of-year tour in 1997, Phil and I had always planned to stay in Britain for a couple of weeks to do a bit of promotional work. Over the next few years it became something of a routine. At the end of our domestic season, or if there was a Northern Hemisphere tour by the All Blacks at the end of the year, we'd always put away some time for personal appearances. One rule, though, was we always had to be back in New Zealand for Christmas.

In 1997, even though I was getting used to being in the limelight back home, I was still pretty new to the kind of showbiz stuff the Brits were looking for. I didn't know what to expect when I fronted up for the British TV programme, *They Think It's All Over*. It was a half-hour sports show which used to screen at about 10p.m. on Friday nights. I'd heard it was a bit off the wall and similar to New Zealand's *Game of Two Halves*. I was invited on as the 'feel the sportsman' guest, where a couple of members of the panel, who are blindfolded, have to try and work out who the mystery guest is — by touch.

Before I got on stage, the panel, which this night included cricketer David Gower, comedian Lee Hurst, boxer Chris Eubank and host Nick Hancock, were discussing who the mystery guest might be. At one point it was suggested it might be a rugby player. Lee Hurst really got the audience going when he said the All Blacks were poofters and that Jonah Lomu himself was just a big poofter. I was behind a screen chucking a ball in the air and when I was finally brought out, Lee and David Gower were given the job of guessing who I was. Lee was going, 'No, it can't be. It can't be.' When he lifted his blindfold and saw me, he was off into the audience. The place cracked up. It was great fun.

I also did *Question of Sport* for the first time in 1997. Since then I've been back two or three times to do the show, despite the fact I really battled the first time around. I'm not really a cricket or a soccer fan. Most of the sports I watch are American — baseball, basketball and football. Anyway, I've always had a ball on the show and the producers seem to like having me back. They even invited me to do the big Christmas special a couple of times, so I guess I must have been doing something right.

Phil Kingsley Jones: Jonah has come a long way since I took him to his first speaking engagement back in 1996. It was in Bulls, of all places. I took Jonah, Gary Whetton and Dallas Seymour down to the little town for a mate of mine who ran the local pub, the Rangitikei Tavern. I did my best to school Jonah up before the speech and even gave him a joke: Two cows in a field and one says to the other, 'What do you think of this mad cow disease?' The other one says, 'Wouldn't have a clue, I'm a chicken.' Well, the pub was absolutely packed and Jonah was the first speaker. He gets up and says, 'Two cows in a field and one says "moo". The other one says, "I was just going to say that."' I'm thinking, oh no, that's the stupidest joke I've ever heard . . . It didn't matter to the Bulls crowd, though. Everyone fell about the place laughing. They must have known Jonah was nervous, but that one gag from the young fella won them over.

I was pretty much injury-free at the start of the 1998 Super 12 season and the doctors seemed to have the kidney condition under control. After missing the Blues' repeat Super 12 victory in 1997, I was itching to get back into action. Even without Sean Fitzpatrick and Zinzan Brooke, the side was still a powerful unit, able to call on heaps of All Blacks. Our campaign started with the dreaded road trip to South Africa. This time around we were due to meet the Sharks first-up in Durban and then the Cats at Johannesburg. The African leg of the Super 12 is always a big ask, but to be fair, the South African sides do it a lot tougher than us each year when they have to come down to play four matches in Australia and New Zealand.

All the South African sides are tough at home and against the Sharks we couldn't even get warm. The harder we tried that day the worse it got. In the end it was Henry Honiball who did the job on us. He kicked all his goals and scored a try himself as the Sharks beat us 24–8. Life without Fitzy and Zinny would not be easy. It's vital for your chances in the Super 12 to get at least one win in South Africa. Against the Cats we were desperate. We got the result. Michael Jones had taken over the captaincy of the Blues after Zinny's retirement and after our nail-biting 38–37 win in Jo'burg — a game I rate as one of the most exciting I ever played in — I could sense some confidence returning to the side. Ice is a completely different sort of person to Zinny or Fitzy. For a start, he's much quieter. Of course, he commanded a lot of respect from the players just because of who he was and what he had achieved in the game. In 1998, though, the old firm was gone. Zinny and Fitzy had always worked in tandem, whereas Michael was sort of a lone figure. The boys knew this. We knew that

Michael would always put his body on the line and would always give one hundred per cent. He'd always get respect. What he needed, though, was support. I think that's the reason we dug so deep against the Cats.

After our return from South Africa we put together another three wins, including one over the Crusaders in Christchurch, before losing to the Queensland Reds. It was a decent hiding, too: 33–18. They're a funny side, the Reds. They've always had the players. Hell, just look at their backs that year – Latham, Horan, Little, Tune, Herbert, Flatley. The trouble with the Reds, though, is that they always seem to run hot and cold through the Super 12. Pity they picked this day in Brisbane to turn in one of their better efforts.

The loss to the Reds was our last in round-robin play. We won our next four matches to finish on top of the table and book a semi-final place against the Highlanders. My form had been a bit up and down throughout the competition, but I felt I was coming right towards the end. I got a couple of tries against the Hurricanes in our final round-robin game and was really up for the Highlanders.

I suppose the semi-final at Eden Park will always be remembered for the controversial decision by the ref, Colin Hawke, to award our full-back, Adrian Cashmore, a crucial try. Joeli Vidiri had thrown the Highlanders winger, Jeremy Stanley, into touch when he didn't have hold of the ball. That allowed Cashy to pick it up and scoot away for the try. I didn't get a really good look at the incident at the time, and while the television replays showed Hawke to be wrong for allowing play to continue, I still see it as one of those things that happen in rugby. I've had plenty of decisions go against teams I've played in over the years. You've just got to accept them.

Hawke's call was always going to be the big talking point after the game, but, to be fair, the Highlanders played out of their skins that day. They just wouldn't lie down and actually gave themselves a chance of winning the match with a couple of minutes to go. I breathed a huge sigh of relief when one of their forwards dropped the vital pass with the goal line wide open. We got home 37–31 to set up a final against the Crusaders. That was the good news. The bad news was that I wouldn't be part of it. I injured my knee in training during the week and would have to watch the final from the grandstand. It was a big disappointment. This was the Blues' third final in three years and I had only been there for one of them.

It was a full house for the final at Eden Park and, really, the match could have gone either way. In the end the Crusaders' defence won out. Even back then you could see the tactical skills of their coach, Wayne Smith. Nothing has changed much in the Super 12 over the years. The team with the best D usually comes out on top. The Crusaders deserved the win.

I've never taken much notice of what's said in the media when it comes to the build-up to Test matches. Whether it be Italy or Australia, I've approached them all the same way. They're internationals and to me they're precious. For the All Blacks there's only one focus – and that's winning. It never concerned me, for instance, that England, our first opponents of the 1998 season, were bringing a lot of uncapped players to New Zealand. Sure, I was interested in the fact that some professional clubs had not wanted to release players for England's Southern Hemisphere tour. It all sounded a bit strange, especially because pro rugby in New Zealand had started so well. Whatever, I find you can lose your focus if you start thinking the next Test will be easy. When England got done by the Wallabies on the way to New Zealand the press really got stuck in and started calling the tourists 'England C'. As I say, it didn't matter to me. They would still be wearing the white jersey with the red rose.

It was a whole new deal for the All Blacks in the opening Test against England at Dunedin. No Fitzy, no Zinny and, unexpectedly, no Frank Bunce. He hadn't made it back to New Zealand from a trip to France on the date he was supposed to and John Hart was pretty dark with him. Even though Frank was in his mid-thirties by then, he was still a key player in the All Blacks back line. Defending or attacking, he was the rock. There were a whole lot of stories doing the rounds about what had gone wrong and caused Frank to be late home. I still don't know the full story. When it comes to Buncey, though, I'd believe anything. The shame was, he never played for the All Blacks again.

Without Fitzy around, Harty had to look for a new captain. When it was announced that Taine Randell would lead the All Blacks I was delighted. I'd been involved with Taine for a long time and he had actually been my captain in the New Zealand Colts team in 1994. At that time Harty didn't have many options and, even though he was still young, Taine had been an All Black since 1995 and had been around the provincial scene for quite a few years. I thought he was a good man for the job.

The scoreboard shows that we hammered the Poms in the first Test at Dunedin. In truth, though, they actually fronted that day. England's biggest problem was that they played a lot of the match with only seven forwards, after their lock Danny Grewcock was sent off for stomping in the first half. Despite this, they didn't give up. England have always played with pride. These guys were no different. There was a World Cup coming up in 1999 and this tour was a chance for some of their fringe players to put their hands up.

I don't often get involved in fights on the field, but there was one bust-up at Carisbrook involving me and the England hooker, Richard Cockerill. I knew from the 1997 tour he had a short fuse, but fortunately this time it was just a bit of push and shove.

At the end of the day, you could have called the battle between me and Cockerill a draw. We both scored tries. My one was especially satisfying as it was the first I'd managed since Wellington in 1996.

I guess it's not too much for the public to expect the All Blacks to improve after a win like the one we got in Dunedin. After all, 64–22 is a pretty decent scoreline. However, in the second Test at Auckland we didn't improve. In fact, we probably went backwards. We won 40–10 and we did outscore England six tries to one, but the performance was ordinary. I didn't have a great first half and it wasn't too much of a surprise when I got subbed off with about twenty minutes to go. I'd like to say I was delighted for my Counties mate, Joeli Vidiri, who replaced me for his first Test cap, but at the time I wasn't very happy.

Opening the season with two Test wins against England should have given us a lot of confidence for the upcoming Tri-Nations series. The truth is, there were some cracks in this All Blacks side. We were a new side with a new captain. We hadn't just lost three experienced players in Fitzpatrick, Brooke and Bunce. We had lost three players who were the best in their positions in the world. Holding on to our Tri-Nations title was never going to be easy.

John Hart obviously wasn't too impressed by my form against England in the second Test. For the first Tri-Nations match, against Australia at the Melbourne Cricket Ground, I was on the bench. Joeli had been in the best form of his life so I couldn't really complain when he was given a start on the left wing. We were good mates at Counties and in the lead-up to the match I offered him as much support as I could. He was nervous all week and I tried to get him to relax and told him to play his natural game. As it turned out, the whole team played badly in Melbourne. The forwards weren't flash and the backs made too many mistakes. It was two tries each, but it was the Aussies' full-back, Matt Burke, who made the difference. He scored all twenty-four points for the Wallabies. Joeli was dragged with twenty minutes to go and I was subbed on. I know after the game he was gutted. He'd made a few mistakes, and he wasn't on his own there, but this was his first run-on Test. It's the one that all players remember. Substitutions happen all the time in the modern game. On this night, though, I felt sorry for Joey. Sorry for myself, as well. It was my first loss in an All Blacks jersey since 1995.

Milestones in rugby come and go. I never really give them much thought, but for the second Tri-Nations match of the year you couldn't really help but get swept up by the hype. The Test at Athletic Park in Wellington was the fiftieth Test between New Zealand and South Africa and I was back in the starting fifteen. I know it's easy to say that the signs were there after Melbourne that this All Blacks team were under pressure, but before the match I was upbeat. Test matches are all about taking your chances. In Wellington we didn't. We didn't kick our goals and we bombed a couple of tries. I'm not taking anything away from the Boks. They played well, especially on defence.

There has been much talk over the years about the fact I've never scored a Test try against South Africa. It's not something that particularly worries me. In saying that, though, I did my best to try and get over in Wellington. I managed to break the Springboks open a few times but, as always, there were two or three defenders there to climb all over me. However, I did have one big win over the Boks at Athletic Park – I took a line-out off the great Mark Andrews. The coaches had discussed the possibility of me going into the line-out during the week, but no one was more surprised than me when the move was called. I don't think the Boks expected me to jump. Whatever, it remains my great claim to fame in the forwards – never lost a line-out in an All Blacks jersey.

We came under a lot of pressure from the media after the

Wellington Test. Some journos were starting to question the team as a whole, but the worst part was the flak new captain Taine Randell was getting. If we didn't start winning I could tell the criticism was going to get even uglier. I was one of just a few players who received any praise for our performance in Wellington. It never made the loss any easier to take. Bugger the raps. Give me the win, any day.

We lost the lot at Jade Stadium in Christchurch – the Tri-Nations and the Bledisloe Cup. It was our third consecutive loss and the sad fact is, the scoreline could have been a lot worse. The Wallabies only got home by four points, but we all knew they were far better than us on the day. Cully and I scored tries at the end, which made the 27–23 result at least look a bit respectable. I can't remember a worse losing feeling after a game. I don't think it was even that bad after the World Cup loss against South Africa. We were trying so hard, all of us.

Taine copped plenty. He was the new captain. He was young and he was the fronter. I mean, what do you say to the country after your team has just coughed up all the cups? What was he supposed to say to the reporters? 'Oh, we've lost a lot of experienced players. We're rebuilding.' No way. The New Zealand public won't buy that stuff. The All Blacks are not judged on how they play. They are judged on whether they win or lose. It doesn't matter whether we win by one point or by a hundred points. The win is what counts. I've never taken my standing as an All Black for granted and I've always appreciated the privileged position the jersey gives you in New Zealand, but it doesn't get away from the fact that the expectation level is massive. It's easily the hardest thing to deal with as an All Black.

There was only pride left to play for in South Africa for our final Tri-Nations game. Despite the pressure and the criticism, deep down we knew we could pull out a big performance at

Durban. Harty made plenty of changes for the match. Four of our greatest players – all-time greats – were dropped: Michael Jones, Ian Jones, Craig Dowd and Walter Little. It was a big call, but with the Tri-Nations gone I think he was looking ahead to the World Cup the following year.

I know everyone laughs when you talk about a game as 'the one that got away'. It's like, who cares? Well, in this match it was true. Up until the final fifteen minutes we played some of the best rugby I've ever been involved in, and against a bloody good Springboks side. They might have scored first at Durban, but after that we just buried them. I had the satisfaction of setting up our first try when I made a break and busted through full-back Percy Montgomery to set up Justin Marshall. After that, everything seemed sweet. The forwards were hungry and we cut out the silly mistakes of the previous three Tests. Right up, that is, until the last quarter. Up 23–5, the game was won, or so I thought. It was at this point that our inexperience cost us. We were excited. We began to rush some of our moves. We should have slowed the pace of the game. Old, experienced heads from the past would have ensured this happened. I know exactly what Fitzy, Zinny and Frank would have said: 'Okay, boys, it's time to truck it up the middle. Set it up. Slow it down. Maul it. Set another ruck. Play it at our pace.' But the old heads weren't there this time. We let the Boks back in and they took control. When they scored their final try we were devastated. It only made things worse later when their hooker James Dalton admitted he never actually scored the match-winning try. We should have saved the season in Durban.

By now the critics were turning on Harty. It wasn't about the team any more. It was about the coach. It's the old story. When everything is going well it's the players who get the praise, but when everything turns to custard it's the coach who cops the flak. Look at the situation with John Mitchell at the end of 2002. He bloods a whole bunch of new players and gets flogged because people say he's devaluing the All Blacks jersey by not picking the best players available. No one moaned when guys like Ali Williams and Keven Mealamu stood up in 2003 and helped win the Bledisloe Cup and the Tri-Nations. But it was different with Harty in 1998. He didn't have a choice. Retirements and injuries forced him to rebuild. I've heard some critics say he should have started earlier. That's crap. We're supposed to win Tests, aren't we? Do we drop our best players for important Tests because they're getting on a bit? I didn't hear too many complaints when the veteran All Blacks did the job in 1996 and 1997. A losing coach just can't win.

Like I've said, milestones and records in rugby come and go. When we lost our third Test to Australia, in Sydney, following the Tri-Nations series, we reached a few more. It was the first time in almost fifty years we'd lost five Tests in a row – the second worst losing run in All Blacks history – and the first time we'd lost three Tests to Australia in one season since 1920. Whatever . . . Even though we led the Wallabies 11–0 at half-time, it was another game we probably didn't deserve to win. I managed a try as we went down 19–14. It was only my second in seven Tests in 1998. That statistic kind of summed up the season for me.

A question that often comes up about 1998 is whether the senior players, myself included, gave Taine Randell enough support thoughout the international season. Looking back, I'd have to say probably not, but it wasn't because we had anything against him or because we didn't feel he should have been made captain. It's just that we were all so used to having Fitzy and Zinny around. We were used to that sort of comfort zone. They fed off each other and if they needed help they asked for it. Taine, I think, felt pretty much alone during 1998. Maybe he tried to do too much on his own and maybe we should have seen the signs after the first couple of losses and offered more support. I think he also had trouble separating his personal feelings from the job of actually leading the players. He took so much of the criticism to heart. I guess that's understandable given the way the season went. He was thrust into the job at a difficult time and he tried his best. What more can you ask?

For a few of the All Blacks in the 1998 side the season still offered some hope after the final Test against the Wallabies. Along with Joeli, Cully and Caleb Ralph, I was off to the Kuala Lumpur Commonwealth Games. Sevens rugby had just been put on the programme for the games and it was something I was really looking forward to. We headed back to New Zealand after the Sydney Test and immediately joined the sevens squad in Auckland. There were fifteen players chosen to travel up to Singapore for the pre-games training camp. There would only be ten of us selected to go on to Kuala Lumpur. We were a talented and tight group. No one wanted to wave goodbye in Singapore.

I was pretty sharp after the Tri-Nations series, but not as sharp as Gordon Tietjens thought I needed to be. His training runs were ruthless and he seemed to give me plenty of extra work. He made it clear he wanted me at peak fitness. The temperature regularly climbed to 38°C in Singapore, but it never bothered Titch. Every day we trained for two or three hours and sometimes we managed to squeeze in games against local pick-up sides. Titch thrashed the hell out of us before those games. He would push the physical boundaries at training and then expect us to perform against the locals. Four seven-minute periods. It was wicked. Those seven-minute spells always seemed a lot longer. I never questioned the timekeeping but . . .

The training was hard, but probably the most difficult time in Singapore came when Titch made the 'cut' for Kuala Lumpur. We'd been through a difficult week together and we'd all become close. There were a few tears at the hotel when the unlucky five headed back to New Zealand. For the rest of us, the real work was about to start. This squad definitely had the 'dream team' look about it. Experience, power and wheels – it was probably the fastest sevens team I've ever been associated with. However, there was one other factor that led me to believe we'd perform well – we were all close mates. The sevens environment has always produced a great bond amongst the players. Yeah, I fancied our chances big-time in Kuala Lumpur.

I loved life in the Games village. Never mind that we were housed in the basement area of our accommodation block (the dungeon, we called it), just walking around the village and mixing with all those great athletes was a blast. I remember one day stopping to talk to Ato Boldon, the great track sprinter from Trinidad and Tobago. He took out a great 100m final at the games – 9.88 seconds. Great time. Nice guy.

Eric Rush: I've travelled a fair bit with Jonah over the years and I know how popular he is right around the world. At Kuala Lumpur, though, it was something else. Everyone at the village – and I mean everyone – wanted his autograph or a photo with the big guy. I couldn't believe it. I know it wasn't the Olympics, but there were still some pretty famous athletes at KL. No one, though, was bigger than Jonah. Hell, when the New Zealand team marched into the stadium for the opening ceremony there were 100,000 people in the ground and it seemed all of them knew Jonah. There was even a 'Lomu, Lomu' chant. It was awesome. Whenever he was out and about his time was never his own. Over the years he has never ceased to amaze me in the way he handles his fame. Nothing has ever been too much trouble for him. I've never once seen him decline an autograph. That's the mark of the man.

The decision to put rugby on the programme for the Kuala Lumpur games must have had the organisers rubbing their hands in glee. The crowds loved it and, for most of the time, we played in front of a packed house. From memory, the ground held about 35,000 spectators. The guy who was running the stadium reckoned they could have filled the place twice over. There were always people hanging about outside looking for tickets, at any price.

The work Titch put into me in Singapore meant that by the time the competition began I was ready for a heavy schedule. We played six matches over three days and Titch started me in all of them. The only game I didn't finish was our opener against Sri Lanka, where the boys ran in thirteen tries — seventy-nine points in fourteen minutes isn't a bad effort. We finished day one with another big win over Malaysia. The fact they never scored a try against us was satisfying, because in a warm-up match they had crossed our line four times. Titch was pretty dark about that. Day two of competition produced a couple more big wins, including a 93–12 thumping of the Bahamas. The heat in KL was a killer, but when you're having as much fun as we were you tend not to notice it so much.

Finals day was always going to be tough. We were drawn to meet Wales in the quarter-finals and, although we got home 38–12, the Welsh never gave up. It was a good shakedown for our semi against Samoa. I hadn't played any sevens all year, but Rushie warned me this one would be tough. The Samoans had pushed New Zealand hard at the Japan sevens and then beaten us in the semis of the Jerusalem tournament earlier in the year. The words of warning were spot-on. We found ourselves down 7–0 at half-time and it was only our fitness and great pace that got us out of trouble. We snuck in front with about two minutes left to play, but right on time the Samoans could easily have taken the game. They made a break that was only stopped by a great tackle from

Rico Gear. You could sum up the character of the New Zealand team in the performance we gave in that match.

The boys were amped for the final against Fiji. There's no doubt they were the gold medal favourites before the tournament began, but for us it didn't matter. We had huge belief. For myself, I was desperate to end the year on a high. A silver medal to go with five losing Tests wasn't an option. Before the final, Rushie got me so wound up I reckon I'd have run through a brick wall – he always knew which buttons to press. He told me just before the game that the Fijians had said I was only good for one run and that I was hopeless on defence. Rushie lit my fuse with those comments. He knew it and I knew it. He then spun Joeli Vidiri a similar story. Joey, of course, would be facing his countrymen. He didn't need much encouragement. Rushie had got inside our heads. It was beautiful.

While the score at the finish was close – 21–12 – this game was completely different to the semi. We led the whole way and we never let the Fijians gain any sort of physical dominance. I had scored eight tries in five games up until the final. It didn't matter that I couldn't get over against Fiji. I was pleased with my work rate. I showed I could defend when it mattered.

Eric Rush: The final against Fiji was the most physical performance Jonah has ever given in sevens. He was awesome. There were two unbelievable pieces of play involving the big guy – one when he just flicked big Bruce Rauqe into touch like he was some sort of rag doll and the other when he made a massive run that basically knocked out Marika Vunibaka and Saimoni Rokini. Powerful, fast and fit. The opposition were scared, man. They were always scared.

The medal ceremony after the final was emotional for all of us and I don't mind admitting there were a few tears when the national anthem was played. Rushie always says his eyes were moist from sweat. Don't believe it. We were all choked up. When my international rugby career began I never dreamed a Commonwealth Games appearance was a possibility. It didn't make up for all those Test losses, but it sure eased the pain. My gold medal is something I will always treasure.

The trip home from Kuala Lumpur was not one I was looking forward to. Mac McCallion, my provincial coach at Counties Manukau, had wanted Joeli and me back for an important NPC match against Southland. In the end I didn't make it. I'd suffered a knee injury in the final and it blew up after the game. Instead, I opted to stay on with Rushie for the final few days of competition. I copped a lot of flak over that decision, but the truth is I couldn't have played even if I had flown home with the rest of the team.

Worse, though, was a situation that had been preying on my mind for several months. My marriage to Tanya wasn't going so good – 1997 had been a tough year on both of us and at the end of it I felt we were starting to drift apart. On top of that, someone else had come into my life. When I got back from the games, Tanya and I talked things through and basically I said to her I didn't think things were going too well. After two and a half years of marriage, we separated. People can make their own judgements now, but the fact is, we were both very young and probably a bit naïve when we got married. The split was tough on both of us because it became so public. Usually I can handle publicity, good or bad, and I accept that when you're in the public eye you're not always going to get the good stuff. Back then, though, it was hard. The media had a field day. It certainly didn't make our split any easier, but nowadays I'd like to think we are still friends. We don't talk often, but we do acknowledge that we were both part of each other's lives. You can't change that.

I got back to New Zealand in time to play in Counties Manukau's final three games. The team had beaten Southland in my absence, thank goodness, and we really needed to win the rest of our matches if we were to make the NPC semis. We had Auckland, Wellington and Canterbury in consecutive weeks. It was a big ask, but we nearly pulled it off. Joeli Vidiri was on fire at the end of the season. He picked up four tries in each of our wins against Auckland and Canterbury, but a draw against Wellington meant we failed by a single point to make the top four.

I've been lucky over the years to travel to some fantastic places and do stuff I could only have dreamed of as a kid growing up in South Auckland. Sure, the days of the long rugby tours were a thing of the past by the time I arrived on the All Blacks scene in the mid-nineties. None of those three-month jobs for the modern-day All Blacks. In fact, a month was about as long as we were ever away from New Zealand, and I can honestly say there wasn't one tour I didn't enjoy. Homesickness never came into it — five years at boarding school had knocked any of those sorts of thoughts out of my head.

I used to lap up the sights and sounds of foreign countries. Even today I'm still in awe of some of the places I've visited. The United Kingdom and Ireland remain special destinations. I fell in love with London from the very first time I landed at Heathrow Airport — so big and so foreign to anything I'd ever seen before. It's the history that really gets you: the buildings, the tradition, even the atmosphere. I suppose it's because I come from a country which is so much younger in that regard.

Another thing about touring Britain which I've always appreciated is the kindness and respect the people have shown me. In England

I've had a pretty charmed run with the tabloids, especially when you consider how some of their own sportspeople have been treated. Maybe it's because I've never really blotted my copybook while I've been on tour.

Because I've never been a big drinker I suppose you could say I've managed to stay out of trouble. But that's not to say I haven't been tempted to take a walk on the wild side now and again. In the early days my favourite touring companions were guys like Eric Rush, Zinzan Brooke and Frank Bunce. Like me, Rushie's not much of a drinker and Zinny, well, he was too much of a professional to ever let his guard down. Buncey was also a real professional, but he loved to have fun and that often meant a drink or two . . . or three. He always used to joke, 'Come across to the dark side, Jonah.' Buncey was a great mate. But Buncey could be dangerous if you let him.

Drinking used to be a big part of rugby tours, and while it's true that the boys still let their hair down at odd times, things have moved on in the past few years. I came into the All Blacks in the amateur era and one thing I've really noticed since the game went professional is that the guys are much more aware of the dangers of binge drinking. In the old days there would always be trays of beer in the dressing-room after a match, and they would disappear fairly quickly. Nowadays, the beer is still there, but so are the sports supplement drinks. They're the first choice of most of the players.

As I became a more senior member of the side and my old mates disappeared from the scene, I found I mixed more freely with all the players. The seniority thing became more of a reason to hang out with the younger guys. The All Blacks environment these days encourages this mingling. I enjoyed making the new guys feel welcome. I got a buzz out of taking them out, showing them some of my favourite spots.

I remember a couple of years ago in Paris a few of the boys were keen to go to a nightclub called VIP. It's not the easiest place in town to get into, and when we arrived there was a massive queue outside the entrance. While I wouldn't say I was exactly a regular at the club, the security guards did know me. 'Hi Jonah, come this way,' they said. The boys were happy about that. When we got inside we sort of just hung out until another security guard came over and asked us if we'd like to come through to a private party in another room and meet Mariah Carey. She was promoting her new album. We got to meet her, had a chat and did the photo thing. It was wicked.

The one drawback of the shorter tours is that you never seem to get the chance to do everything you want. Training in the professional age is full-on when you're touring – up to three sessions a day – so it doesn't leave a lot of time for sightseeing. Nights are often taken up with sponsorship commitments. A lot of the guys will spend their days off playing golf – it's become a big go in recent years. I play a bit, but my main passion on tour has always been listening to music and shopping for old and new sounds. Whenever I'm in London I always search out the top music shops – Tower Records, HMV, Virgin, you name it.

For quite a few years the All Blacks 'music committee' was basically comprised of just me. I loved it. I have a wide interest in music and I could generally cover all the bases for the guys. Even today I listen to all sorts of different stuff – hip hop, R&B, and even the old rock stuff. The whole All Blacks team got to see *Buddy* – the musical based on the life of Buddy Holly – at the Strand Theatre in London's West End a couple of years ago. Brilliant.

The promotional trips through the UK have produced a few amusing moments over the years. One of the funniest happened on the way to Leicester at the end of 1998. I was driving and I had my fitness trainer, Lee Parore, in the front seat and Phil in the back seat. We weren't far out of London when I heard the scream of a police siren. I looked down at the speedo and thought, *I'm cool, we're only doing about 60mph.* Next thing, this copper signals me to pull over. He comes up to the window and looks in: 'Name and driver's licence, please.'

'My name is Jonah Lomu,' I said as I handed over my licence.

'Oh, umm, Mr Lomu. Ahh, Jonah. Well, it's very nice to meet you. I don't suppose there's any chance of an autograph?'

I've never quite worked out why he stopped me in the first place. Surely it couldn't have had anything do with the fact that I was Polynesian, driving a brand-new Mercedes Benz, wearing a black singlet, a gold chain around my neck and a bandana on my head? Nah, couldn't be.

Another memorable trip was to the Seychelles at the end of 1998. Phil had been approached by the legendary Miss World pageant organiser, Eric Morley, to see if I'd be interested in judging the contest. I got a bit of bad press about accepting the invitation, but I have no regrets. It was a great experience and Phil and I had a ball. There were heaps of celebrities invited as both judges and entertainers and I got to hang out with Ronan Keating and the guys from Boyzone, as well as Errol Brown, the former lead singer of Hot Chocolate. It didn't matter that none of them were rugby freaks, we still hit it off from the start. One of the other judges of the contest was Canadian Formula One driver, Jacques Villeneuve. We went to dinner one evening and talked motor racing the whole night.

Speed is my drug. For as long as I can remember I've loved cars — exotic cars, fast cars. Professional rugby has allowed me the opportunity to pursue this passion. In fact, I've lost track of how many cars I've owned over the years and even today I'm not really sure how many I've got garaged around the country. The first car I ever owned was a Mazda 323. It was given to me early on in my rugby career after I did a promotion for a dealership. After that, there was no stopping me. The first car I bought was a 3 Series BMW. Then came Holden Commodores, Fords, Nissans, Audis. You name it, I've been all over the show. For a while there I just couldn't resist the temptation to go out and try and buy every car that took my fancy. It caused Phil and my accountant, Ian Duff, a fair bit of grief. They'd say 'No!' I'd say, 'Whatever . . . ' and go out and put them on hire purchase. Then I'd hope like hell they wouldn't find out. They always did. Phil and Duffy would almost always end up going down to the car yards to pay them off.

Nowadays I like to help build cars. I've got a Chevrolet C1500 truck which I've been working on for about four years. It's a low rider. The motor has been customised with a 454-cubic inch big block, Holley four-barrel carburettor, twenty-inch rims, a hydraulic tilt tray . . . I'm forever calling my car mates looking for parts. I've even put an X-Box console in it.

Then there are my genuine boy racers like the 1967 Chevy Camaro. It's a fully tubbed out, fully blown drag racer. My Nissan Skyline GT-R 34 is pretty special, too. I think there were only a couple of thousand of them ever made. According to the plate I've got, mine was number six off the production line. It's my pride and joy — an N1 GT racing block, JE pistons, Corilla rods and twin Garrett turbos. Nice. It came straight from the factory in Japan with a 2.6l engine, but I've done heaps of modifications and changed almost everything. The original diff, for instance, had a 3.9 gear ratio; it's now geared at 4.5. The car's a real cop magnet, but in all honesty I don't speed on the open road. I get my adrenaline rush on the racetracks and drag strips. I've had the Skyline right off the dial at the Pukekohe racetrack in South Auckland, going 320km/h. Yeah, that thing can really move. The licence plate says MOW YA.

I enjoy all forms of motor racing, but perhaps the biggest buzz is drag racing. I find it refreshing, good for the mind. I know a lot of people say it's just straight-lining, but in actual fact there are heaps of things that can go wrong before you reach the end of that line. I've had a little bit of success at the Meremere Dragway and that's encouraged me to think about taking up the sport seriously in a few years' time.

I've been well looked after by sponsors when it comes to cars. Ford, of course, have been extremely generous to me and the All Blacks for a number of years, while in Britain I've been really spoiled. In recent years the British car company TVR have given me one of their beautiful sports cars to drive every time I've wanted one. At the end of 2002 the company blew me away when I got to drive the Tuscan Speed Six – the very same car used by John Travolta in the movie *Swordfish*. I mean, what can you say? I've been to their factory in Blackpool where all the cars are made by hand. Mind-blowing.

Along with cars, my other hobby is music. For me, the two go hand in hand. When I get into a car and turn on my sounds I'm in a world of my own. It's my time, my space and it's cool. That's why dB drag racing – that's dB for decibel – is also a passion. It's a relatively new sort of thing. Two cars line up with a microphone to see which audio system can produce the loudest volume. Thanks to my association with Fusion Electronics I've been able to chase my dream of trying to break the world record for the loudest car audio system. I've got my own range called FJL and the record is getting closer. Last year the boys at Fusion broke the Australasian record using FJL gear in a little Vauxhall Chevette – two fifteen-inch speakers, four amplifiers, 169.1 decibels. Awesome. They're going to have a crack at the world record at Nashville in November and they're chasing 174 decibels. The boys want to make a statement and it'd be wicked to see the record broken with my Fusion range.

Ready for France, 1994 — first jersey, first test. It was an emotional time.

I've got fullback John Timu in support as I confront French fullback Jean-Luc Sadourny in the first test of the '94 series against France at Lancaster Park, Christchurch. Too bad 'on the line' is out.

Hard out in the second 1995 World Cup pool match, against Wales. Chasers are Wayne Proctor (left) and Gareth Thomas.

I've got big Gavin Hastings in my sights as I break against Scotland in the World Cup quarter-final at Loftus. Rob Wainwright looks to make the tackle.

I didn't sleep a wink the night before the 1995 World Cup semi-final against England. I was running on pure adrenaline throughout the entire match and I know something special was happening only a few minutes into the game.

A tackle's as good as a wink...catching up with Tony Underwood in the World Cup semi-final.

The try against England at Cape Town,
perhaps the one people will always
remember me for.

Springboks wing James Small shakes my
hand after the final.

Me, Fitzy and Jeff Wilson with the Bledisloe Cup after our win over Australia at the Football Stadium in Sydney in 1995. It was our last Test as amateurs.

It was cold and it was wet, but it didn't stop the All Blacks crushing the Wallabies at Athletic Park in the opening Tri-Nations match of 1996. Here I give Joe Roff the big fend while Scott Bowen tries to hang on.

In South Africa for the 1996 Test series. Rushie yelled, 'Let's do it!' 'Ka mate, Ka mate…'

On the 1997 tour of Britain. No tries this day, but it was still a huge thrill to play for the All Blacks at Manchester United's 'Theatre of Dreams'. England No. 16 is Austin Healey.

In the black corner Jonah Lomu, and in the white corner Richard Cockerill. Playing against England at Dunedin, 1998.

Heading for the try line against
Australia at Jade Stadium in 1998.
Wallaby tackler is Tim Horan.
We lost the lot that day — the
Tri-Nations and the Bledisloe Cup.

Stepping carefully against Australia
in the final Tri-Nations match of
1999 at Stadium Australia. It was a
world-record crowd for a rugby
match — and it was a record losing
margin for the All Blacks.

Not quite what it appears…
Lawrence Dallaglio has hold of
my jersey after I score my second-
half try against England. Upset-
looking team-mates are, from left,
Andrew Mehrtens, Tana Umaga
and Jeff Wilson.

Three Scotsmen get in on the
tackle during the World Cup
quarter-final at Murrayfield.

I got two tries against France in the
semi-final of the 1999 World Cup
at Twickenham. It wasn't enough.
The French finished all over the
top of us and ended our dream.

Attacking against the Wallabies at Stadium Australia in the opening Test of the 2000 Tri-Nations series. Some critics rate the match as the greatest ever played. Wallaby defender is Chris Latham.

Scoring against England in our narrow loss at Twickenham in 2002.

Jonathan Kaplan's arm eventually went up to signal my first try... umpteen replays later.

Anyway, back to the Miss World pageant and chatting to Jacques Villeneuve that night was one of the highlights of the trip. Phil enjoyed the evening, too, but if the truth is told, his highlight was probably just making it to the contest!

Phil Kingsley Jones: The big boy nearly killed me on that trip. We flew from Auckland to Los Angeles and then on to London. At Heathrow we had to change terminals for a British Airways flight to Rome. That's where the problems began. Our bags had been offloaded and the airline staff couldn't find them. When they finally turned up we had about ten minutes to get to the gate. Jonah packed all the bags on a trolley and just said to me, 'Run!' I had a crook hip back then and I hadn't done any running for years. It didn't worry Jonah that I was coughing and spluttering as we legged it to the gate. At one point we raced up this escalator. It was me first, with him following. He just picked up the trolley, bags and all, and sprinted to the top. People watching couldn't believe it.

In the finish, I got to the gate just before Jonah, only to be told that if we had bags there was no way they could let us on. Just as they finished telling me this, Jonah came around the corner with the trolley. 'Jeez,' this bloke said as he looked Jonah up and down, 'Is that who I think it is?' 'Yes, it is,' I said. 'Shall you tell him we're too late or shall I?' They opened the luggage hold and let us on.

I was exhausted by the time we arrived in Rome and was looking forward to a peaceful flight on Seychelles Airlines. Not likely. When we got on board the captain made a special fuss about Jonah being on board. He then went on to tell all the passengers that the plane was the only one owned by the airline. 'It's pretty old,' he said. 'We've recently had one of the wings tightened up with a bit of tape. No cause for concern, though, I'm sure we'll make it.' Happiness was landing in the Seychelles.

CHAPTER THIRTEEN

RIDING THE PINE

I was furious when I stormed into the offices of Number 11 Management. I sat down and spilled my guts out to Phil. After being excluded from the first World Cup training camp of 1999 – the now famous 'SAS boot camp' at Hobsonville – I decided I'd had enough of the All Blacks life. I wanted out. John Hart and his fellow All Blacks selectors had judged that I hadn't measured up to the fitness levels they required and, along with a couple of other players, I was not welcome at the camp. This was World Cup year. This was my dream and all I could see was the door being slammed in my face.

Phil tried to calm me down, but I didn't want to know. 'Get me out of my contract!' I shouted. 'This is just crap!' Phil was also upset that I hadn't been invited to the camp, but he was, as always, realistic. He said that it wasn't the end and that I'd just have to work harder to get my fitness up to the standard the selectors required, but I wasn't listening. Rugby league. Anything. Just get me outta here!

In the end Phil had to call in my accountant, Ian Duff, to lay everything out. It wasn't going to be that easy to just walk away from my rugby career and from all that we'd built over the past few years. I was fuming, but I was also beginning to get the picture.

It was get fit or get out. If I didn't do something myself, then I might not be in a position to make my choices about my future. They could very well be made by other people.

John Hart: We picked a World Cup training squad at the end of 1998. We set the players clear standards and they were regularly tested throughout the summer. When we sat down to do the analysis there were three players – Jonah, Isitolo Maka and Joeli Vidiri – who were clearly not up to the standards we had set. We had little choice but to exclude them.

In Jonah's case you could say maybe that was a bit harsh, given who he was and what he'd been through, but the message had been made clear to all the players. If they hadn't done the work they wouldn't be considered for the camp. The other point is that unfit players simply wouldn't have coped with the physical demands of the camp. If they had been included the result might well have meant they would have been sent home early. That scenario would have been no good to anyone. We were trying to instil discipline and teamwork. I know Jonah was upset at the time, but I'm sure that now even he would have to admit that he simply hadn't done the work.

The truth is, that while I was dark with everyone at the time, privately I kicked myself for letting my fitness slip in early 1999. John Hart, of course, was right. I hadn't done the work over the summer and I hadn't achieved the standards that were set for all the players. I was pissed off, but after a couple of days I calmed down and set myself some personal goals. I was going to make it. I was going to get to the World Cup. I accepted that there couldn't be one set of rules for me and another set for other players.

Probably the most talked about fitness test at that time was the 3km run. I hated it. I've never had a problem with the strength and speed tests but that run used to do my head in. The All Blacks selectors were clear about what they expected from me: thirteen minutes thirty seconds. It's not a really quick time for some players, but for me it was the magic mark and believe me, back then it was a big call — a real big call. At the time trials before I was shut out of the Hobsonville camp I had stopped the clock at eighteen minutes. I had a lot of work to do. Harty gave me about three weeks to get my stuff together.

With a lot of help and encouragement from All Blacks fitness trainer, Marty Toomey, I worked my butt off over those three weeks. I trained six days a week and I went hard. The Ho Chi Minh Trail through the Auckland Domain again became my stomping ground. I clocked up more kilometres in that short space of time than I'd ever done before. I had never once run thirteen minutes thirty seconds for 3km and there were times, lots of times, when I doubted I'd ever make it, but at the back of my mind was always the thought of the World Cup . . . the thought of missing out.

I still remember the morning Marty rang and said, 'We'll go for it today.' The venue was the North Harbour Bays Athletics track on Auckland's North Shore. The time was 1p.m. and when I arrived I was raring to go. When Marty asked if I wanted to run a warm-up lap, I said, 'No, let's just do it.' I told Marty I wanted a fourteen-minute pace to start off. At about the halfway mark he said, 'We're behind time.' We picked it up a bit, but it wasn't until the second to last lap that we got serious. With about 200m to go, Marty yelled, 'You're still behind! You're going to have to boot it, boy!' I sprinted hard over those last 200m, hoping like hell I'd cracked it. At the finish I was exhausted, but at the same time relieved. 'You made it!' Marty said. 'Thirteen minutes . . . twenty-nine seconds.'

I became a Chief in 1999. The Super 12 was entering its fourth year and the powers that be in Wellington decided that Counties Manukau would no longer be part of the Blues franchise and instead would become part of the Chiefs. I had enjoyed my time with the Blues and I think I could have made a case for staying with them, perhaps through the draft system, but the challenge of going to a new team, under my old Counties coach, Ross Cooper, was one I looked forward to. It's about being happy in the environment. I knew I would be comfortable with so many of my mates at the Chiefs.

Another knee injury just before the start of the Super 12 meant I missed the Chiefs' opening three matches. It wasn't a good beginning for me or the team. We were thrashed in our opening game at Christchurch against the reigning Super 12 champions, the Crusaders. By the time I returned for the match against the Blues, all the team had to show for their efforts were a couple of bonus points from close losses to the Reds and the Waratahs. My return to the team didn't help things much. We were beaten by the Blues in Hamilton and I had to look at my jersey a couple of times when I was tackled to remind myself that I was now a Chief. At Rotorua a week later we lost to the Highlanders and after five rounds of the competition we were dead last on the table.

The turning point for the Chiefs came against the Brumbies at Canberra. We were written off before the match, even though the Brumbies were struggling as much as us and had only won a couple of their games. This was Bruce Stadium, though. The Brumbies at Bruce are hard. At half-time in the match I could see the season going down the drain. We were behind on the scoreboard and even though we were still in touch with the Brumbies we were definitely being outplayed. Ross Cooper had a face like thunder when he walked into the changing rooms. He didn't say much. He didn't have to. As he walked out we all knew we had let him and ourselves down.

For one of the few times in my career I lost my rag with the players. Normally I say very little at half-time. This time I went ballistic. I said it was time for us to front. No more talking about what might have been: 'Let's go out and show these jokers what we can do!' I've never regarded myself as any sort of motivator, but I knew we were capable of a lot better than what we'd showed in those first forty minutes. In the second spell we played some of our best rugby of the season. The final score was only 16–13, but it was a win and a huge morale booster for the rest of the season.

We beat the Hurricanes, the Cats and the Sharks and then left for South Africa knowing that two wins might just give us enough points to sneak into the semi-finals. As it turned out, we managed only one – a cliffhanger against the Bulls in Pretoria – but still returned to New Zealand with seven valuable Super 12 points, although it was not enough, unfortunately, to grab a place in the semis. Won five, lost six. We knew we could have done better.

I didn't just become a Chief in 1999, I also became an adidas man. My personal contract with Reebok had actually expired at the end of 1997 and in 1998 I was pretty much a free agent. I had enjoyed the association with Reebok, but things got a bit strained towards the finish. It seemed that everywhere I went I had to be on guard to make sure I was wearing the right gear and doing the right thing by Reebok.

Phil Kingsley Jones: In the end, Reebok's patience probably wore a bit thin. I was becoming more and more like a policeman, watching all the time to make sure Jonah was following his contractual obligations. He was photographed playing golf in Britain at the end of 1997 wearing Mizuno gear and in Japan we got in a bit of strife when he appeared in some Canterbury gear. On top of everything else, Reebok were demanding more and more of his time for personal appearances. The company had been great for Jonah, but in the end it all got too hard. The Reebok contract had originally been signed for three years and at the end of 1997 we still had a year to run. Eventually we shook hands and ended the association. The arrangement was that they could use anything of Jonah they already had 'in the can' but he wouldn't be required to make any personal appearances. I can't speak too highly of Reebok. They were honourable to the end.

I signed with adidas in April 1999. The announcement was made at my old school, Wesley College. The deal was for two years with a two-year right of renewal. The financial arrangments were, of course, confidential, but I must say I did get a bit of a surprise when I saw one Sunday newspaper come out with a story saying that I'd signed for $10 million. Where do they get their info? It certainly didn't come from Phil or me and I know adidas were quick to jump in and rubbish the piece. I can't believe the papers can print this stuff when they've got nothing at all to back it up.

The sponsorship deal fitted perfectly with the All Blacks set-up in 1999. The New Zealand Rugby Union had also done a deal with adidas. They would become my major gear and boot sponsor from the middle of the year. It was more than just a sponsorship thing, though. Adidas would be a principal partner of the NZRU and I would be part of it. I would never again have to worry about what I had on my back or what boots I was wearing. I was adidas to the core. Over the years, they have been a fantastic company to work with. They've got a great stable of high-profile sports people right around the world; top athletes like David Beckham, Ian Thorpe and Martina Hingis, and I've become friends with a number of them. Adidas have always treated me well and no one was happier than me the following year when we renewed our contract for another four years.

The All Blacks faced a long season in 1999. It began in June with Tests against Samoa and France and would be followed by the Tri-Nations in July and August. Then, of course, was the World Cup through October and, hopefully, November. The country's top players tuned up for the international season with a trial match in Christchurch. New Zealand versus New Zealand A. I was in the top side, but I was only on the bench. Tana Umaga and Christian Cullen were on the wings, while Jeff Wilson was given a start at full-back. Harty was obviously experimenting before the World Cup. Despite all the extra work I'd done, including that time trial, I think he still believed I wasn't as fit as I could be. In fairness, though, the chosen three had all been in great form through the Super 12. I would be used as an 'impact player'. It's a term that has become very popular since rugby went professional; it was also a term I would have to get used to for the next couple of months.

Todd Blackadder is one of Canterbury rugby's all-time favourite players. He's a legend in red-and-black country. Sixty minutes into the match at Christchurch, Joeli Vidiri crossed for a try to New Zealand A. The gap had been closed to 19–11 to the All Blacks and three of us – Toddy, me and Mark Hammett – got the message to start warming up. As we ran up and down the sideline the crowd went wild. The Christchurch crowds have always been good to me, but I knew where their loyalties lay this day. Twenty thousand people started screaming, 'Toddy, Toddy'. Mark and I turned to the Canterbury captain and said, 'Jeez, you better go on first, Toddy. It'll take all the pressure off us.' Thankfully the All Blacks held on for the win.

Harty stuck with the back three of Wilson, Cullen and Umaga for the first test of the season against Samoa at Albany. I was back riding the bench. When I came on again for Cully after sixty minutes, the All Blacks already had the game won. We were in awesome form. I scored from virtually my first touch of the ball when the boys worked me on to the outside of Brian Lima and gave me a clear sprint to the line. Jeff Wilson scored a couple of minutes later to pick himself up four tries for the match. I don't know what it was about Auckland's North Shore, but Goldie loved that ground. He averaged something like five tries a Test at the Albany Stadium. While the final scoreline of 71–13 makes it look like the game was just a walk in the park, it was actually a really physical clash. There has always been a real bond between the Samoan players and the All Blacks. Many of us are friends and often there are brothers and cousins lining up against each other. It always adds a bit of spice to the games. That night, for instance, Tana's brother, Mike, was playing full-back for Samoa.

My improving fitness still wasn't enough to convince Harty that I was ready for the season's first big Test, against France. Instead, straight after the Samoa match I bolted down the southern motorway to link up with the New Zealand A team in Hamilton. From the All Blacks subs bench to, you guessed it, the subs bench for the As. We beat the French and I scored another try when I came on, but it was all getting a bit depressing. I wouldn't be heading for Athletic Park for the All Blacks–France test. This time I was off to Canberra with New Zealand A, but how far down the rung had I slipped?

There were a couple of pieces of good news to come out of the match against ACT at Canberra, though. I picked up two more tries in our big win, but more importantly, I would not be required for the two matches against the Australian Barbarians and instead would be flying home the following morning. Flying home to join the All Blacks training camp at Queenstown.

One player in red-hot form for the All Blacks in early 1999 was Tana Umaga. He scored two tries against Samoa and followed up that effort with a hat-trick against France in Wellington. He was everywhere — everywhere in No. 11. Tana and I were mates, we still are, and I was rapt for him. I hadn't shaved the two 'Is' into my eyebrow all season. I thought a lot about the jersey. I wanted No. 11 back.

Tana Umaga (All Blacks wing/centre 1997, 1999–2003): I remember being asked in 1999 what it felt like to be keeping Jonah out of the All Blacks starting line-up. The answer was that it was a weird sort of feeling. Like everyone back then, I was a huge fan of his. He was quicker than me, bigger than me and he was a lot stronger. He did things on a footie field that no one had done before — and haven't done since. In the nicest possible way, Jonah was a rugby freak. In saying that, I still had to concentrate on my own game. I was happy to be part of the Test scene and delighted that the selectors had confidence in me. I tried to make the most of my opportunities without worrying about whether Jonah would eventually be back to take the jersey.

Harty spoke to me before the opening Tri-Nations test in Dunedin and explained the selectors' thinking. At that stage of the season they saw me as an impact player and they believed I had some more work to do before I could be considered as a Test starter. Against South Africa I would again be on the bench. I wasn't over the moon about the decision, but at least John had taken the time to explain things to me. I didn't agree with all his decisions that year, but I always appreciated the fact that he spoke to me. A coach who communicates with his players gets my nod.

At Carisbrook, with the All Blacks up 16–0, I came on for Tana with twenty minutes to go and within a few moments I was straight into the action. I'd really got myself pumped on the sideline and when Andrew Mehrtens put up a huge punt I thundered down on the Springboks full-back, Percy Montgomery. I don't think he expected me to arrive as quickly as I did and he only just managed to get his pass away to Breyton Paulse. It wasn't long after that when my eyes lit up again as the Springboks coughed up ball from a ruck just outside their 22m. Jeff Wilson slipped me an inside pass and I broke the first line of defence and then got around Breyton Paulse. Here was my opportunity to break that try drought against the Boks. I charged down the grandstand touch and had the line in my sights when they hit me. In the end I think there were four or five of them hanging off me. It was like bang . . . bang . . . bang. They came from all directions. I loved it. I've always loved the physical confrontation. As I struggled to stay on my feet, I began to lose all sense of direction. I knew I was close to the try line, but it wasn't until the Boks forced me into the corner flag that I realised how close I'd come to scoring. The Boks have this thing about me and the try line.

The final result – 28–0 – against the Boks was massive and the boys, especially Taine Randell, who had suffered so much in 1998, cherished that victory. Holding South Africa scoreless in a Test is a rare thing. Maybe the new adidas uniform we wore that day was a good omen. It was said to be 'state-of-the-art' gear and it caused a bit of a stir when it was first shown to the New Zealand public. It was all black, with no collar and tight-fitting, but the boys never had a problem with the change. It was still black and it still had the silver fern over the left breast. That's all that ever counts.

We had managed three tries in our win over South Africa. Against Australia at Auckland a couple of weeks later we could only get one. Sure, the 34–15 win looked impressive on the scoreboard and the boys were always in control, but it was the boot of Andrew Mehrtens that did the damage. I've played a lot of Tests with Mehrts, and his coolness under pressure has always amazed me. Against Australia he belted over nine penalty goals

— a world record-equalling performance we were told later — and a conversion for twenty-nine points. He just couldn't miss. Ten from ten. Freakish. As he was lining up his last shot at goal late in the second half I yelled, 'How about a blindfold this time, Mehrts?'

I've watched Andrew's style closely over the years and I know the experts will tell you that good goalkicking is all about timing. That's true. Mehrts is a great golfer. The timing thing with him is a given. To me, though, a lot of his success comes down to the fact that he is so relaxed behind the ball. In fact, he told me once he doesn't concentrate that hard about the ball itself. I've seen him looking around at things going on in the ground and often he'll just be chatting away as he's preparing to line up the shot. It's the same when he's running the back line. Cool, relaxed and a quick brain . . . Mehrts has got a great rugby brain.

I'd come off the bench for fifteen minutes against Australia at Eden Park. Against South Africa at Loftus I got about fifty. Daryl Gibson suffered a back injury in the first half and when I replaced him the whole back line was reshuffled. The most interesting move saw Cully go to centre. We didn't know it then, but it would become a familiar sight later in the season. The Boks didn't have a great day in Pretoria. We pressured them into a lot of mistakes and with Mehrts firing, at altitude, we beat the South Africans comfortably. Three wins from three. We were beginning to shake off the bad memories of 1998.

Against all predictions, mine included, Australia upset South Africa the following week at Cape Town. The narrow win by the Wallabies effectively handed us the Tri-Nations trophy. Beautiful. All that was needed now was a win in Sydney to give us back the Bledisloe Cup. Then we'd be nicely set up for the World Cup a month or so down the track.

John Hart: I know how frustrated Jonah felt about being on the bench during the Tri-Nations, but the selectors always believed he'd fight his way back to peak fitness for the World Cup. It was never part of our plans to use him as an impact player once we got to Britain. We knew that providing he was one hundred per cent physically he would perform for us on the world stage. He has always been a big-match player, a tournament player. In saying that, I have nothing but admiration for the way he reacted to his role as a bench player through 1999. Of course he would have preferred to start each Test. Who wouldn't? But he never complained. Not once.

After we returned from South Africa there was a three-week gap before our final Tri-Nations match. It gave me a chance to get some real game time for Counties Manukau and it also meant I would get to play my first Ranfurly Shield match. Injuries and a variety of other circumstances meant that I had never been in a challenging side, but the Ranfurly Shield is still New Zealand's biggest sporting prize and I was fizzing before the match against Waikato. Conditions at Rugby Park in Hamilton that day were shocking. It never stopped raining the whole time and the ground was a bog even before we ran out. No worries for the locals, though, as their huge pack ground out the victory. I had desperately wanted a big game before the final Tri-Nations Test and, even though we lost, I got plenty of opportunities to test the Waikato defence, especially in the first half. It wasn't just my work rate what pleased me in Hamilton. For the first – and only – time in my first-class career I took a shot at goal. It might surprise a few people to learn that I didn't have a bad sort of place-kick back then. Nothing that would challenge Mehrts, of course, but I could always get a fair bit of distance. We had been awarded a penalty about 45m out from Waikato's line and I banged away what I thought was a fairly stylish left-footer into the wind. A few of the guys reckoned it fell short of the crossbar. I'm positive it shaved the left-hand upright.

They turned up in their tens of thousands for the final Tri-Nations Test of the year. They sang 'Waltzing Matilda' and the records tumbled at Stadium Australia. A world-record crowd of 107,000 and a record losing margin for the All Blacks in a Test match. We got absolutely stuffed at the new Olympics stadium and the 28–7 loss cut us deep. It couldn't have come at a worse time. Six weeks out from the World Cup and it seemed all the hard work we had put in to repair the damage of 1998 had disappeared.

I watched on from the bench in the first half as the Wallabies just overpowered us. It was so frustrating. They beat us in the tight and they beat us in the loose. Their phase play – that damn Brumbies style with George Gregan running the show – was awesome. Recycle, recycle, recycle. It was relentless and there were no mistakes. In many ways, their performance reminded me of the hiding we had dished out to them at Athletic Park in 1996. They could do nothing wrong.

By the time I got on just after half-time the Aussies had cleared out to a 22–7 lead. I had a couple of cracks in the second half, but they didn't come to anything. There was only a try apiece in it at the end, but there was no denying who were the better side on the night. For once Méhrts couldn't steer us home. He scored a try and kicked the conversion, but the game belonged to Wallaby full-back Matt Burke. Seven penalty goals, a conversion – and the Bledisloe Cup.

The pain of the loss to Australia was eased a bit when Harty gave me the word I'd be in the World Cup squad. Even during my time on the bench I'd tried to block out any negative thoughts about the World Cup. I just hoped I'd be there and hoped I had shown enough on the field to convince the selectors I was worthy of a place in the thirty-man squad. We were only a month or so out from the tournament and in that time there was a camp scheduled at the rugby institute in Palmerston North. It was the final tune-up for the World Cup and for me, particularly, it was exciting. I always enjoy the buzz of assembling for an All Blacks tour.

Having missed the big camp at Hobsonville and heard some of the boys talk about the SAS nightmare, I figured this one would be standard training sessions and the normal briefings. I never dreamed there would be a Hobsonville 'refresher' thrown in. We were told one morning that we were off on a promotional road trip – to Taupo, the scene of my own hell training camp back in 1995. This time around, though, I'd enjoy the place. The boys grabbed their shorts, T-shirts and runners and chucked a few videos on the bus. We were a pretty upbeat bunch as we headed up the middle of the North Island. When we turned off just past Waiouru Army Camp there were a few strange looks exchanged on the bus. We were heading to the middle of nowhere and it didn't take long to realise this wasn't going to be some pleasant day out. What we'd been brought to was a mini version of the Hobsonville camp. There were a few groans as one of the SAS boys jumped on the bus. His name was Sam and he was well known to the other players. 'Welcome back, boys,' he grinned. It was like they'd all seen a ghost. I swear thirty heads went down: oh no, not again . . .

Hiking, paddling, sprinting, carting logs up hills . . . I wouldn't say I exactly enjoyed the experience in Waiouru, but it did give me a feel for what the guys had been through a few months earlier. I did have a bit of a scare when I strained my Achilles tendon running up a hill. It wasn't too serious, though, and while it kept me sidelined for a couple of days, I wasn't in the mood for complaining. I was counting off the hours until the start of the World Cup. It was my focus and it was my dream.

CHAPTER FOURTEEN

NON, NON, NON . . .

What went wrong against France? I've asked myself that question hundreds of times since the awful day at Twickenham in 1999. At half-time we held the lead, but things were a bit quiet. Too quiet. This was the World Cup semi-final and we should have been talking things up. We should have been talking about the pace we wanted to play the game at in the second half. We should have talked about how we were going to dictate things — about slowing the game down. We should have been helping Taine Randell. We should have talked about a lot of things . . .

After the first forty minutes it was clear we were in for a battle. Hell, the warning signs were there for everyone to see when they opened us up through the middle to score their first try. Even though I thought we were controlling things pretty well, and Andrew Mehrtens was kicking his goals, they just kept coming back. I've heard people talk about this 'sixth sense' thing. I don't know much about that, but as the half rolled along I got this funny feeling about the French. I wanted to do my bit. I wanted some work. I wanted to shake off that feeling. I remember screaming early on, 'Give me a crack! Give me a go!' Finally, with about twenty-five minutes up, that moment arrived. And it was sweet. Josh Kronfeld, the other half of the old Double J firm, started the move and when I got a neat flick pass from Christian Cullen I wasn't going to let it die. For once the French defence was disorganised. My marker had raced up on me quick and when I got past him there was nothing going to stop me. There were one or two Frenchmen hanging off me as I crashed over. We took a 17–10 lead into the break. And then . . . then came the quiet.

Where was the yap? Where was the fizz? We all knew what had to be done. We all knew the French weren't out of it. And me? Me, of all people knew it was never over against the French until it was over. Remember 1994, Jonah. We needed a second half battle plan. Instead we went into our shells. Four minutes into the second half the French fell off their tackles and the game should have been over. I worked a double-round move with Jeff Wilson from inside our half and then busted through the midfield for my second try. We were out to 24–10. Fourteen points up. Two converted tries clear. All Blacks don't lose matches from that position, so maybe I'd got it wrong at half-time. Maybe the silence was meant to be. This can't be that hard. Control. Roll. Kill the clock. The lid was on the French coffin . . .

Even after four or five years, what happened in the second half seems almost unexplainable. It was unreal. The French quite simply caught fire. I have never seen another team do anything like what they did to us in that second half. Out of this world. What about the three tries they scored? What about those magic touches and switches of play? They owned the ball – and they buried us. Every time they kicked a goal or scored a try we told ourselves it was just a matter of regaining control. Trouble was, they were out of control. The harder we tried, the worse it got. Jeff Wilson's late try saved us from the mother of all hidings – 43-31. The end.

Gutted. Sick to the stomach. How many ways can I put it? I stayed on the field after the game to shake hands with the French and congratulate them. Of course, I was hurt by the loss. Losing in black is always painful, but playing for the All Blacks is also a privilege and an honour. You never lose the memory of the losses, but to me they are outweighed by the memory of wearing the jersey. In the end you've got to learn to accept a loss. Being a humble winner is easy. Being decent, being gracious in defeat, is a lot harder. I was taught early in my career that an All Black doesn't drop his head and walk away after a loss.

I was a senior All Black in 1999. I told the players to stay back and give the French the credit they deserved. They had played out of their skins. Most of them walked off, but I couldn't do that. When the All Blacks win, the opposition stay back to congratulate us. When the roles are reversed why can't we do the same? For all that, it's not for me to judge the actions of the other players. A lot of them were young and they hurt, and that hurt was probably just too much to bear. Don't get me wrong. I felt the loss as badly as anyone. I would have swapped my two tries against France – two of the best tries I ever scored in international rugby – for a one-point win.

You could hear a pin drop in the dressing room after the match. It was a very lonely time. The World Cup was over and the dream had come crashing down. It's always at these moments that the players think about the team and what the jersey stands for. It's an empty feeling, the emptiest feeling in the world, and it's something that is so hard to explain. It's only later when everything starts to sink in that you think about the reaction back home. Sure, we knew the knives would be out and that we'd cop plenty from the media, but for those few moments in the Twickenham dressing room it was only about the team.

I'll never forget the looks on the faces of the workers at Los Angeles Airport when they saw the mural of the All Blacks front row on the side of the big 747. A painted plane. They couldn't believe it. We couldn't believe it when we first saw it in Auckland. That was the hype of the 1999 All Blacks World Cup campaign. That was the level of expectation. I might be a bit out of step with some people, but I thought it was an awesome way of showing support for the World Cup team. It's easy to sit back now and say it was over the top, flying into London with our 'patch' on display for the whole world to see. It was a bit freaky, but it was also pretty cool.

The painted plane might have come as a bit of a shock to the players, but one thing that never surprised us was the planning that went into the 1999 World Cup campaign. Harty and our manager, Mike Banks, had worked for months before we left for Britain to ensure everything ran smoothly. Our base was Pennyhill Park Hotel in Bagshot. It was about 40km from London and perfect. It offered us everything we needed: peace and quiet, a training ground close by and heaps of leisure facilities. A nine-hole golf course is great, but a television set in the bathroom is wild. This place was flash.

While we enjoyed the out-of-the-way surroundings of Pennyhill Park, we couldn't get away from the fact that everyone at the World Cup was gunning for the All Blacks. Our first opponents were Tonga, but most of the early talk was about England, who would be our second opponents in pool play. They were a bloody good side. We knew that before we left New Zealand. The Pommy media rated them big-time and we were ripe for the picking. Mmm. The Tongans, too, fancied themselves. Their coach, Dave Waterston, had been around the international scene for a few years. He'd helped Kitch Christie with the Springboks back in 1995 and he wasn't shy when it came to talking up his team's chances. For a Kiwi, he was pretty mouthy. His team wouldn't take a backwards step. They weren't afraid. They could win. I'm into my drag racing and Waterston's comments reminded me of a saying we have in the sport: 'The bullshit stops when the light goes green'. We couldn't wait for the green light. The team was starting to bond. Our stay at Pennyhill Park was drawing us closer.

It was relief and it was joy when Harty named his opening side of the World Cup. I was back in the starting line-up. Back on the left wing after five games off the bench. I hadn't shaved my eyebrow for months. Not since my last starting Test. For this game, against my Tongan brothers – well, at least some cousins – my signature '11' would be back in place. The game would be special for me, not only because it was against the country where my family's roots lie, but also because it was the first ever All Blacks Test against the Tongans. I'm no different from the other Pacific Islanders in the All Blacks. I would go hard, maybe a little harder than normal, but the result was what counted. It was another Test for New Zealand.

The 'dream back four' that so many people had talked about for so long was named for the Tongan game. Jeff Wilson at full-back, Tana Umaga and me on the wings and Christian Cullen at centre. John Hart had battled with the centre spot ever since Frank Bunce's departure at the end of 1997. Cully is a brilliant rugby player, but Cully at centre? That was a huge call. We got what we expected from Tonga at Bristol. They came out smokin'. I knew they'd reserve some special attention for me, but in the end it was Tana Umaga who wore the best shot of the day. There had been a lot of borderline stuff going down – high shots that were only just legal, late tackles that were just late. The hits were coming from all directions. Then Tana copped a wicked head-high. It was an absolute shocker and he was fuming. When he got up he just turned around to the boys and said, 'We're not putting up with any more of this bullshit!' We had been rattled. They had achieved what they set out to do. We just looked at each other – okay, let's put 'em away.

Discipline under John Hart was strict and the players always knew exactly where they stood with team management if they stepped over the line, so we couldn't exactly try and match fire with fire. Still, we weren't going to stand for any more crap in the second spell. At one point I stiff-armed the Tongan full-back, Josh Taumalolo. It wasn't deliberate. It was one of those instinctive things that happens when a player chops back on your inside. I threw my arm out and caught him with a classic coat-hanger. When he got up he gave me one of those 'what the hell was that for?' looks. I just said, 'If that's the way you guys want to play it . . . ' It didn't help that Josh was my cousin.

Our half-time lead was only 16–9. We knew we were better than that. In the second half we ran in four more tries and came away with a 45–9 win. I got a try in each half and, while the team hadn't performed anywhere near as well as we'd wanted, I was satisfied with my own 'starting' effort. After the game there was talk, mainly amongst the media, that we had been intimidated and that we had been scared of the Tongans. That's rubbish. Their tactics had put us off our game in the first half, but the only thing we were scared of that day was the red card in the referee's pocket – and a mouthful from John Hart afterwards.

Without trying to get ahead of ourselves, we all knew that a win against England would be a massive boost for our chances of making the World Cup final. England versus New Zealand was always going to be the game of the pool round. Win this one and we would have a pretty good run into the semis. Lose? We didn't think much about losing. Apart from veteran prop, Craig Dowd, coming in for Kees Meeuws, who had been injured against Tonga, Harty made no changes for the big one at Twickenham.

We didn't need the media guys telling us before the game how good this English side were. You only had to look at their recent record and, of course, all that experience they had up front. Their forward pack was full of hard-arses. On paper they were a bloody good unit. Like I say, though, we weren't fazed by the media hype. We were always confident going into that game. We'd done our homework and, despite the hiccup against Tonga, I really believed we were in good shape.

I reckon I can always pick the mood of the opposition by the looks in the players' eyes as we perform the haka. They stood firm and they looked staunch. The English that day had come to play. By kick-off I was itching to get it on. For me, there's something special about playing England. Maybe it's because they're always talking themselves up. Maybe because it's the 'mother country', the home of the game. Whatever, playing England really spins my wheels. We beat England that day at Twickenham, not because of a couple of big runs I had or the try I scored. The truth is that I never saw that much ball. We beat England because we defended like we had never defended before. The English threw everything at us but our D was unbelievable. They won plenty of ball, but they couldn't crack us. I have never been so proud of the way our line held that day. I wouldn't have a clue about the final tackle count, but one thing is for sure, we made a heap more than the English.

Territorially, England bathed us in the first half, but we still managed to go to the break 13–6 up, thanks to Mehrts's boot and a try by Jeff Wilson. I was rapt for Jeff. It was his fiftieth Test. There were no negative thoughts at half-time. None at all. We were in front and that was all that mattered. The English are great talkers on the field. It was especially noticeable in the second half. As they closed the gap on us and eventually levelled at 16–16, the chatter was upbeat and it was non-stop. For us, the talking was all about our defensive lines and the need to keeping digging it in. This wasn't about the attack of the 'dream back four', this was about making tackles. It was about survival. Our forwards were criticised at the end of the 1999 season for being too soft. It makes me laugh how some critics remember only what they want to. Against England that day our forwards were awesome.

Like a lot of people, I guess, my clearest memory of the match is the try I scored halfway through the second spell. It started when we forced a turnover just inside our half and the ball came out to Andrew Mehrtens. 'Hit me, Mehrts, hit me!' I screamed. Good old Mehrts. He fired out one of his specials and I knew it was on. I got on the outside of Jeremy Guscott with a bit of a flick and I straightened down the left-hand touch. The English players were scrambling and when I got past their winger, Austin Healey, who I caught flat-footed with an inside feint, the line was begging. Matt Dawson had a crack, but I backed myself to get through him. It was Dan Luger who finally grabbed hold of me as I crossed the line. Too late. The try had been scored. Then all hell broke loose. As I planted the ball there were arms and legs everywhere. Then, whack. I copped a beauty on the side of my head from Lawrence Dallaglio. I was filthy. 'What the hell was that for?' I yelled. 'I'm over the bloody try line!' I didn't realise then that he had been hit from behind after I scored, but I still believe there was no need for him to drop down on my head with his forearm.

I'm not usually a player who goes for the verbals. This time, though, I was really pissed off. Dallaglio had only just returned to the English team after a newspaper had set him up in that famous drugs 'sting'. The news was still hot in Britain. As I got up, and in between the pushing and shoving, I fired a shot at Dallaglio. 'Trouble with you, mate, is that you've been doing too many "lines" – too many drugs,' I said as I ran back to position, tapping my arm. I was disappointed in Lawrence at the time. I know he was probably really frustrated that I'd scored, but that shot he gave me wasn't necessary. He told me later that someone had shoved him and he hadn't meant to clobber me. Whatever. I actually like the guy and I accept now that it was just one of those things. Life's a bit short to be holding grudges about incidents that happen on the footie field.

The England game had been hard and physical. Our final try saw the score blow out to 30–16, which was probably a little flattering. We only had five days until our final pool game, against Italy, and we were absolutely knackered when we came off the field. After the game, as we soaked in those fantastic Twickenham baths, I could sense there was an air of confidence developing in the team. The boys were relaxed and happy.

I've always been big and I've always had an appetite to match my size. There's no denying that on my day I can tuck it away with the best of them. Let's take taro, for instance. It's a root vegetable and, for many people in the Islands, it's a staple food. Because of the size and muscularity of many Polynesian people, taro are often jokingly referred to as the Pacific Islands steroid. Who knows? I got addicted to the stuff when I was young and I still love them. Taro are much bigger and heavier than potatoes and the texture is quite fibrous, but when I was growing up, I could comfortably put away a plateful of boiled taro – for me, that's about three or four, weighing up to 1.5kg each.

I discovered fast food in my early teens. While it's fair to say that I've cut down in recent times, there have been many stories over the years about my eating habits. Some of them are completely true and some of them contain just an element of truth. One of the funniest ones happened early on in my rugby career. I was at an All Blacks trial and a few of us headed down to the local McDonald's for a 'quick bite'. I was the first to order. The bill came to NZ$45. I think the other guys thought I'd ordered for them as well – that's until I turned around and asked them what they were having. Quick bite? Yeah, right.

Kentucky Fried Chicken was always a favourite when I was growing up, and I've had a few legendary sessions courtesy of the Colonel, and I've always had a bit of a weakness for pizza, too. A couple of years ago, when one of the big chains introduced a NZ$14.95 eat-all-you-can night, I thought I had it made. One night John and I and a couple of our cousins decided to put the offer to the test. At the end of dinner, the tally was about thirty large pizzas between the four of us. The manager of the restaurant was filthy. As we were leaving he came over and told us never to come back. Banned. I didn't think we'd done anything wrong . . .

However, with the arrival of professional rugby, fast food became a bit of a no-no on tour. Still, there were always times when the boys managed to slip out quietly for a feed and during the 1999 World Cup in Britain I remember a few of us heading down to a McDonald's in Worcester. I was hungry – super-hungry. Justin Marshall was sitting opposite me and he couldn't believe his eyes when he saw my tray. 'You'll never get through that, Jonah. That's impossible,' he said. An hour or so later I had finished and Marshie was absolutely astonished. He was fishing through all the wrappings to see if I'd hidden any food. From memory, the count was two Big Macs, two Quarter Pounders, two Filet-O-Fish, two McChickens, fries, large drink . . . oh, and a twenty-piece pack of McNuggets, too.

Anyway, back to the World Cup and a score of 101–3 doesn't sound too good in anyone's language, but after we posted the ton against the Italians at Huddersfield they were in a surprisingly good mood. On the scoreboard they'd been wasted, but they never stopped trying. I like that attitude. As long as I've been around, the All Blacks have always admired the never-say-die attitude that some of the weaker rugby nations have taken against us. One of their players said to me after the game, 'Oh, that's the sort of rugby we dream about. If only we could play that way.' It's pretty special to think the Italians regarded just playing against the All Blacks as an honour. I scored two of our fourteen tries against Italy, including one when I was called in for a planned move off the back of the scrum. I actually finished the game at No. 8 after Taine Randell went off injured. It was an interesting experience after all those years in the backs, but I wasn't in a hurry to put up my hand again.

The All Blacks were expected to flog Scotland in the quarter-finals. Nice thought, but in the rain at Murrayfield we played poorly. We got out to a good lead at half-time and then we took the foot off the pedal. At 25–3 we were in a comfortable position. Maybe we already had our eyes on the semi-final. Who knows? We made too many mistakes in the second spell and allowed the Scots to score two tries. I had been well marked all game, but I did manage to get our only try of the half when I got on the outside of my marker, Cameron Murray, and ran about 40m to score. The media trotted out a lot of theories about our poor performance against the Scots. One of them was that the team had been distracted from the job because of the few days we'd spent at Nice on the French Riviera after the Italian match. None of the players thought it was a big deal. It had always been planned and it wasn't as if we weren't going to be training. The only difference was that we were out of the World Cup spotlight – or so I thought.

Up until our short stay in France I had never had much experience of the European paparazzi. Sure, there had always been media around, but I'd never been stalked or hounded by photographers. That's why I never thought much about asking my girlfriend, Teina, to spend some time with me in Nice. On top of that, and despite some newspaper stories, I had never been told by team management that wives or girlfriends weren't allowed to

245

travel across to France. Yes, there were rules when it came to partners, but I stuck to them. She wasn't staying at our hotel and she wasn't going to interfere with any training sessions or meetings.

The paparazzi ambush happened in a flash. One minute Teina and I were walking quietly along the street and the next they were everywhere – cars, a van and even a motorbike, all of them carrying photographers. When team management got the news I'd been photographed with Teina there were a few questions to answer, but it was far from the big deal the press tried to make it out to be. There was no yelling or screaming. Once I'd explained that Teina wasn't staying at the team hotel and that she wasn't interfering with my training, nothing more was said. I have no regrets about having Teina in Nice. I only saw her in my free time. We enjoyed each other's company in the time we spent together and I had no trouble switching back on when it came to doing the things that were expected of me as an All Black. I don't think anyone can have a crack at me for my performance at the World Cup, before or after the French Riviera.

I don't think any of us were prepared for the kind of reaction we got after we lost the semi-final to France. I'd been around long enough to know how tough the New Zealand public and media can be after an All Blacks loss. This time, though, it was different. Of course, there was all the usual stuff. 'Oh, they shouldn't have played Cullen at centre.' 'Justin Marshall should have started the game.' 'How does an All Blacks side lose from that position?' This sort of stuff you expect. New Zealanders are passionate about the game and after a loss everyone has an opinion. I can handle that. I expect that. What the All Blacks didn't expect was the personal attacks after the semi. They hurt like hell.

Taine Randell had copped more than his share of criticism in 1998. After the semi the critics laid into him again. He made a comment about the All Blacks not really being up for the match against South Africa – the game that would decide third and fourth position. I'm sure it was something he regrets saying. Like all of us, he was just wrecked after the semi. He took the loss very personally. The play-off for third and fourth place at a World Cup is not exactly the easiest game to get yourself up for, but it was still a Test, a Test against South Africa. I know Taine well and I know he wasn't being disrespectful to the jersey or to the South Africans.

Things got worse – much worse – after we lost the play-off match in Cardiff. What the hell were we doing in Cardiff? This wasn't how it was supposed to end. We didn't play well against the Boks. As far as I was concerned, though, we did try. Of course, it was hard to get up for the game, but I never felt, as some critics did, that we never tried. We lost by four points to the reigning world champions. The loss to France had knocked us badly. Mentally we were shot, but we did try, and on the day we weren't good enough. We finished second . . . and we were fourth in the world. It was New Zealand's worst performance at a World Cup.

John Hart resigned after the match. I felt sorry for him. After all the bullshit he took in 1998 he never backed down from the challenge. He accepted the job in 1999 and he did it to the best of his ability. He didn't cost us the World Cup. The players lost the match against France, not John Hart. He was everyone's hero in 1996 and 1997 when we were unstoppable. He was everyone's hero when we led the French 24–10. Fifteen All Blacks played those last thirty minutes against France, not John Hart.

Sure, I had my problems with Harty throughout the four years he coached the All Blacks. I never agreed with everything he did. There were things about his style I didn't like, but so what? There were things I didn't like about Laurie Mains's style, as well. John Hart did a lot for New Zealand rugby. People forgot that very quickly. He was willing to try anything to get the best out of his players. Those mind games were a bit different and I'm the first to admit I had trouble coping with all that 'head' stuff. For instance, I struggled with some of the things Harty would tell the media about why I was dropped for a particular game, especially after being told something completely different face to face. But the one thing he did for me in 1999 was to give me that real hunger and the desire for the World Cup. I wasn't happy about sitting on the bench through the Tri-Nations. I hated it. I've got no doubt, though, that if he hadn't had me on the bench I wouldn't have been the player I was at the World Cup. I hit that tournament running. I have Harty to thank for that.

When the All Blacks returned to New Zealand, the knives had been sharpened big-time. The worst criticism was reserved for Hart and Randell. It was unbelievable and it never stopped. It was like some sort of play where the curtain wouldn't come down. I am a proud New Zealander, but let me just say that I was ashamed of my country at the end of 1999. I don't have a problem with All Blacks, myself included, being criticised for the way they might have played, but I can't handle personal attacks. Hell, the All Blacks coach was even spat at. This isn't the New Zealand way. The players were accused of being spineless and gutless. Well, let me say finally that we weren't proud of what happened at the World Cup, but spineless and gutless? No way!

CHAPTER FIFTEEN

WELLINGTON BOOTS

The offers I received to play professional rugby in Britain after the 1999 World Cup were unbelievable. The money some clubs were talking was enormous and I don't mind admitting the temptation to throw away my career in New Zealand was something I really wrestled with. Before the tournament started I told Phil I didn't want to be distracted by the talk of contracts and overseas offers. I wanted to concentrate solely on rugby. After the Cup we were bombarded. In some ways, losing against France probably swayed my final decision, but for days after the tournament I couldn't make a decision. As my girlfriend, Teina, and I toured around Britain, with Phil not too far behind us, the question over where my rugby future would lie hung in my mind. Should I stay? Should I go?

Of all the offers I received, the one from Bristol was the most attractive. Out of this world, in fact. Around a million pounds a season, cars for Teina and me, a choice of where we could live and a full-time managing job for Phil. There were, of course, many other offers. How about Italy, Jonah? What about France? When the Bristol offer was put on the table I thought I'd made my mind up. Yeah, this is a great deal. This has got to be good for me. Phil would say each day, 'Well, what's it to be? Bristol or the Blacks?' And each day my answer became less and less enthusiastic. You see, there was a bottom line. For all the big money that was being talked and the promise of a secure life after rugby, it always came back to the same thing. It always came back to the jersey. Winning a World Cup in the black jersey was what I wanted most. It was the fix.

Phil Kingsley Jones: Jonah was effectively a free agent after the World Cup. His contract with the NZRU had expired and I honestly believed he would make a new career for himself somewhere in Europe. In the end, the whole All Blacks thing got to him. He loves New Zealand and he loves the All Blacks. Maybe if they'd won the World Cup he might have gone. I mean, the money was mighty attractive. Hell, Bristol were so keen to sign him that at one stage they even offered a two-game deal which was worth six figures. Staggering. When he finally made the decision he wanted to stay in New Zealand, I rang the NZRU and we did the whole negotiation bit on the phone. I told them what I wanted and they agreed straight off. When we got back to New Zealand, CEO David Rutherford was there to meet us. The deal was signed at Auckland Airport.

After giving away any thoughts of playing offshore I decided I still needed a fresh challenge in my rugby. The Hurricanes offered that challenge. My girlfriend, Teina, was from Wellington and a move was always on. No pressure, though. Teina would have been quite happy to have moved up north. In fact, she would have been happy if I'd decided to make a career in Britain. The Hurricanes mightn't have been the most successful Super 12 side around, but they had a hell of a lot of exciting players, especially in the backs. There was Christian Cullen, Tana Umaga and Alama

Ieremia and the thought of playing alongside them in Super 12 was a huge attraction.

Phil did the deal with the NZRU for me to transfer to Wellington and link up with the Hurricanes. There were no dramas. When it came to Wellington and national championship rugby we also got a good result. Phil had a great relationship with their CEO, David White. He told Phil he only had limited resources. That didn't matter to us. The money at provincial level wasn't a big deal. In fact, during my whole professional career with Counties Manukau, I was never paid by the union. From 1996 to 1999 we never charged the union a cent. Provincial unions in New Zealand struggle. You've got to want to play for your union. As it turned out, we finished up with a complimentary hospitality box at the brand-new Westpac Stadium – a box for Phil and I to use for as long as I played for Wellington. What can I say? Phil's used it a lot more than me . . .

Teina and I needed a house. I bought one on the cliffs, at Maupuia on the Miramar Peninsula, with awesome views of the city and the inner harbour. Over the years it's been a good talking point for people. The colour – some people say mustard, others are less kind – makes it stick out and I know a lot of taxi drivers point it out to passengers on the way to and from the airport. That never worried me. What used to get up my nose a bit, though, was the constant stream of sightseers when Teina and I first moved in. Whatever. We learned to get used to it.

My first rugby assignment of 2000 was the Wellington round of the IRB World Sevens. The series began in December 1999, but because of all my commitments I hadn't been available for any of the previous tournaments. In fact, Wellington was the only leg of the series I was able to participate in throughout 2000. It was something all the boys had looked forward to. A new tournament and a brand-new stadium. Somewhere around 50,000 people turned up over the two days in Wellington and the atmosphere was almost as electric as the Hong Kong event.

We had little trouble making it through to the final, but that's where things came unstuck. Against our traditional sevens rivals, Fiji, we got outclassed. I didn't perform well at all. Christian Cullen, myself and Caleb Ralph had been included in the New Zealand side pretty much on reputation, whereas most of the other guys had been on the circuit. We desperately wanted to win that first tournament in Wellington – we wanted to show the home supporters what we were capable of and repay them for their support – and it was disappointing.

The fans at Westpac Stadium have been magic over the years. Despite the fact the Hurricanes haven't always been easy to follow, the people just keep turning up. For the first game of Super 12 there was a full house to watch us put away the Sharks. The crowd expected a big performance. They wanted fireworks from the backs and we didn't disappoint them. The back three of Cully, myself and Tana got all five tries. One of mine came after I raced through a gap and chip-kicked the Sharks full-back, Justin Swart – something that's not normally part of my game. I don't know who was more stunned, the crowd or me. As I dropped the ball onto my toe I suddenly thought, what the hell am I doing? Anyway, it worked perfectly and the ball bounced nicely for me to collect it and dive over. Shit. Chip and chase. All right! I've copped a bit of stick over the years for my kicking. I actually don't think I'm as bad as some of my critics reckon. Hey, I'm not crash hot, but I can punt off both feet and my dropped goals always work beautifully . . . at training, anyway.

Of course, criticism is something I've had to put up with for almost all my first-class career. 'Jonah can't kick.' 'Jonah's no good on defence.' You get used to it. To be an international sportsman you've got to be pretty thick-skinned. One particular remark that did make me smile, though, came from Queensland Reds coach, John Connolly, at the start of Super 12. He reckoned I was 'only half a player'. I don't know Connolly from a bar of soap and I'm not sorry about that. I'd like to think that his comment was just part of the mind game stuff so many coaches seem to drag out these days. I suppose you could say I got the last laugh on Connolly when the Hurricanes whipped the Reds in New Plymouth, although I'm not sure whether I was awarded five points for the try I got that day or whether it was only worth two and a half. You'd have to check with Connolly . . .

My hopes of a good performance in Super 12 2000 suffered two big setbacks after the Queensland game. I missed the Canes' next three matches after damaging medial ligaments in my knee. Coupled with that I also had a problem with my heel. Neither injury required surgery, but both needed time. Worse was to come. I returned to the side for the big matches against the Blues, Crusaders and Brumbies, and although we won only one of these games – a ripper against the Crusaders at Wellington – we were still well in the hunt for a semi-final spot. The Hurricanes had recorded five wins from their first seven games and a win against the Waratahs in Sydney was important in terms of momentum and a view to the semis.

I blame Phil for what happened to me in Sydney. Oh, the Hurricanes got the win all right. It's just that I wasn't there to see out the whole game. For the first and only time in my first-class career I was red-carded. Ordered from the field – and I couldn't believe it. The referee was South Africa's Andre Watson, a man I have a lot of respect for, but I reckon he got it wrong in Sydney. I had been yellow-carded early in the first half for a spear tackle on Nathan Grey and spent ten minutes in the bin. I didn't have too much of a problem with that first card. Like I've said, there's such a fine line when it comes to spear tackles. Hit 'em hard and up they go . . . What I did have a problem with was Phil's advice before the match. Phil, the manager, Phil, the bloody coach, said, 'What you have to do today, Jonah, is hit the bastards harder. Get your arms up and drive low into them with your whole body. Doesn't matter if they've just passed the ball. If you're committed, then stick with it. Hit the bastards hard.' Oh, gee, thanks Phil. I've knocked Grey arse-up and he's come down head-first. Yellow card. Ten in the bin. Thanks very much.

The red card came just before half-time. I went to tackle one of the Waratahs players just as he was passing the ball. Watson ruled I had gone in to deliberately knock the ball down. 'Professional foul,' he said. 'They would definitely have scored a try. You're off.' I rang Phil after the game. 'Gidday, coach. Yuh satisfied?' Phil still laughs about it. Despite having lawyer and Hurricanes assistant coach Bryan Williams, defending me, I received a two-match suspension. I was hot about it and decided to appeal the decision. The appeal hearing was a joke. Phil and I fronted the judicial committee and practically before we'd had a chance to sit down, one of the members of the panel said, 'Why are you appealing? Don't you know we could give you a longer suspension?'

Phil and I were stunned. Why was I appealing? Because I thought I was innocent, that's why. It wasn't the Grey tackle that I was upset about. It was the professional foul call, the one that got me the red card, which I couldn't cop. I turned to Phil and said, 'We're screwed already.' 'Yeah,' he agreed. 'But when we walk out, don't let them think they've won. Don't give them any satisfaction.' The suspension was upheld and it cost me any further part in the Super 12. I was disappointed, but decided that I'd head off on the road trip to South Africa to support the boys anyway. The Hurricanes lost both matches and missed out, making the semi-finals by only three points. The second half of Super 12 had turned into a real anticlimax.

I needed games before the start of the international season. Injuries and suspensions had meant I'd only played six matches in Super 12. I turned out once for my Wainuiomata club in Wellington and then received an offer to play for the UK Barbarians. When Phil put the idea to the All Blacks management they took a bit of persuading, but in the end they gave me the green light. The new coach, of course, was Wayne Smith. I was rapt when he was appointed to take over from John Hart. I knew Smithy well and I had enjoyed his style when he was part of the All Blacks coaching set-up in 1998–1999. He was hugely respected by the players, especially the Canterbury boys who'd had him as Crusaders coach, and we all thought he was the right man for the big job.

As usual, the Barbarians club managed to put together a useful side. We played Ireland at Dublin in a game that celebrated the 125th anniversary of the Irish Rugby Union. We trailed the Irish for most of the game and only got up in the last minute to win. They call these sorts of games festival matches. I'm not so sure about this one. There were some huge hits going in. For Phil, the highlight of the game was seeing his son, Kingsley, who actually captained Wales in the late 1990s, playing on the same team as me.

Phil and I had to leave for home virtually straight after the game, but what should have been a straightforward trip to the airport turned out to be an absolute mission. I love the Irish and they've always taken a special interest in me, but I wasn't prepared for the reception I got outside Lansdowne Road. Phil and I were lucky to make it to the car. Our driver reckoned he'd never seen a mob like it. They were shouting and screaming and knocking on the car windows. Still, it's nice to feel wanted.

It wasn't too much of a surprise to me when Wayne Smith appointed Todd Blackadder All Blacks captain. I'd toured with

Todd and I'd played under him a couple of times in 1997. With Todd Blackadder, what you see is what you get. Great guy, inspiring leader and a wonderful rugby brain. I've got no doubt that he is one of the key reasons the Crusaders were so successful in the late 1990s and 2000. However, one thing that did amaze me was all the crap he had to put up with when he was named captain. His critics didn't believe he deserved to hold his locking position in the team, let alone captain the side. I don't agree. He wasn't tall by today's standards, and he wasn't flashy, but Toddy worked his butt off every time he pulled on the black jersey. He wasn't the 'money man' in the line-out, but he always got his share of ball. He had a huge work rate and a great tactical understanding of what was required at international level, as well. Todd Blackadder remains one of the finest captains I ever played under.

The All Blacks warmed up for the Tri-Nations with matches against Tonga and a two-Test series against Scotland. Tonga were nowhere near as motivated for the game at Albany as they had been for the pool match in the World Cup the year before. We nailed them all over the park. From memory, the forwards scored as many tries as the backs as we racked up a hundred points, but it wasn't my night against Tonga and there was a bit of criticism that I hadn't got myself involved enough – a hundred points, but no tries for Jonah. Like I said, I have become used to criticism, especially about my work rate. Yes, we were running in tries from all over the place and, yes, maybe I didn't get myself involved enough. It was around this time that Smithy had a few little one-on-ones with me. He talked about my work rate and how we could improve things. Smithy's one of the game's great thinkers and tacticians. He put the idea into my head that I was attached to the fly-half by an imaginary 2m rope. It was to get me used to the idea of coming into the back line from all over the field, to stop me drifting. He was also a firm believer that his blindside wing should always be in a flat position on the inside of the fly-half. Not only did it give you the opportunity to enter the back line from anywhere, it was also an ideal position to hide, if you like, and keep the opposition guessing.

Smithy was right on the money, both in the style of his approach and also in the tactics he devised. In the first Test against Scotland, at Dunedin, I made up for my quiet game against Tonga with three tries. Stay with the breaks, Jonah. Stay close and the chances will come. Again we created space — space to burn — and I was there to captitalise on plenty of opportunities which came my way. My first try was especially satisfying after a great bust up the middle by Alama Ieremia. I took a pass from Pita Alatini just inside the Scots' half and knew the try was on once I got on the outside of my marker, Craig Moir. Their full-back, Chris Paterson, made a desperate late lunge, but just as I thought I'd done enough to shrug him off, his arms slipped down my legs and he clipped my ankles. Cully was steaming up on my inside, but I couldn't throw the pass. Instead, I somehow managed to get back to my feet and scramble over as the last of their cover arrived. Dunedin was Happy Hurricanes Day. Cully, Tana and I scored six tries between us. The Scots were a bit more competitive in the second Test at Auckland and the scores were closer. It didn't matter. With a new coach and a new captain we'd achieved our goal for the first part of the season. The big stuff would start in Sydney.

Going into the first match of the Tri-Nations we were confident — confident in ourselves and confident in the coach and the game plan. Smithy had done his homework and identified the areas where he thought the Australians were vulnerable. Really, though, our plan was simple. It was to attack at every opportunity. That night in Sydney, Stadium Australia was packed with yet another world-record crowd — 110,000 — for a rugby Test. Could the game live up to the pre-match hype? It didn't really matter to me. Whether it was one point or twenty, just give me the win.

Everything before the game felt right. We had trained well and we were relaxed. From the moment Tana intercepted a Chris Latham pass a minute after kick-off, we were on a roll. It was like nothing I'd ever experienced. Oh, England in 1995 was special, but here . . . here we were just on fire. I set up Pita Alatini for a try after a big charge down the left wing, and with a penalty goal from Andrew Mehrtens and another try by Christian Cullen we were out to a 24–0 lead – all this in the first eight minutes. I remember thinking, shit, this is just crazy! The whole team were stunned. God knows what the hell was going through the Aussies' minds – I mean, they had hardly even touched the ball.

I still ask myself how we let Australia back into the game. They were a fantastic unit, but at 24–0 down, they should have been dead and buried. The fact they came back at us is a tribute to their mindset – that bloody Australian never-say-die mindset. They poured on the pressure and really squeezed us hard in those next thirty minutes until half-time. The 24-all scoreline left us a bit shell-shocked in the dressing room, but Smithy remained upbeat. He had great faith in us. There was no panic. He just told us to open things up again. Run everything.

In certain games you can sense that things aren't going to go your way. I never felt that in Sydney. Even after the Wallabies grabbed the lead at 35–34 with about seven or eight minutes to go, I still believed that if we were patient we could do it. We just needed something to go our way. We were deep into injury time when the break finally arrived. Alama Ieremia punched hard at the Aussie defence, dragging in a bunch of defenders on their 22m and set up the ruck. I knew we had the Wallabies stretched out left. I could hardly contain myself. Forget the patience stuff. As Byron Kelleher passed to Taine Randell, I started screaming, 'Give it to me! Give it to me!' His lobbed pass dropped perfectly into my arms and I set sail for the line. Only Steve Larkham to beat and only a couple of metres to work in. I had to stay on his outside and all the time I was aware I was getting dangerously close to the touchline. Larkham's attempted tackle hardly slowed me and it was really just a matter of keeping my balance as I tiptoed down the chalk. The try took a moment or two to register, but when it did . . . man, it was so sweet – 39–35 and the Wallabies' first loss as world champs. Beautiful.

They still call that game the greatest test ever played. I don't know. It was certainly a hell of a match and I don't think I've ever played in one quite like it. For the sheer intensity, for the speed and the skill level, it is probably pretty hard to top. Entertaining, too. Yeah, the crowd loved it, but for all the joy and excitement after the game, there was still a feeling amongst the boys that the job was only half done. The win in the Tri-Nations opener was the leg-up we wanted in our hunt for the Bledisloe Cup. Before we got that chance we had to face the Springboks at Jade Stadium.

That day at Christchurch I scared the hell out of Percy Montgomery – and he coughed up a try. I thundered after a kick by Andrew Mehrtens and, as I zeroed in on Percy, I just screamed at him. He cracked and he got the wobbles. Instead of trying to pick the ball up, he just aimed his boot at it and kicked it – straight into Cully's hands. Thanks very much. Montgomery's an interesting footballer. When things are going well he can be the best full-back around. If you can get the Boks under pressure, though, and in doing so turn up the heat on Percy, then it's usually curtains. Never give Percy time. In Christchurch he got none. Cully grabbed a double against the Boks and while I missed out (again!), I took a lot of satisfaction from the game. Smithy had worked hard with me on both attack and defence and, while I had a few of those awkward moments defending, I was pretty happy with the way things were going.

With wins over Australia and South Africa under our belts, victory over the Wallabies in Wellington would have given us the Tri-Nations title and the Bledisloe Cup — to me, the bigger prize of the two. I've never needed any special motivation to play against Australia. The intense rivalry between the All Blacks and the Wallabies has always been enough to get me up, but a couple of days before the match, one of the Australian media guys really lit my fuse. At a press conference he asked me how I felt about Ben Tune coming off the bench and back into the Wallabies line-up. Ben's a fine winger and he'd been off the scene for a while with injury. I think I gave him the standard answer — 'I'm looking forward to marking Ben again.' — but he wouldn't let it go. 'Well, you know, he has always looked after you well and he's one of only a few players to sit you on your arse.' Pardon me? I asked him where he was going with the question and he came straight back. 'Yeah, he's torn you up heaps of times.' He was baiting me. I was pissed off, but managed to hold my temper. 'Well, I'll have to try to remedy that this weekend,' I replied.

The Wellington Test, the first ever at Westpac Stadium, will always be remembered for the penalty goal John Eales nailed at the end of the match. Just after half-time, though, I got my chance to make that journo eat his words. Before the game I had wised up our centre, Alama Ieremia, that I wanted a crack at Ben. The Aussies were obviously keen to get him back into the action as soon as possible and with only about a minute of the second half gone, Ben got his first touch. As the Wallaby move began to unfold just inside our half, Alama yelled at me, 'He's on his way!' I came off my wing at pace just before Tuney got the ball. He was Alama's man, all right. Instead, though, he hesitated just long enough to let me through. Bang! I caught Ben smack in the sweet spot. It was a huge hit, so big that I could hear the wind being forced out of his lungs. Hi, Ben. Welcome back to test rugby . . . It wasn't really personal. I have huge respect for Ben. I just needed to make a point to the bloke in the press box.

We lost the Test at Wellington because we made a mistake right at the finish. We cocked up a line-out, then gave up a penalty. As I stood under the goalposts and watched John Eales line up the shot I was just about sick. This shouldn't be. I have always tried to be a good sportsman, but inside my head I was praying for him to miss. Blow wind, blow. Make him miss. Make him fall over. Oh, shit . . . We were the better team in Wellington. I have no doubt about that, but in the end that penalty summed up what Test match rugby is all about — pressure. We didn't cope with it. We should have held them out. In Sydney we had forced the result through pressure. Here it was our turn to crack.

Todd Blackadder copped a lot of shit for the loss. It was like that whole Taine Randell thing all over again. Blame the captain. Hell, hadn't he been the man who had led the Crusaders to three Super 12 titles in a row? Hadn't he just led the All Blacks to five straight Test wins? We lost by a point to the world champions because we made one mistake. As All Blacks, that's probably unforgivable. I accept that, but I don't accept the fact that the captain that day was the sole person responsible for the loss. I couldn't believe the way his captaincy was scrutinised after that game. The behaviour of certain sections of the crowd at the end of the game just made things worse for me. They began throwing bottles at referee Jonathan Kaplan. He had awarded the penalty goal deep into injury time and some supporters obviously felt hard done by. Whatever, it didn't excuse what happened. Norm Maxwell had to protect Kaplan from the bottle-throwers as he left the field. It was the first time I had seen this sort of thing happen in New Zealand. It was very sad.

I'm not going to pretend the final match of the Tri-Nations was one of my better efforts. I was off my game in Johannesburg. I didn't see a lot of ball and this sometimes causes me to lose a bit of concentration. Apart from that, though, the Boks were definitely hungrier at Ellis Park. I got the impression after we arrived in South Africa that this game was do-or-die for them. They had lost their first two matches to us and the Wallabies and the press were giving them a hard time. At one point they got out to 33–13 and we were looking down the barrel. At the final whistle we had pulled it back to 40–46, but it wasn't a game I remember with much fondness.

Wayne Smith (All Blacks coach 2000–2001): There was a lot of comment early on in the season about Jonah's low work rate. He was criticised about his defence generally and his inability to turn and take kicks. When we sat down and talked about it I found he was receptive to feedback and always willing to work harder to improve his game. For me, his dedication to improvement was a standout feature of the 2000 season. He started the international year slowly, but showed that he was prepared to work at the weaknesses in his game. He ended up having an outstanding season, playing a major role in two of the best Bledisloe Cup Tests ever played. The thing that has always struck me about Jonah is that he is such a selfless individual. That might surprise a few people who have this impression that he's a sporting superstar concerned only with the trappings that go with that. Not so. Jonah Lomu is a team man — one of the givers in the sport.

The All Blacks were still on Test duty when the NPC first division kicked off in August. By the time I played my first game, Wellington had already knocked over two of the big guns, Canterbury and Otago. Four games later we were holding a crisis meeting. We got dicked by North Harbour at Albany and after that Norm Hewitt got us together for a big honesty call. He was angry when he fronted the boys and he accused us of playing for ourselves and lacking guts. He wasn't alone in his views. Two of the younger members of the side also had a crack. They wanted to run more. They wanted to smash opposition players. Jerry Collins and Rodney So'oialo wanted Wellington to win – and they wanted it bad. Jerry was especially vocal. Even back then I knew that he had what it took to make it at the highest level. Since making it into the All Blacks, he has shown that he's a man who prefers to let his on-field actions do the talking. 'There's no bloody use just speaking about it,' he told the team. 'Let's just get out there and do it!'

The Wellington coach was Dave Rennie. He was a good bloke and I personally believe that technically he was very sound. Dave's assistant was Hurricanes coach Graham Mourie, one of the greatest All Blacks captains of all time. You couldn't help but respect Goss for where he'd been and what he'd achieved. The trouble was, the two coaches were trying to get us to play a style of game that wasn't really suited to the sort of players in the squad. It was a mixture of the Brumbies' and Crusaders' style of play, and very much defence-oriented. We were ball carriers – forwards and backs. We were a physical outfit – a lot of Polynesian and Maori players – and we wanted to run at the opposition, and run hard. To their credit, Dave and Graham listened to our views and came up with another game plan. I'm not sure what would have happened if they hadn't taken our thoughts on board . . .

We became a very close unit after that meeting, winning our

final three matches in round-robin play and booking ourselves a semi-final against Auckland. I could really sense something special was building within the side when, after being down 7–11 at half-time, we gutsed out a 28–21 win over Southland at Invercargill. Against Waikato in our final round-robin game, we really put things together. Our loosies were outstanding. Jerry Collins, Rodney So'oialo and Kupu Vanisi were doing what they wanted – they were smashing the opposition. We hammered Waikato 48–23.

One problem that stuck with us right through the season was our poor discipline. There were some people who even suggested this area of our game was simply part of the Hurricanes and Wellington culture. That's ridiculous. What team ever goes out looking for yellows or reds? In fact, all through the NPC we talked about our discipline and the need for us to keep cool heads. The Wellington guys are super-competitive and sometimes we did over-step the mark, but I also think that once you've been labelled a bit of a wild outfit the referees always look that much harder.

It was disappointing that all the talk about our ill discipline went out the window in our semi-final against Auckland and again we found ourselves with a couple of players in the sin bin. Being reduced to fourteen men for twenty minutes of the match should have hurt us. In the end it didn't. Our forwards just laid into Auckland. Jerry showed that day just what a hard-arsed footballer he is. He had done all his talking after the North Harbour game and against Auckland his physicality was unbelievable. The consequences for the Auckland players running straight at Jerry were frightening. Out on the wing I was just in awe – the guy was only nineteen.

At the start of the NPC, Wellington were being looked at as outsiders for the semi-finals. Exciting backs, average forwards. In the end, the backs did score the tries, but it was the forwards who got us through to the final. The win over Canterbury in the final is right up there as one of the highlights of my rugby career. In the All Blacks you're always expected to win. With Wellington it was so completely different. We were the underdogs in virtually all the key games in the NPC. It all came down to belief in ourselves — and for that Wellington owes Norm Hewitt a huge debt. Over the years he's had his share of critics and I know he upset a lot of people when he released his controversial biography in 2001. In NPC 2000, though, he captained from the front and throughout the whole campaign he was never prepared to accept second best. Even a broken arm midway through the second half of the final against Canterbury wasn't enough to force him from the field. At that stage we were ahead 34–15. The lead looked solid enough, but maybe Norm knew something we didn't. In that final quarter Canterbury threw everything at us and at full-time there was only five points in it. Wellington's title. My proudest day in provincial rugby.

I finished up with nine tries in the NPC and certainly one of my fondest memories is of the second try I scored against Canterbury in the final. I was marking the Fijian winger, Marika Vunibaka. I took a pass about 60m out and had a running battle with Marika all the way to the goal line. The first time he came at me he went straight for my upper body. I pushed him off and headed wider. He had another go, but again came in too high. After I pushed him off for the second time I was almost at the line. This time he went for my legs, but it was too late . . .

I'm never rude to Doc Mayhew. Like, we're great mates. So I suppose he got a bit of a shock when I told him to piss off at Paris on the All Blacks end-of-year tour. I had gone down in the second half of the first Test after colliding with a Frenchman's knee. We were ahead 15–12. 'Come on, Jonah, I think you've broken your cheekbone,' Doc said. 'Piss off. I'm staying put,' was my reply. My face hurt like hell. The loss against France at the 1999 World Cup still hurt like hell, too. We were playing for the Dave Gallaher Trophy – Dave Gallaher, a New Zealander who had given his life for his country in the First World War. I wasn't leaving the field for anything or anyone. In front of 80,000 French supporters we dug deep for Dave Gallaher and we dug deep for ourselves: 39–26. Like Toddy Blackadder said after the game, 'It was Armistice Day. We had the poppy on our jerseys. We did ourselves proud.' Doc Mayhew was proved right after the game. My cheekbone was broken. In fact, he's pretty much always right and I have so much respect for him, but I like to think that respect is reciprocated.

Dr John Mayhew: I've been around athletes my whole working life and I can say in all honesty that Jonah is the most freakish I've ever come across. Physically he is also the strongest, by a considerable margin. The sad thing is, he played so much of his international career with a huge handbrake, medically speaking.

'I'll never forget one amazing feat of strength he displayed at Burnham Military Base in Christchurch, back in 2001. We had been invited into the officers' mess at the conclusion of an All Blacks training camp and were having a few quiet drinks. At one point this huge fellow strolled in – quite obviously a weightlifter. He must have been 140kg and his muscles were absolutely rippling. He walked up to this giant anvil in the middle of the room and stopped while the officer in charge laid down a challenge: "If any All Black can lift this, there'll be free drinks for you all – every time you visit." Then this big guy grunted and groaned and showed us how it was done. Staggering. This was a seriously big weight. We were in awe of him and, it seemed, there were no All Blacks ready to take up the challenge. About ten minutes passed when one of the players nudged me: 'Look, Doc, Jonah's over by the anvil.' The big guy was in street clothes. There was no announcement. There was no bravado. There were no grunts or groans. He just squatted down and arm-curled the thing. Strong? Jonah Lomu? You better believe it.

I flew home and watched the All Blacks lose the second Test at Marseilles from my home in Wellington. In many ways that game summed up our season. We had played South Africa twice, Australia twice and France twice. We beat them all . . . once.

CHAPTER 16

WINNING IS A RUSH

I looked at him lying on the deck. Like the rest of the boys, I thought he was mucking about. 'Come on old man, get up. What's the matter? Can't you hack it any more?' It's a bit of a game we like to play in sevens. We take the piss out of each other all the time. When a player goes down in a tackle or gets a knock and takes a bit of time to get up, he cops a serve from the other guys. Eric Rush always leads the charge. Rushie is the king of the piss-take, but this time the king wasn't getting up. I couldn't believe what I was seeing. The great man was lying on the ground and the pain was written all over his face. He wasn't just hurting, he was in absolute agony. Rushie wasn't getting up.

We were only a few minutes into our final pool match of the day, against England, at the 2001 World Cup Sevens in Mar del Plata. I missed the actual incident, but later Rushie told me he'd landed under Karl Te Nana and one of the Poms. The impact had smashed his right leg. His thigh bone was wrecked. His lower leg bone was wrecked, as well. I looked at his leg, and the awful sight of the bone sticking out of his sock, and I forced back the tears as they stretchered Rushie – New Zealand rugby's Mr Indestructible – from the field. His dream was over. He had desperately wanted to win this World Cup. In a career that went right back to the late 1980s, this was the only sevens prize that had eluded him.

We went on to win the game against England. We had played reasonably well on the first day of the tournament, beating three of the lesser sides, and on the second day we opened with a win against Chile. Even though I had prepared well for the World Cup and was fully fit, coach Gordon Tietjens decided to use me in fits and starts early on. Against England, though, it was different. This was my old enemy. I had started this game and I made a vow to myself when Rushie went off that I would try and do it for him. We all wanted to do it for Rushie. I hadn't scored a try in the tournament before this game. I hadn't cut loose. Now, I was amped. In the finish I got my try. We got the win. It wasn't pretty, but we made the quarter-finals and nothing was going to stop us.

Despite the win over England, we were all feeling pretty sorry for ourselves when we returned to the hotel. The win against the Poms had done bugger all for our morale. We had been thinking about Rushie for hours after the England game and the sight that finally greeted us upon his return later that night did little to lift our spirits. He was in plaster from his hip to his ankle. He would spend just one more night with the team before flying back to New Zealand.

I was Rushie's room-mate in Mar del Plata and I was determined to do all I could to make his final night as comfortable as possible. When he told me he was hungry I rang room service and ordered up a large plate of steak and chips. Normally, red meat is off limits to the sevens boys. Titch is a hard man when it comes to diet. I sat on my bed and watched Rushie wolf down his meal. I was envious, and Rushie knew it. 'Jeez, Jo [Rushie always called me Jo], this is a bloody good feed,' he said. 'Mmm . . . you'd love this steak.' He was right. The smell was driving me crazy. Finally, he said, 'Here you go. I can't finish this last piece. You have it. Don't worry, I promise I won't tell Titch.' I must have kept my eye on that last piece of steak for at least a couple of hours, but I couldn't bring myself to eat it. We still had a job to do. We had a World Cup to win. The rule was simple: no red meat. In the end I ducked downstairs and grabbed a plate of spaghetti and some toasted sandwiches.

After Rushie drifted off to sleep I decided to keep watch. It was just like the night of the 1995 World Cup semi-final against England. I had so much racing through my mind. Rushie had told me the doctors had said he might never play rugby again. The thought of that was too awful. We would win this World Cup for Rushie. I did not close my eyes all night . . . The lobby of the Sheraton Hotel the following morning was like a funeral scene. As we farewelled Rushie many of the boys were in tears. We did a haka and that set Rushie off. He just broke down. I was the last person to say goodbye. As I tried to hold back the tears he whispered to me, 'Jo, it's time for you to show the boys what you're made of. Show everyone what you can do. Go hard.' I told him I couldn't guarantee that we'd win the tournament, but I did make him a promise. I would run until I dropped.

After Rushie left we headed to a local park for a bit of a walk and a team meeting. We talked about what the tournament meant to us and what victory would have meant to Rushie. I had my say. I told the guys I wasn't the fittest man in the side, not by a long way, but I repeated what I had said to Rushie – I would go hard.

Our quarter-final match was against Samoa. They were a good side back then, but on this day they were no match for us. We were in the zone. We belted them 45–7 to set up a semi-final against Argentina. Titch had warned us about Argentina. He warned us of their passion and he warned us how they would lift with massive home-town support. On finals day there were 30,000 people in the stadium and I reckon ninety-nine point nine per cent of them were cheering for Los Pumas.

It never pays to think too far ahead in a sevens tournament. It's always one game at a time, but in Mar del Plata it was hard to believe that if we made the final our opponents would be anyone else but Fiji. We got a hell of a shock when the Aussies knocked them over in the first semi. The Fijians had all their stars on board – Waisale Serevi, Marika Vunibaka, Vilimoni Delasau – and they'd come to win. They weren't happy when we passed them on the way out for our match against Argentina. There was no way we wanted the same fate. We hooked into the Argentinians from the start. We used our pace and our power . . . and we used Rushie. He was never far from our thoughts on finals day. Five tries to one. Bring on the Aussies.

We prepared for the final against Australia in pretty much the same way we always prepare in sevens. Team talk, warm-ups and music – always lots of music. Karl Te Nana, who had taken over as captain from Rushie, slipped me a Tupac Shakur disc at one stage and we gave the old rapper the full noise. We were in the dressing room next to the Russian boys. They couldn't get over our pre-match routine. The expressions on their faces were classic as they poked their heads in to see what was going on. Is this the World Cup of rugby sevens or are we in a nightclub? We prayed before the final. It's a thing we've always done in sevens. Doesn't matter whether you're a believer or not. We just do it. We come together. It's bonding time. We prayed for ourselves and we prayed for our friends and our families back home. We also prayed for Rushie. The Aussies that day didn't have a prayer. There was too much emotion in the New Zealand side.

I got a lot of credit for our win in the final. Yeah, three tries was a personal highlight, but it was a team effort. I know that's a cliché. Too bad. It's the way it was. I was proud of the way the young guys stepped up. We only led 12–7 at the break. We needed composure in the second half. We needed patience. Those young guys delivered. Rodney So'oialo and Mils Muliaina were barely into their twenties, but they looked like All Blacks in the making.

Gordon Tietjens: Jonah might downplay his part in that World Cup win, but from my perspective he was quite outstanding. He literally grew another leg after Rushie got injured. In the semi-final against Argentina he just blew them apart. In the final he was even better. On fire. I'll never forget his first try. He received the ball about 70m out and just went for it down the right-hand touchline. All that power and pace that some people thought he'd lost. He got around Richard Graham and then smashed through Brendan Williams. Jonah Lomu was back.

There were three main missions for the New Zealand sevens team in 2001. The World Cup win in Argentina meant we had completed the first one. That left the defence of our IRB World Sevens Series title and, within that tournament, the big prize for the New Zealanders of the Wellington Sevens. The boys were just so desperate to win at Wellington. Trouble was, most of the players who returned home with gold from Mar del Plata couldn't be selected for their home event. For the likes of Brad Fleming, Mils Muliaina, Roger Randle and Rodney So'oialo, it was straight back to their Super 12 sides. I think that was unfortunate and, at the time, I couldn't see why they weren't able to be released for a two-day tournament. I mean, Super 12 hadn't even kicked off. I was lucky. I still had a clause in my contract with the NZRU that allowed me to play sevens for New Zealand. It would have been a great gesture by the franchises to have released the other players for Wellington. Man, we were world champions. We wanted to strut our stuff and nothing replaces that feeling you get playing in front of your home crowd.

However, even without many of our World Cup stars, it's hard to offer excuses for being tipped out of the Wellington Sevens at the quarter-finals stage. Sure, the draw meant we ended up with Fiji in the quarters, but we still had talent to burn — certainly enough to win that game. It wasn't to be. The Fijians were hurting from their early exit in Mar del Plata. Now, it was our turn. I had a chance to win the game in the dying seconds. I was ankle-tapped only a couple of metres from the Fijian line, but as I tried to scramble over, the ref ruled I'd knocked the ball on. I disagreed. I had tried to squeeze the ball free. There was no knock-on. What can I say? He had the whistle. The end. Our misery was made worse when we got done by Samoa in the Plate semi-final. We felt pretty bad. There had been so much expectation. We had let ourselves down and we had let the big crowd down, too.

On paper you would have thought the Hurricanes were a good chance in Super 12 2001. We had the backs — hell, we had the backs every year — and the forwards had a really good look about them. The loosies were as good a unit as any in the competition. Filo Tiatia, Rodney So'oialo and Jerry Collins. Hard to argue with that. In the tight we had guys like Norm Hewitt, Gordon Slater, Kevin Yates, Paul Tito and Dion Waller. Solid.

After Wellington's NPC win the year before, everyone expected Norm to be named captain for the Super 12. The coaches, Graham Mourie and Bryan Williams, had other ideas. I don't know why they replaced him. I can only guess they wanted a player they could have more control over, someone who wouldn't question their decisions all the time. Norm always questioned. He wasn't a smart-arse. He just knew the ropes, because he'd been around the first-class scene for a long time. In the end, they gave Gordon Slater the job. Graham obviously knew Gordy well from their time in Taranaki and maybe he felt he could relate better to him. I dunno. Norm said in his book the team were a bit pissed off when he was replaced. I never detected that. Goss and Bryan were the bosses. We just had to get on with the job.

A knee injury kept me out of the first match of Super 12, but I went on to play the next nine games on the trot. It wasn't the happiest time in my career. Many of us struggled with Graham's coaching style. There was too much blackboard stuff. In fact, there was too much stuff altogether. The boys just never seemed to have any time to themselves. A normal day would begin around 8a.m. We'd train for a couple of hours, then it was out to the police college at Porirua for some gym work. After that it was video analysis, followed by lunch and then more training. Often we wouldn't finish until after 6p.m. This was every day except game days and Sunday, our recovery day. By the time game day had rolled around we were getting sick of each other. We needed space. Goss just didn't seem to understand this. I had my share of disagreements with the coaching staff that year, too.

In terms of results, the Hurricanes went backwards in 2001. Won five, lost six. The old discipline problems came back to haunt us and our inconsistency was there for everyone to see. It's still hard to explain how in consecutive weeks in the middle of the season we could knock over the Crusaders and the Brumbies and then, in our second to last game, go out and get thrashed by the Chiefs. It's not very often I look back on a rugby campaign without any fondness. The Super 12 of 2001 was, unfortunately, one of those campaigns. I was glad when it was over.

Before the international season began I again accepted an invitation to play for the UK Barbarians. I was criticised for that decision. It was nothing new. It seems that whenever I do something a bit different I get caned in the media. Sure, the Baabaas pay well and, yes, the invitation did come in the middle of the season, but the bottom line has always been that I never accept an invitation to be part of an overseas team without first gaining permission from the All Blacks coaches. Wayne Smith didn't have a problem with me taking part in the two matches, against Scotland and England. In fact, he was supportive, especially once I told him that Phil had arranged for Rushie to come along and act as my personal trainer.

Rushie is one of the great trainers. He always keeps himself super-fit. It's the reason he's been able to stay at the top of the sevens tree for so long and also why he's recovered from injuries that would have ended the careers of other players. On the Barbarians tour, he worked me as hard as I've ever been worked. While most of the other guys in the side would use their spare time to go shopping or sightseeing, Rushie would have me out running or in the gym. I had made a commitment to Smithy that I would return to New Zealand at peak fitness and I wasn't going to let him down. There was no way that was going to happen with Rushie running the show.

The day the Baabaas played England, Rushie received a call from Gordon Tietjens asking if there was a chance I could make myself available for day two of the London Sevens. The sevens boys had suffered a few injuries and I was only too happy to lend a hand. Phil and I were criticised for that decision as well. The fact is that Titch had actually registered my name before the start of the tournament. The NZRU had agreed to let me play if I was needed. Hell, it was just one day. Sometimes you just can't win . . .

I wasn't considered for the opening match against Samoa, but I was back in the side for the Test against Argentina in Christchurch. It was a strange day in many ways. Jeff Wilson was back on the right wing and Anton Oliver was the new All Blacks captain. I didn't have a problem with either selection.

When Jeff decided to take a break from rugby in 2000 I was disappointed because I've always enjoyed playing with him, but I wasn't surprised. Like me, he'd been around for a long time and had come into the All Blacks at an early age. I don't know too many guys who would have made the call to take a year out. That's Jeff, though. He's strong-willed and when his mind is made up, that's usually it. Maybe his body was telling him something. Who knows? I respected his decision and I was rapt when he came back.

Anton Oliver led the All Blacks to a big win over Argentina at Jade Stadium, 67–19. I didn't get on the scoresheet, but I did enjoy myself. There was a good feeling within the team and Anton led the side just as I thought he would. He's a straight shooter and he's a hard man. He would never ask a player to give any more in the black jersey than he was prepared to give himself. It was a decent win and when we backed up the following week against France and came away with another win, everything was looking great. Jeff and I both got tries. The old firm was back in business. My training with Rushie was paying off. I felt fit and was pleased with my work on defence as well as attack. Bring on the Tri-Nations.

We travelled to Cape Town for the tournament opener and we came away with a win. I did it tough in the first half and remember touching the ball only a couple of times. I didn't see much more of the action in the second half, but it didn't matter. Tony Brown kicked us home 12–3 and that's what counted. Points in South Africa are not easy to come by. I'm always happy to take an away win first up. The Aussies weren't as lucky the following week when they were beaten in Pretoria.

Everything, it seemed, was set up for the All Blacks in the first of the Bledisloe Cup Tests in Dunedin. We went into the game as hot favourites. The Aussies' record at Carisbrook was not great. A lot of the critics had the game won for us before kick-off. I'm not a great man for stats, but I was aware that the Dunedin Test was my fiftieth for the All Blacks. Even though we play a lot more Tests these days, the milestone was special. When I led the team onto Carisbrook I was a proud man.

I got a try against the Aussies that day and I received a special presentation. I would have swapped them both for a win. We were well beaten. Two tries apiece mightn't look too bad on the scoreboard, but there was no doubt the Aussies were the better team in Dunedin. We made too many mistakes against a side who had obviously been fired up by all the critics who had written them off. The Bledisloe Cup dream was gone for another year.

We kept our Tri-Nations hopes alive with a win over the Springboks at Eden Park, but the season, I guess, was wrecked when we lost to the Wallabies at Sydney in the last minute. It was a game we could have won, but how many times have I said that? Even though the Aussies took a good lead into the half-time break, I still felt we were in the match. We got ourselves into a winning position at 26–22 late in the game and it was an absolute arse-knocker when Toutai Kefu scrambled over for the winning try. Sure, we had our problems again with the line-outs, but really it was that Wallaby steel under pressure that sealed our fate. The match was John Eales's last for Australia. He turned down chances to shoot for goal at the finish and he backed his team to force the win through a try. I liked John Eales and I respected him as a player, but I wasn't the only All Black who breathed a sigh of relief when he decided to hang up his jumper.

None of us knew it at the time, but the match also signalled the end of Wayne Smith's All Blacks coaching reign. I think that final Tri-Nations loss was almost too much for him to bear. When he said publicly that he wasn't sure about whether he was the right man to coach the All Blacks, it sounded like a death wish. It was sad. Smithy was a man who always showed his emotions. He took the losses personally and he wore his heart on his sleeve. I don't regard that alone as a fault. Maybe it came down to self-doubt and, I suppose, the powers that be just couldn't wear that. In New Zealand rugby it's just not a good look. It's seen as a weakness.

I'm often asked who I regard as the best coaches I've ever had. Generally I don't like to nominate favourites. I've taken lots on board from all the coaches I've had down the years, but with Smithy it's fair to say you had the complete package. Technically he was superb and his people skills were fantastic. I reacted really well to his one-on-ones. What more can I say? Even though we lost twice to Australia in 2001, I felt he was starting to mould a good side. For me, Smithy was close to the ultimate coach and I felt deeply for him when he wasn't reappointed.

As if the pain of losing to the Wallabies in the dying seconds wasn't enough, the Wellington guys had to put up with another heartbreaker in our Ranfurly Shield challenge against Canterbury late in the season. I played in only five of the NPC matches and, while we didn't perform nearly as well as we had the year before, the Shield was there for the taking. We led Toddy Blackadder's boys 29–12 with only about twenty minutes to go. We were slaughtered in the penalty stakes, but again it came down to composure under pressure. Final score: Canterbury 31–Wellington 29. That hurt.

John Mitchell and Robbie Deans were appointed to run the All Blacks after Smithy took the bullet following the Tri-Nations series. They selected a heap of new players for the end-of-year tour of Ireland, Scotland and Argentina. I was relieved to get the call. Others, like Taine Randell and Jeff Wilson, weren't so lucky, but they weren't rung by the selectors to say they wouldn't be required for the tour, which I thought was a bit lousy. I think in the finish even John Mitchell would agree that he probably made a mistake there. Between them, Taine and Jeff had played more than a hundred tests for the All Blacks and they deserved that call.

The critics gave us a hard time for our performances on tour, and it's true that we did struggle early on in all three Tests, but we won. Isn't that what it's about? Would those same critics rather we had played well and lost? A try in each Test left me satisfied with my own efforts. I was impressed by the new coaching duo and I had a good feeling about going into 2002 under Mitch and Robbie.

CHAPTER SEVENTEEN

A BAD YEAR AT
THE OFFICE

After the end-of-year All Blacks tour I was determined to try and get my 2002 Super 12 season off to a good start. My relationship with the Hurricanes coach, Graham Mourie, hadn't been that hot so I thought I'd try and work on improving things. It wasn't to be. I arrived late for Hurricanes training. Well, that's what the media said, anyway. There was a real stink over it. The most disappointing thing for me was that when the Hurricanes management were asked about my absence from early season training, they said they didn't know where I was — didn't know why I wasn't there. As far as I was concerned, that was a crock.

I had been told by the All Blacks management to take a break after the end-of-year tour. The manager, Andrew The Colonel Martin and coach John Mitchell had recommended, as they did with all the All Blacks, when I should re-enter training with the Super 12 squad. The window they gave me was a little after the Hurricanes actually started pre-season training. Phil and I took the opportunity to do a bit of promotional work and I basically took it easy for a while. I didn't blame the media for having a crack at me. I knew the rules and I also knew the Super 12 coaches had the final say about when they wanted their players back, but I was bloody annoyed with the Hurricanes' management. To the best of my knowledge they were fully aware of the situation and I was never told I couldn't have a break.

It came as no surprise to me when I was named on the bench for the Hurricanes' opening match against the Blues. By the time I did get onto the field the game was already gone. It was embarrassing. In front of our ever-faithful home crowd in Wellington we got belted 60–7. One media report said it was the Hurricanes' worst performance in Super 12. That's probably right. After the match there was a fair bit of talk amongst the players. We had to lift – and we had to do it quickly. We were about to hit the road for our two matches in South Africa. In the end, we managed a bonus point win against the Bulls in Pretoria before getting flogged by the Stormers at Cape Town.

The season was only three matches old, but already I wasn't enjoying my footie – and I don't think I was on my own there. It just wasn't fun any more. The same old problems kept surfacing. It was all too intense. There was not enough time between training sessions. In 2001 and 2002 with the Hurricanes it always came down to the same thing. The players needed some space. I'm sure Goss thought he was doing the right thing, but he struggled to read the players' body language. Technically, I think he was astute. He could also be a great guy away from the training field. I just don't think he realised at the time what he was doing. Our coach was strangling us. As I've matured as a person and a player I've learned to accept what the coach says. I've taken the view that he knows best. With Goss, though, I lost my nut on more than one occasion.

Despite the internal problems, there was still too much talent in the Hurricanes side of 2002 for us to fall over completely. We staged a mid-season revival and won four of our next five games. Our best win came against the Brumbies, the reigning Super 12 champions, at Canberra. The loosies were magnificent. Rodney

So'oialo, who had only had one full game for us up till then, came
into the side at No. 8, and Jerry Collins moved to the flank to
partner Kupu Vanisi. They were up against Peter Ryan, George
Smith and Owen Finegan. On the night it was no contest. We
blitzed the Brumbies.

The win gave us a shot at making the semis, but that chance
all but disappeared in the next match, against the Waratahs in
Sydney. It's a game I'd prefer to forget. I'm sure Christian Cullen
thinks the same. We both stuffed up, big-time. First, Cully got
across for what looked like a sensational try, but the video replay
showed he had dropped the ball as he was trying to force it. Then
I tried to take a ball close to the line from Paul Tito and dropped
it as well. I had been caught in two minds. It had looked like the
forwards weren't going to free up the pill so I went in to help
'clean out'. Just as I moved in, Paul popped the pass and I couldn't
hold it. It was one of those nights and we lost 19–13. Cully and
I got ripped up in the media for our mistakes, but that was fair
enough, I guess.

A week later when the Crusaders came to town, we just couldn't
foot it with them. To make things worse, we got smashed by the
Chiefs in our final game. That match in Hamilton was the only
one I missed all season. It didn't make me feel any better. It was
my worst ever Super 12. One try in ten games kind of summed
up my season.

As if the failure to make the Super 12 semi-finals wasn't enough,
many of us players watched on in disbelief as the World Cup
sub-hosting fight played out in the media. Personally, I was gutted
when we lost the chance to host part of the tournament. To me,
there is nothing quite like playing for the All Blacks at home.
Once the battle was lost I knew I would never pull on a World
Cup jersey in New Zealand. Sad. Unlike a lot of people, though,
I'm not prepared to dump all the blame on the rugby union CEO,

David Rutherford, and chairman, Murray McCaw. I know both men and I also know how passionate they were about New Zealand rugby while they held those positions. I think the NZRU board should have stood up earlier and said, 'Hey, they were acting on our wishes.' Instead, both guys were hung out to dry and were basically forced to resign. Not fair. I wasn't surprised when other members of the board got tipped over by the provincial unions later in the year.

All Blacks coach John Mitchell made it plain to everyone at the end of 2001 that he wasn't going to pick players on reputation. When it came to selection for the first part of the international season – one-off Tests against Italy and Fiji and a two-test series against Ireland – it was pretty clear that three Hurricanes – myself, Christian Cullen and Tana Umaga – were all going to have to prove ourselves to John. All three of us were in and out of the starting line-ups for the first four Tests. Cully got starts against Italy and Fiji, while I came off the bench against the Italians and in the first Test against Ireland. Both times I replaced Doug Howlett on the right wing. Despite only getting about forty minutes of game time, I was reasonably happy with my form. Against Italy I scored a try and then, in a really tight Test against Ireland at Dunedin, I helped set up a nice try for Leon MacDonald.

I'm not sure if Mitch liked what he saw or not, but for my first run-on Test of 2002, against the Irish in the second Test at Auckland, I was picked to start on the right wing. It wasn't something that we'd talked about that much. The call was made by the coaches and I was happy enough just to be picked, especially after it was agreed I could still wear my No. 11 jersey. John and Robbie Deans always believed that wingers should be able to play both right and left sides of the field. I think they believed they were enhancing my role within the team by getting me comfortable playing on the right. That was just fine by me.

The final Test before the Tri-Nations series was against Fiji. Everything should have gone right in that game. The old Hurricanes firm was back in action. Cully was at full-back. Tana, who had played only in the first T test against Ireland, was at centre, and I was named on the left wing. We were at home in Wellington and, although the stadium wasn't full, there was a great buzz amongst the crowd. For me, though, everything went wrong. Before the game I was feeling the strain of a difficult season — feeling the strain like never before. It had started during the Super 12, in the course of the build-up to the Brumbies game. Mentally, I had just lost it in Canberra. That day I came close to completely cracking. Everything seemed to be closing in. Of course, my kidney condition wasn't getting any better. In fact it was getting worse. There was also strain in my relationship with Teina, which just added to my problems. Usually I can handle the pressure and all that public expectation, I can handle the fact that my body sometimes lets me down, but my head . . . ? Oh, man, I was way outside of my comfort zone.

I had a shocker against Fiji. The harder I tried the worse it got. My game was going to the pack. My head wasn't right. When that happens, then nothing's ever going to work. So much of my rugby has been about instinct. Against Fiji my head took over and there was way too much going on. My opposite number, Norman Ligairi, ran around me twice. I missed other tackles and never really got involved. While I was pretty much missing in action for the whole night, the rest of the team played well. It was a difficult game, because of some of the rough stuff that was going down, but I don't use that as an excuse for my own efforts. I had to get my mind sorted — or I had to get out.

The All Blacks selectors showed faith in me by naming me in the twenty-six-man squad for the Tri-Nations. I got on the paddock only once in the whole series and that was for just twenty minutes against South Africa, at Wellington, but I was grateful to be there. The selectors could just have easily given me the flick after Fiji. Instead, they stuck with me. I had stayed quiet about the problems I was having with my mental state – problems that had affected my game all season – but I should have spoken up.

I owe John Mitchell and Robbie Deans for the encouragement they gave me during that campaign. Both men were honest with me. They knew exactly what areas I had to work on. They genuinely wanted me to perform. One night over dinner Mitch said to me, 'Don't worry, Jonah. We'll work with you. We will get everything sorted.' I desperately needed to hear that. At times I received more attention from both of them than I probably deserved. Mitch and Robbie were right to bench me for the Tri-Nations. In the past I would have been super-bitter. This time around, though, their advice and support helped me overcome a hurdle I hadn't struck for a long time – the hurdle of self-doubt.

John Mitchell (All Blacks coach 2001–2003): Robbie Deans and I just felt so sorry for Jonah after the Fiji game. When we walked into the dressing room it was obvious that he was really down. It was very sad to see how his game had degenerated in that short space of time. Leading into the Tri-Nations he just didn't seem to be his normal energetic self. We were looking for wingers who had consistent work rates and who were reliable with their skills. At that stage Jonah just wasn't offering us that. Nevertheless, both Robbie and I worked hard with him on an individual level. It wasn't just because it was Jonah Lomu. We tried to do that with all the players. We knew what he was capable of when he was right. We were anxious for him and anxious to help him improve his game.

When Wellington beat Canterbury in the opening match of the NPC, I thought my season might be turning for the better. I came off the bench that day as we got home 33–24. However, the great start to our season took a dive when Southland rolled us the following week at Invercargill. I don't think we were ever destined to win that game. Southland were just so determined. I knew things were bad when their flanker, Ben Herring, scored from his own team's kick-off. He intercepted our very first pass. Not a good look. Inconsistency cost Wellington again. One match we were on fire, the next we were ordinary. In the end we missed making the semi-finals cut by just a couple of points.

At the end of the NPC I didn't have much to look back and smile upon. In the entire season I had scored only four tries in twenty-two matches. I honestly believed I was a goner for the All Blacks Northern Hemisphere tour. In fact, I don't believe I should have even been considered for selection. And that's honest. I didn't need Mitch or any of the other selectors to talk to me about form or about reputation. I had come off a terrible season. Simple as that.

When the touring squad was announced there were some massive surprises. The selectors had decided to rest many of the country's leading players and there was a huge debate about how, by doing that, they were devaluing the All Blacks jersey. Maybe I was lucky that this debate turned the media's attention away from me, because the selectors went on record as saying that, of the twenty-six players chosen, twenty-five were picked on form and merit. One player was picked on reputation. They had given me a lifeline.

John Mitchell: I met with Jonah just prior to the tour and made my views clear to him as to exactly what we were looking for. I said that I felt his time was running out and that the tour was really important for him in terms of the 2003 World

Cup. Again, it came down to his work rate, particularly inside the ball carrier and his availability in the wide channel. His selection wasn't a loyalty-based thing at all and I certainly wasn't asking him for any sort of on-field repayment. The fact is that I don't think in my lifetime I'll ever see a more talented, more instinctive, or more powerful player than Jonah Lomu. He had a gift for the game that I have never seen in anyone else. Both Robbie and I just wanted to see him enjoy himself on that tour and play to the best of his abilities. The coaches and selectors wanted him to succeed. Everyone wanted him to succeed.

I was very much the senior player on the All Blacks tour at the end of the year. Of course, I had graduated to the back seat of the bus well before the tour, but Mitch and Robbie had made it clear that they wanted me to take a more active role in the running of the team. They wanted me to set some examples for the younger players — hell, there were plenty of them — and they wanted me to help out captain Taine Randell wherever I could. What could I say? They had showed faith in me. I would do everything possible to repay that faith — on the field as well as off it.

First-up, we faced England at Twickenham. It was always going to be a huge ask. I mean, just look at their pack — Johnson, Grewcock, Dallaglio, Hill, Vickery — an unbelievable amount of experience. We went into the Test with a pack which included four brand-new All Blacks and a total of eighty-five caps between the entire eight. Jeez, Taine had forty-eight of those alone. We got beaten by three points at Twickenham. Beaten by a team that everyone had told us were the best in the world. The performance by the All Blacks that day is one of the gutsiest I've ever been involved in. We struggled in the line-outs and the scrums, we made a heap of mistakes and we turned over way too much ball. With only twenty minutes to play it was 31–14 to the Poms. We should have been down for the count, but in that final quarter the boys dug deep. We got it back to 31–28 and actually gave ourselves a chance of winning. Losing that final line-out on our throw right on their line was heartbreaking.

As far as my own game went, I don't think I could have given much more. This was England, man. The wheels were spinning before kick-off. I got a try in each half and they both came from planned moves. Robbie Deans told me before the match, 'Stay wide, Jonah. No matter what, stay wide and the boys will get it to you.' With about fifteen minutes gone we were pounding the English line. I stayed wide. The ball came left at speed and the boys put on all the moves. Before Dougie Howlett gave me the final pass we'd used cuts and dummy runners to confuse the English defence. I got the ball about 15m out and just dropped my shoulder into Jason Robinson and went straight through him and Mike Tindall. The ref didn't award the try straight away. I wasn't worried because I was in no doubt I'd grounded the ball. Umpteen replays later, Jonathan Kaplan's arm went up.

We were in desperate trouble before I got my second try. The opportunity came once again after our forwards had been hammering away at the goal line. This time, though, the ball was sent right. At 31–14, we had to score. I came off my wing and crashed the midfield. After I went through Tindall and fended off Ben Cohen we were back in the game. That try was followed by a great little dab by halfback Danny Lee. The conversion by Andrew Mehrtens got us to within three points. I know it's easy to say now, but I honestly believe that if we had won that final line-out of the game we would have beaten England. We finished right over the top of them.

As much as we like to serve it up to the English, I must say I've always enjoyed playing against them and then socialising with them after the match. The England team of that year were a very good unit, professional in every way. I have always admired their forwards and after the game I couldn't help but think they would be serious contenders for the 2003 World Cup. The backs that day were as well organised as any English back line I've ever played against, especially the goalkicker. I think his name was Wilkinson . . .

Again, it was old-fashioned guts and a lot of All Blacks pride that got us through the Test against France in Paris a week later. The French pack really worked over our young forwards. Our line-out got monstered in the second half and we were forced to do a lot of defending. It didn't help that the Aussie referee, Scott Young, handed out three yellow cards to the All Blacks. That's effectively thirty minutes of the game that we played with only fourteen men. Against a side like France it made the final score-line of 20–20 look that much better. Tana did the damage for us in Paris. His try was magic, but it was his tackling that broke the French backs. In the second half they lived in fear of his big hits.

On the morning of the final Test, against Wales, I wasn't feeling great. To start with, it was just a bit of discomfort. As the day wore on, though, I was beginning to feel really sick. During the warm-ups I started throwing up. I thought I must have picked up some sort of stomach bug. Just before kick-off I was worried. Shake it off, Jonah. Time to grunt up. I couldn't shake it off, though. The game remains a blur. Literally. I was light-headed and I was getting double vision. When we came off the field I knew we'd won, but that's about it.

Once I got into the dressing room things got even worse. I wasn't cold but I was shaking uncontrollably. After I showered, I grabbed Doc Mayhew. 'Doc, I'm crook. I can't stop shaking.' He found a security guard and together they virtually carried me back to the hotel. At one point someone asked me for an autograph. I took the pen, but I was shaking so much I couldn't even sign my name. By now I had bad pains in my stomach. When we got back to the hotel, Doc ran a bath for me. He gave me some painkillers and helped me into bed.

I managed to get some sleep and, although I was still shaking in the morning, I was feeling a little better. Adidas had some work scheduled for me in Macclesfield in Cheshire. They're great sponsors for both me personally and for the All Blacks and I didn't want to let them down. I managed to get through the promotion okay, but that night everything turned to custard. The pain was back. This time, though, it was pain like I had never experienced before. My head also began to throb and I started throwing up again. The hotel staff called an ambulance and I was taken to the Macclesfield Hospital.

I was a mess when I arrived. I couldn't lie still. A nurse started asking me about the pain and I just said, 'Gimme something. Please. Anything.' After the first shot of painkillers I felt no better. 'This ain't working,' I said. 'Gimme some more.' Finally, the doctors arrived. They checked me over and they took some blood. It was quite a few hours later before they returned. 'Mr Lomu, about those blood tests we ran on you. Well, your kidney function tests don't seem right. The levels are all wrong.' Oh nooooo . . . tell me something I don't know . . . 'Doc, just forget about the kidneys,' I interrupted. 'I know all about my levels. Concentrate on my stomach. Just do what you have to do. Cut me open. Chop out whatever's causing the pain!'

Eventually they opened me up and found I had a strangulated intestine. I think it was a pretty straightforward sort of operation in the end. Anyway, they told me I'd have to stay in hospital under observation for at least forty-eight hours. No sweat. Later, a couple of the nurses asked me when I'd be moving to a private hospital. 'What for?' I asked. 'I like it here.' The hospital staff were great.

I had my laptop computer with me and, of course, a few DVDs. At one stage the nurses turned my bed around so they could watch the movies, too. We joked and laughed all the way through *Dirty Dancing*. Debbie Tunnicliffe from adidas UK also stayed with me the whole time I was in hospital. I'll never forget that.

Phil and I thought hard about staying on in Britain after my operation. We had a fair bit of promotional work booked and neither of us wanted to let anyone down. In the end we decided to continue. Four of us set out 'on tour' in a two-car convoy. Me and Knockie Hurren, Phil's great friend from New Zealand, were in a brand-new TVR. Beautiful. Phil was with Kevin Lane, another mate, in a VW Passat. I was lead car and I couldn't help thinking as we drove around Britain that this was how it had all started back in New Zealand. On the road again with Phil. A couple of times he took the wrong turning. That's typical, I thought, He could never keep up. Probably had Elvis on full noise, talking non-stop – and still driving like a nana . . .

EPILOGUE

Auckland, February 2004

Everything in my life at the moment is a day-by-day proposition. My medical condition hasn't worsened since the whole neuropathy thing kicked in last year, but it hasn't got a whole lot better either. We've made more changes to the dialysis regime – we've even changed machines a couple of times – but the one thing that's become very clear is that the need to transplant has become critical. I've got to get my legs right. I've got to stop any further damage to the nerves. The trouble is, the waiting list for a kidney transplant isn't getting any shorter – three, maybe four years in New Zealand unless you have a live donor. Like I said at the start of the book, I try and stay positive, and I wait.

Helping me to stay in that frame of mind is the support I've received from right around the world. It's been phenomenal. I've got bags full of mail from well-wishers – they're precious and I will keep them for the rest of my life. The 'hits' on jonahlomu.com have been coming in just as fast. Awesome. Fiona and I have been overwhelmed. Even though I haven't played rugby for nearly a year, the invitations to travel to different events both in New Zealand and overseas, and to speak at functions, have flooded in. I'm doing what I can.

It was always a given that my team-mates would stay in touch while I've been off the scene. It's the All Blacks way; it's the way the 'club' works. I get calls all the time from former coaches and players. I got a chance recently to catch up with the Hurricanes when they were in Auckland for a pre-season game and I had a long chat with Tana Umaga.

Back in Super 12 2003, Tana had called on me as a senior player to try and do more for the team — to go hard on the field, to talk more and support the younger players. I just wasn't well enough. Tana looked at me a couple of times during that handful of games as if to say, *Are you really trying as hard as you can?* I couldn't blame him. I've never been one to talk much about my illness and no one really knew how bad I was back then. I have great respect for Tana. He always gives his best on the field. I wanted to do my bit for him and the team. He is a great friend, as well as a great ambassador for the game. It was good to catch up with him; good to talk things over.

Tana himself says, 'None of us knew how bad "big guy" was in Super 12 2003. He never liked to burden anyone with his problems. That's always the way it's been with Jonah. As captain of the Hurricanes I *was* hard on him. "Come on," I'd say, "the team needs you — *I* need you." When I found out the extent of his illness I felt terrible. I rang him to say how sorry I was — sorry I had demanded more from him when he already had this massive problem. "No worries," he said. That's typical Jonah. For every player in the Hurricanes it then became a question of what we could do for the man who for so long had wanted to do so much for everyone else.'

While I no longer have a rugby-playing contract, I *have* just re-signed with adidas. They have shown great support and loyalty, even though they are fully aware of my medical condition. They are keen to use me in a sort of ambassadorial role in the meantime and I know they will stand behind any decisions I have to make in the future. They have been great sponsors for both me and the All Blacks.

Like the rest of New Zealand, I was devastated when the ABs lost to Australia in the World Cup semi-final. I honestly thought the boys would do it this time around. I guess on the day we just didn't front. I have been there before and I know how bad they would have felt. They went into the match as favourites and came out of the tournament with nothing. It hurts like hell. In the end, the best team won the World Cup. England took a hugely experienced side to Australia. They were at the top of their game, and while some of the footie might not have been the prettiest to watch, in the end it's not about *pretty*. It's all about winning. Good luck to them. They deserved it.

My future in the game quite obviously remains uncertain. I recently discovered there is another procedure for transplanting kidneys. It involves more invasive surgery than the standard operation, but instead of leaving the new kidney exposed, it is placed higher up in the body; placed basically over one of my existing ones. It is more protected by the ribs. It gives the doctors more comfort. It gives me comfort.

If a kidney can be found; *if* the neuropathy can be reversed; *if* I can be restored to full health, then I'll give rugby another shot. I know they're big 'ifs', but the game is still my life. I'll be 32 in 2007 – that's World Cup year. I love rugby and I love Paris. Like they say, watch this space . . .

Jonah Lomu
First-class career
Statistics compiled by Geoff Miller

Game	Date	Venue	Team	Opponent	Score	Other*
1994						
1	4:5:94	Levin	Counties	Horowhenua	108–12	3t
2	22:5:94	Gisborne	Possibles	Probables	54–31	
3	24:5:94	Pukekohe	Counties	Hawke's Bay	46–15	1t
4	14:6:94	Napier	Probables	Possibles	29–17	1t
5 (1)	26:6:94	Christchurch	NEW ZEALAND	France	8–22	
6 (2)	3:7:94	Auckland	NEW ZEALAND	France	20–23	
7	10:7:94	Te Kuiti	Counties	King Country	38–14	1t
8	31:7:94	Port Macquarrie	NZ Colts	NSW Country U21 Development XV	76–3	2t
9	3:8:94	Sydney	NZ Colts	NSW Country Development XV	60–10	3t
10	6:8:94	Sydney	NZ Colts	Australia U-21	41–31	
11	13:8:94	Dunedin	Counties	Otago	29–24	2t
12	21:8:94	Pukekohe	Counties	Wellington	29–3	1t
13	27:8:94	Takapuna	Counties	North Harbour	6–36	
14	3:9:94	Pukekohe	Counties	Taranaki	38–14	
15	10:9:94	Pukekohe	Counties	Waikato	8–15	
16	25:9:94	Pukekohe	Counties	Auckland	15–18	
1995						
17	1:4:95	Wanganui	Presidents XV	Divisional XV	22–71	2t
18	8:4:95	Dunedin	North Island	South Island	55–22	2t
19	16:4:95	Hamilton	NZ Harlequins	Waikato	96–25	3t
20	29:4:95	Whangarei	Probables	Possibles	64–26	2t

*t = try (+) = replacement (-) = left field

297

Game	Date	Venue	Team	Opponent	Score	Other*
21 (3)	27:5:95	Johannesburg	NEW ZEALAND	Ireland	43–19	2t
22 (4)	31:5:95	Johannesburg	NEW ZEALAND	Wales	34–9	
23 (5)	11:6:95	Pretoria	NEW ZEALAND	Scotland	48–30	1t
24 (6)	18:6:95	Cape Town	NEW ZEALAND	England	45–29	4t
25 (7)	24:6:95	Johannesburg	NEW ZEALAND	South Africa	12–15	
26 (8)	22:7:95	Auckland	NEW ZEALAND	Australia	28–16	1t
27 (9)	29:7:95	Sydney	NEW ZEALAND	Australia	34–23	1t
28	19:8:95	Pukekohe	Counties	King Country	24–15	1t
29	27:8:95	Pukekohe	Counties	Canterbury	41–39	1t
30	2:9:95	Invercargill	Counties	Southland	25–21	
31	24:9:95	Pukekohe	Counties	Otago	38–43	2t
32	30:9:95	Wellington	Counties	Wellington	33–8	1t
33	8:10:95	Pukekohe	Counties	Otago	32–41	1t
34 (10)	28:10:95	Bologna	NEW ZEALAND	Italy	70–6	2t
35	1:11:95	Toulon	New Zealand	French Barbarians	34–19	
36	4:11:95	Beziers	New Zealand Roussillon	Languedoc	30–9	(+)
37	7:11:95	Bayonne	New Zealand	Cote Basque	47–20	
38 (11)	11:11:95	Toulouse	NEW ZEALAND	France	15–22	
39	14:11:95	Nancy	New Zealand	French Selection	55–17	2t
40 (12)	18:11:95	Paris	NEW ZEALAND	France	37–12	1t

*t = try (+) = replacement (-) = left field

CAREER STATISTICS

Game	Date	Venue	Team	Opponent	Score	Other*
1996						
41	1:3:96	Palmerston North	Blues	Hurricanes	36–28	
42	10:3:96	Christchurch	Blues	Crusaders	49–18	It
43	15:3:96	Canberra	Blues	Brumbies	34–40	It
44	2:4:96	Auckland	Blues	Highlanders	51–29	
45	7:4:96	Auckland	Blues	Northern Transvaal	30–26	2t
46	20:4:96	Auckland	Blues	Chiefs	39–31	It
47	26:4:96	Brisbane	Blues	Reds	13–51	
48	7:5:96	Johannesburg	Blues	Transvaal	22–34	
49	11:5:96	Durban	Blues	Natal	30–23	
50	19:5:96	Auckland	Blues	Northern Transvaal	48–11	2t
51	25:5:96	Auckland	Blues	Natal	45–21	It
52	1:6:96	Napier	Presidents XV	NZ Barbarians	72–18	2t
53 (13)	7:6:96	**Napier**	**NEW ZEALAND**	**Western Samoa**	**51–10**	
54 (14)	15:6:96	**Dunedin**	**NEW ZEALAND**	**Scotland**	**62–31**	It (–)
55 (15)	6:7:96	**Wellington**	**NEW ZEALAND**	**Australia**	**43–6**	It
56 (16)	20:7:96	**Christchurch**	**NEW ZEALAND**	**South Africa**	**15–11**	
57 (17)	27:7:96	**Brisbane**	**NEW ZEALAND**	**Australia**	**32–25**	
58	13:8:96	Port Elizabeth	New Zealand	Eastern Province	31–23	It
59	20:8:96	Potchefstroom	New Zealand	Western Transvaal	31–0	
60	27:8:96	Kimberley	New Zealand	Griqualand West	18–18	
61	5:10:96	Pukekohe	Counties Manukau	Wellington	40–22	(+)

*t = try (+) = replacement (-) = left field

Game	Date	Venue	Team	Opponent	Score	Other*
62	12:10:96	Te Kuiti	Counties Manukau	King Country	65–33	1t
63	20:10:96	Pukekohe	Counties Manukau	Canterbury	46–33	
64	30:11:96	Twickenham	NZ Barbarians	England	34–19	

1997

Game	Date	Venue	Team	Opponent	Score	Other*
65	21:9:97	Pukekohe	Counties Manukau	Otago	16–14	(+)
66	27:9:97	New Plymouth	Counties Manukau	Taranaki	11–10	(+)
67	12:10:97	Pukekohe	Counties Manukau	Southland	85–17	2t
68	18:10:97	Hamilton	Counties Manukau	Waikato	43–40	
69	26:10:97	Christchurch	Counties Manukau	Canterbury	13–44	
70	11:11:97	Pontypridd	New Zealand	Wales A	51–8	1t
71	18:11:97	Huddersfield	New Zealand	Emerging England	59–22	2t
72 (18)	22:11:97	Manchester	NEW ZEALAND	England	25–8	
73 (19)	29:11:97	Wembley	NEW ZEALAND	Wales	42–7	
74 (20)	6:12:97	Twickenham	NEW ZEALAND	England	26–26	

1998

Game	Date	Venue	Team	Opponent	Score	Other*
75	28:2:98	Durban	Blues	Coastal Sharks	8–24	
76	7:3:98	Johannesburg	Blues	Golden Cats	38–37	
77	14:3:98	Auckland	Blues	Highlanders	41–22	1t
78	21:3:98	Auckland	Blues	Chiefs	25–23	
79	27:3:98	Christchurch	Blues	Crusaders	31–24	1t
80	4:4:98	Brisbane	Blues	Reds	18–33	

*t = try (+) = replacement (-) = left field

CAREER STATISTICS

Game	Date	Venue	Team	Opponent	Score	Other*
81	13:4:98	Auckland	Blues	Waratahs	47–25	
82	19:4:98	Pukekohe	Blues	Northern Bulls	34–24	1t
83	26:4:98	Auckland	Blues	Western Stormers	74–28	
84	16:5:98	Wellington	Blues	Hurricanes	45–34	2t
85	23:5:98	Auckland	Blues	Highlanders	37–31	
86	13:6:98	Hamilton	New Zealand A	England	18–10	(–)
87 (21)	20:6:98	Dunedin	NEW ZEALAND	England	64–22	1t
88 (22)	27:6:98	Auckland	NEW ZEALAND	England	40–10	(–)
89 (23)	11:7:98	Melbourne	NEW ZEALAND	Australia	16–24	(+)
90 (24)	25:7:98	Wellington	NEW ZEALAND	South Africa	3–13	
91 (25)	1:8:98	Christchurch	NEW ZEALAND	Australia	23–27	1t
92 (26)	15:8:98	Durban	NEW ZEALAND	South Africa	23–24	
93 (27)	29:8:98	Sydney	NEW ZEALAND	Australia	14–19	
94	27:9:98	Pukekohe	Counties Manukau	Auckland	45–29	
95	3:10:98	Pukekohe	Counties Manukau	Wellington	29–29	
96	10:10:98	Christchurch	Counties Manukau	Canterbury	49–42	1t

1999

Game	Date	Venue	Team	Opponent	Score	Other*
97	26:3:99	Hamilton	Chiefs	Blues	18–29	
98	3:4:99	Rotorua	Chiefs	Highlanders	16–27	
99	10:4:99	Canberra	Chiefs	Brumbies	16–13	
100	16:4:99	New Plymouth	Chiefs	Hurricanes	24–21	1t

*t = try (+) = replacement (-) = left field

301

Game	Date	Venue	Team	Opponent	Score	Other*
101	24:4:99	Pukekohe	Chiefs	Cats	44–42	
102	30:4:99	Hamilton	Chiefs	Sharks	32–19	
103	8:5:99	Cape Town	Chiefs	Stormers	9–16	
104	14:5:99	Pretoria	Chiefs	Bulls	39–31	1t
105	11:6:99	Christchurch	New Zealand	New Zealand A	22–11	(+)
106 (28)	18:6:99	Albany	NEW ZEALAND	Samoa	71–13	1t (+)
107	20:6:99	Hamilton	New Zealand A	France	45–24	1t (+)
108	3:7:99	Canberra	New Zealand A	A.C.T.	51–29	2t
109 (29)	10:7:99	Dunedin	NEW ZEALAND	South Africa	28–0	(+)
110 (30)	24:7:99	Auckland	NEW ZEALAND	Australia	34–15	(+)
111 (31)	7:8:99	Pretoria	NEW ZEALAND	South Africa	34–18	(+)
112	15:8:99	Pukekohe	Counties Manukau	Southland	31–10	1t
113	21:8:99	Hamilton	Counties Manukau	Waikato	11–27	
114 (32)	28:8:99	Sydney	NEW ZEALAND	Australia	7–28	(+)
115 (33)	3:10:99	Bristol	NEW ZEALAND	Tonga	45–9	2t
116 (34)	9:10:99	London	NEW ZEALAND	England	30–16	1t
117 (35)	14:10:99	Huddersfield	NEW ZEALAND	Italy	101–3	2t
118 (36)	24:10:99	Edinburgh	NEW ZEALAND	Scotland	30–18	1t
119 (37)	31:10:99	Twickenham	NEW ZEALAND	France	31–43	2t
120 (38)	4:11:99	Cardiff	NEW ZEALAND	South Africa	18–22	

*t = try (+) = replacement (-) = left field

Game	Date	Venue	Team	Opponent	Score	Other*
2000						
121	25:2:00	Wellington	Hurricanes	Sharks	40–23	2t (–)
122	4:3:00	New Plymouth	Hurricanes	Reds	43–25	1t
123	31:3:00	Wellington	Hurricanes	Blues	14–25	
124	7:4:00	Wellington	Hurricanes	Crusaders	28–22	2t
125	21:4:00	Canberra	Hurricanes	Brumbies	28–47	1t
126	29:4:00	Sydney	Hurricanes	Waratahs	27–20	(–)
127	28:5:00	Dublin	UK Barbarians	Ireland	31–30	
128 (39)	**16:6:00**	**Albany**	**NEW ZEALAND**	**Tonga**	**102–0**	
129 (40)	**24:6:00**	**Dunedin**	**NEW ZEALAND**	**Scotland**	**69–20**	3t
130 (41)	**1:7:00**	**Auckland**	**NEW ZEALAND**	**Scotland**	**48–14**	
131 (42)	**15:7:00**	**Sydney**	**NEW ZEALAND**	**Australia**	**39–35**	1t
132 (43)	**22:7:00**	**Christchurch**	**NEW ZEALAND**	**South Africa**	**25–12**	
133 (44)	**5:8:00**	**Wellington**	**NEW ZEALAND**	**Australia**	**23–24**	
134 (45)	**19:8:00**	**Johannesburg**	**NEW ZEALAND**	**South Africa**	**40–46**	
135	27:8:00	Wellington	Wellington	Northland	24–30	1t
136	2:9:00	Wellington	Wellington	Taranaki	41–13	1t
137	8:9:00	Wellington	Wellington	Auckland	19–24	
138	16:9:00	Albany	Wellington	North Harbour	7–24	
139	24:9:00	Pukekohe	Wellington	Counties Manukau	45–29	1t
140	30:9:00	Invercargill	Wellington	Southland	28–21	2t
141	7:10:00	Wellington	**Wellington**	Waikato	48–23	1t
142	13:10:00	Auckland	Wellington	Auckland	48–23	1t
143	21:10:00	Christchurch	Wellington	Canterbury	34–29	2t
144 (46)	**11:11:00**	**Paris**	**NEW ZEALAND**	**France**	**39–26**	

*t = try (+) = replacement (-) = left field

Game	Date	Venue	Team	Opponent	Score	Other*
2001						
145	3:3:01	Wellington	Hurricanes	Bulls	26–20	1t
146	9:3:01	Wellington	Hurricanes	Stormers	15–27	1t
147	17:3:01	Durban	Hurricanes	Sharks	21–39	
148	23:3:01	Bloemfontein	Hurricanes	Cats	15–18	
149	31:3:01	Christchurch	Hurricanes	Crusaders	41–29	1t
150	6:4:01	Wellington	Hurricanes	Brumbies	34–19	1t
151	14:4:01	Napier	Hurricanes	Highlanders	35–33	
152	27:4:01	New Plymouth	Hurricanes	Waratahs	42–17	
153	4:5:01	Wellington	Hurricanes	Chiefs	27–51	
154	24:5:01	Edinburgh	UK Barbarians	Scotland	74–31	4t
155	27:5:01	Twickenham	UK Barbarians	England	43–29	1t
156 (47)	23:6:01	Christchurch	NEW ZEALAND	Argentina	67–19	
157 (48)	30:6:01	Wellington	NEW ZEALAND	France	37–12	1t
158 (49)	21:7:01	Cape Town	NEW ZEALAND	South Africa	12–3	
159 (50)	11:8:01	Dunedin	NEW ZEALAND	Australia	15–23	1t
160 (51)	25:8:01	Auckland	NEW ZEALAND	South Africa	26–15	
161 (52)	1:9:01	Sydney	NEW ZEALAND	Australia	26–29	
162	15:9:01	Wellington	Wellington	Counties Manukau	47–0	2t
163	21:9:01	Whangarei	Wellington	Northland	37–16	
164	29:9:01	Christchurch	Wellington	Canterbury	29–31	
165	6:10:01	Auckland	Wellington	Auckland	13–26	
166	20:10:01	Wellington	Wellington	Otago	10–28	
167 (53)	17:11:01	Dublin	NEW ZEALAND	Ireland	40–29	1t
168 (54)	24:11:01	Edinburgh	NEW ZEALAND	Scotland	37–6	1t

*t = try (+) = replacement (-) = left field

Game	Date	Venue	Team	Opponent	Score	Other*
169 (55)	1:12:01	Buenos Aires	NEW ZEALAND	Argentina	24–20	It
2002						
170	22:2:02	Wellington	Hurricanes	Blues	7–60	(+)
171	2:3:02	Pretoria	Hurricanes	Bulls	37–18	
172	8:3:02	Cape Town	Hurricanes	Stormers	13–40	
173	15:3:02	Wellington	Hurricanes	Sharks	40–17	
174	22:3:02	Wellington	Hurricanes	Cats	30–21	
175	30:3:02	Palmerston North	Hurricanes	Reds	22–18	
176	5:4:02	Dunedin	Hurricanes	Highlanders	10–19	It
177	14:4:02	Canberra	Hurricanes	Brumbies	20–13	
178	27:4:02	Sydney	Hurricanes	Waratahs	13–19	
179	4:5:02	Wellington	Hurricanes	Crusaders	20–48	
180	26:5:02	Twickenham	UK Barbarians	England	53–29	
181 (56)	8:6:02	Hamilton	NEW ZEALAND	Italy	64–10	It (+)
182 (57)	15:6:02	Dunedin	NEW ZEALAND	Ireland	15–6	(+)
183 (58)	22:6:02	Auckland	NEW ZEALAND	Ireland	40–8	
184 (59)	29:6:02	Wellington	NEW ZEALAND	Fiji	68–18	
185 (60)	20:7:02	Wellington	NEW ZEALAND	South Africa	41–20	(+)
186	16:8:02	Wellington	Wellington	Canterbury	33–24	(+)
187	24:8:02	Invercargill	Wellington	Southland	20–22	
188	30:8:02	Wellington	Wellington	Northland	51–18	
189	7:9:02	Albany	Wellington	North Harbour	19–17	It
190	6:10:02	Tauranga	Wellington	Bay of Plenty	74–20	It (+)
191	12:10:02	Wellington	Wellington	Auckland	27–47	(+)

*t = try (+) = replacement (-) = left field

Game	Date	Venue	Team	Opponent	Score	Other*
192 (61)	9:11:02	Twickenham	NEW ZEALAND	England	28–31	2t
193 (62)	16:11:02	Paris	NEW ZEALAND	France	20–20	
194 (63)	23:11:02	Cardiff	NEW ZEALAND	Wales	43–17	

2003

Game	Date	Venue	Team	Opponent	Score	Other*
195	7:3:03	Wellington	Hurricanes	Stormers	33–18	(–)
196	14:3:03	Durban	Hurricanes	Sharks	35–20	(+)
197	21:3:03	Bloemfontein	Hurricanes	Cats	28–21	(+)
198	29:3:03	Wellington	Hurricanes	Chiefs	24–14	(–)
199	9:8:03	Porirua	Wellington	Taranaki	17–27	(–)

New Zealand Record

Opponents	P	W	D	L	Tries
Argentina	2	2	-	-	I
Australia	13	6	-	7	6
England	7	5	I	I	8
Fiji	I	I	-	-	-
France	8	3	I	4	4
Ireland	4	4	-	-	3
Italy	3	3	-	-	5
Samoa	2	2	-	-	I
Scotland	6	6	-	-	7
South Africa	12	7	-	5	-
Tonga	2	2	-	-	2
Wales	3	3	-	-	-

*t = try (+) = replacement (-) = left field

INDEX